W9-BLI-594

THE
EPIC
OF
MAN

THE

EPIC

OF

MAN

BY THE
EDITORS OF
LIFE

TIME INCORPORATED

NEW YORK 1961

TIME INC. BOOK DIVISION

Editor
NORMAN P. ROSS

Copy Director
WILLIAM JAY GOLD

Art Director
EDWARD A. HAMILTON

Chief of Research
BEATRICE T. DOBIE

•

Editorial staff for *The Epic of Man*:

Editor
COURTLANDT CANBY

Designer
LEONARD JOSSEL

Text
LINCOLN BARNETT, *Senior Writer*
ROGER BUTTERFIELD, WALTER KARP, HUBERT KAY,
HILLIS MILLS, JOHN OSBORNE, GERALD SIMONS,
CARL T. SOLBERG, RICHARD L. WILLIAMS, JACK WINOCOUR

Chief Researcher
CLARA E. NICOLAI

Researchers
PEGGY BUSHONG, SHEILA OSMUNDSEN, MARY ELLEN MURPHY,
BARBARA BALLANTINE, MARION L. STEINMANN,
ANN H. EISENBERG, ROSE JOURDAIN

Picture Researchers
MARGARET K. GOLDSMITH, JOAN T. LYNCH, SUE E. THALBERG

Art Associates
ALBERT J. DUNN, ROBERT L. YOUNG, ARTHUR J. DUNN

Art Assistants
JAMES D. SMITH, JOHN M. WOODS, ARTHUR A. GOLDBERGER

Paintings and Maps
FEDERICO CASTELLON, XAVIER GONZALEZ, KENNETH S. FAGG,
SIMON GRECO, CARROLL JONES, STANLEY MELTZOFF, ANTONIO PETRUCELLI,
BOB RILEY, ALTON S. TOBEY, RUDOLPH F. ZALLINGER

Photographs
JAMES BURKE, LARRY BURROWS, JOHN DOMINIS, DAVID DOUGLAS DUNCAN,
ALFRED EISENSTAEDT, ELIOT ELISOFON, ANDREAS FEININGER, FRITZ GORO,
YALE JOEL, DMITRI KESSEL, DAVID LEES, RALPH MORSE, CARL MYDANS,
FRANK J. SCHERSCHEL, HOWARD SOCHUREK, JAMES WHITMORE

Copy Staff
MARIAN GORDON GOLDMAN, *Chief;* REBECCA CHAITIN,
DOLORES A. LITTLES, ESTHER KAPLAN, CLARICE GARRISON,
ANNE HUMPHERYS, NANCY WILDER, JUDY SCHER, CLARK WISWELL

•

Publisher JEROME S. HARDY

General Manager JOHN A. WATTERS

•

LIFE MAGAZINE

Editor
EDWARD K. THOMPSON

Managing Editor
GEORGE P. HUNT

Publisher
C. D. JACKSON

This book is based on a series of articles entitled *The Epic of Man* which appeared in LIFE from 1955 to 1957. They were prepared under the direction of Senior Editor Kenneth MacLeish and Art Director Charles Tudor and were written by Lincoln Barnett. Much new material has been added, and many of the illustrations and photographs are here published for the first time. The following individuals and departments of LIFE Magazine helped in producing the book: Albert Rosenfeld, Science Editor; Nancy Genet and Joann McQuiston, Assistant Editors; Nancy King, Reporter; Ray Mackland, Picture Editor; George Caturani, Chief of the Foreign News Bureau; Thomas N. Carmichael, Chief of the Domestic News Bureau; Doris O'Neil, Chief of the Picture Library; and Content Peckham, Chief of the Time Inc. Bureau of Editorial Reference.

CONTENTS

THE HUMAN

PLAINS Indian tales often begin with the set formula: "Once there was a poor orphan." Perhaps the phrase does in truth reflect man's eternal vision of himself. He yearns for the lost safety of the old instinctive world he has abandoned. Perhaps, in moments of reflection and nostalgia, there is also evident in the phrase the iron determination of the orphan to win—by magic, by all means that come to hand—his Eden of contentment, his Utopia, the place of peace so long dreamt of by his great visionary teachers. Yet, alas, no more restless and unruly pupil ever sat before great masters than our own human species of today.

"It doth not yet appear," said St. John in the New Testament, "what we shall be." *The Epic of Man* is the account of a still uncompleted but tremendous journey—the journey of man out of darkness into the light of civilization, out of mindless ignorance into a shuddering knowledge of himself and the inescapable fact that the power he has learned to draw from nature has given him, as yet, no comparable mastery over himself.

A rich and enriching chronicle, *The Epic of Man* traces the human story through the long reaches of prehistory to the borders of recorded history. Section I, *The Emergence of Man*, gives an account of man's earliest years on earth as the anthropologists have so far been able to reconstruct them. In Section II, *The Coming of Civilization*, the story of ten of the world's first great civilizations is unfolded. Section III, *Living Societies of the Past*, presents isolated groups of people—the primitive Aborigines of Australia, the Caribou Eskimos of Canada, the Berbers of the Dadès River Valley in Morocco, the Newars of Nepal—which have survived in the modern world little changed from that earlier world of prehistoric man and early civilization which forms the central subject of the book. The cultures of these people, who now face the challenge of modern technological civilization, are reminders of how far the journey of man has carried him.

The history of man's evolution on this planet is a short history by geological standards, yet it covers approximately 15 million years of time. Five thousand years of intermittent written records cover man's known history, then trail off into the silence of the Stone Age hunter's world. For the rest of the 15 million years of human evolution, during which our bodies and our brains were drastically altered, we have today only a few handfuls of broken teeth, a few battered skulls, the magical carvings and paintings of dead hunters, and a paucity of rude tools to tell the story of the way we crawled upward from the jungle darkness, and of the way our bodies were transformed in the course of that long journey. The science which has revealed this story, insofar as we have been able to piece it together, is a recent science. Because it has been based upon the study of human remains that are infrequently discovered, and often in remote, uncivilized areas, progress has not been rapid, nor are we in a position at the present time to recount fully every aspect of the emergence of man from the animal world about him.

Because we are men, because we are curious, and because we are enormously aware of time and its relation to man in the universe, we have learned to search consciously for the shaped flint, and out of hard-gained anatomical knowledge, to restore the features of beings (I hesitate even to use the word *men*) whose like will never be seen upon the earth again. And we have learned to reconstruct the complex features of lost civilizations from the buried fragments that have survived their ruin. The restoration of those vanished faces, of those forgotten cultures, the ability to get from them significant aspects of the human adventure depends first upon the use of archaeology as a kind of detective science. The painstaking findings of archaeologists and paleontologists have been incorporated in the paintings in *The Epic of Man*, which reconstruct scenes in the lives of fossil men and ancient civilizations. The photographs that accompany these paintings provide a visual record of the actual discoveries made by the archaeologists.

TO lend coherency to the archaeological record, to what would otherwise be a collection of mere unrelated facts, a guiding principle is required. This guiding principle is, of course, evolution. By its demonstration of the community of descent of all living forms, the theory enables us to recognize across the gulf of time the altered faces of precursors which would otherwise remain meaningless and unrecognizable. And just as our bodies may be read as a projection from the mysterious past, so human cultures are seen to be subject, also, to certain rules of development, reflecting their origin from the even more mysterious interplay of unique, individual minds. Some cultures may dream millennia away in small and simple circumstances close to the earth, as is true of certain remote peoples today. Again, a twist of technology, the force of a religious drive, may create a gigantic growth which after centuries of creative effort freezes into a hardened mold of custom or collapses in ways which seem quite unpredictable.

The story of man, as can be seen from the pages that follow, may be read from many diverse angles. It may be seen as the consequence of an unspecialized forelimb, no longer used for walking and thus left free to explore and meddle with the surrounding universe. It may be read as the result of the transmission, by the symbol-using brain, of the social consciousness through time; or as a succession of economic stages, allowing for the increasing division and specialization of labor. Or the germ of the story may be found in that curious potential which seems to allow the brain of *Homo sapiens* to grasp any principle, any intuition which enables him to modify and transform either his exterior environment or his interior world of dreams. Man is, in fact, a dream animal, and this book is an account of some of the more important of his dreams—dreams of power, whether spiritual or temporal; dreams of the creative artist who has

ADVENTURE

brought into being all of the fallen beauty that we see in these pages, exhumed from dead temples and from ruined shrines.

It is possible to state the core of what is different about the life of man as distinguished from that of his animal relations and associates by pointing out that the latter dwell in a kind of timeless, instinctive present. Man, by contrast, has entered history. He rises and he falls, he remembers and forgets, he builds and destroys. But in the remembering and forgetting, in the building and destroying, he is slowly, and now more rapidly, altering the face of the planet beyond recall.

The animal world makes evolutionary adaptations based on biological selection. In his earliest phase, when man achieved an upright posture and a foot adapted to progression on the ground, he was pursuing a very old evolutionary pathway: that of adaptive radiation into a grassland environment. Bipedal though he was, he would have seemed no more unusual than certain big, flightless birds that had once inhabited the air. His brain was anthropoidal in size and seemed no dire threat to anyone. Many of his fellow grassland primates indeed seem never to have become men at all. But one group, perhaps rather late in its development, entered and adapted itself to the most remarkable corridor of existence ever penetrated by a living creature upon the earth. If I may put the matter dramatically, *ancestral man had entered his own head,* and he has been adapting ever since to what he finds there. This is why I said earlier that man is essentially a creature who lives on dreams. The difference that has arisen between man and the other animals lies in a cunning distinction between the words *adaptation* and *adaptability*.

The mole is *adapted* to a specifically restricted environment to which a lengthy specialized evolution has confined him. He can survive nowhere else. This restriction, with varying limitations upon freedom of movement, is true of all of earth's creatures from gorillas to garter snakes. When man began to express and differentiate his outer and inner worlds through the use of symbols—language, in other words—he had "adapted," by something that happened in his brain, to infinite *adaptability*. He could now shape and differentiate and define his world and transmit that knowledge to others of his kind. More, he could express what he felt about it. He could project himself into tomorrow's hunting situation by devising traps for the unsuspecting creature still living in its instinctive present. Or man could remember and express what happened yesterday or last year, and derive lessons from the experience. He could devise tools, improving and multiplying them as the mind dictated.

THE fading of the old instinctive world cannot have been easy; indeed we still suffer from those wounds today. Sometimes, like a pet dog in the kitchen growling over an undisputed bone, we are afflicted by unreasoning aggressions. Fears come in the night, fears that in early man were enhanced by ignorance—ignorance of sun and moon and water, so that all things soon lay under the spell of spirits generated in his own mind. Witchcraft and magic long preceded the world of science. Indeed it must have been a narrow crack that man squeezed through when he entered his own mind. Our good fortune lies in the fact that man was not lost totally from reality amidst the glooms of his own powerful imagination.

After hundreds of millions of years of evolution, nature had succeeded in producing, in the brain, an organ whose success had added to the staid course of biological heredity an inconceivably rapid method of adjustment through what might be called social heredity—the oral and written transmission of ideas from person to person and group to group. Man's adaptability, as contrasted with the animal world of biological adaptation, had become his supreme instrument of survival. Star measurer, deviser of great ethical systems, he was and he still is, however, a creature floundering from one medium to another. Deep written in his body is the old world of the ice, the tiger and the cave. Like the puppy in the kitchen, he is still capable of growling over bones; he is a power lover without having mastered the final lesson that true power consists in the mastery of oneself.

IN *The Epic of Man* lies the story, insofar as it is known, of man's escape from nature's trap of narrow specialization, of his far march across ice ages, of his building a variety of civilizations out of the ideas in his head as well as with the tools in his hands. Here, above all, is the story of his mental projection upon his tools and implements of all those special features nature has slowly evolved in creatures limited to a hundred special environments. Man, by science, can duplicate them all or discard them at will. He can fly or swim, roll with the wheel, bring light into the midnight darkness of his streets. All this he can do with the selfsame body, while increasingly he spins the substance of the future out of the same mind that painted mammoths on the walls of ice age caverns. Man is paradoxically the supreme generalized animal by reason of a supremely specialized brain. It is his cities that are now his true specializations, his cities that lie vulnerable to extinction under the silent winging of the satellites.

Man has been steeped and ripened in ages of ice and rain. Like most of nature's great innovations, there is an orphan obscurity about him; he is marred, transitory, an evolutionary miracle moving from a world within nature toward something of which only his best minds can entertain gleams and visions.

"The route that we pursue in time," the philosopher Henri Bergson once remarked, "is strewn with the remains of all that we began to be, of all that we might have become." Here, stated succinctly, is the true effort of the archaeologist; namely, to give man just this vision of himself, just this warning and even just this hope: that with a true knowledge of the past he may wander less blindly among the shards and attic rubble of past failures and perceive, perhaps, the Utopia for which he seeks.

LOREN EISELEY
Professor of Anthropology
Provost, University of Pennsylvania

A MAGDALENIAN HUNTER who has been stalking reindeer is ready to make the kill with his spear. The Magdalenians, a highly developed *Homo sapiens*, lived in Europe some 13,000 years ago. They could sew clothing and perfected the barb-headed spear. For most of half a million Stone Age years, from his beginnings as a human animal until the invention of agriculture about 6000 B.C., man, a hunter, ate the flesh of other animals.

THE EMERGENCE OF MAN

In the Old Stone Age he developed physical versatility and the skills that have made him master of the earth

ALONE among all creatures on earth, man has a sense of destiny. He is haunted by the conviction that he is more than an animal. Yet he cannot deny his unmistakable kinship with myriad lesser forms of life which share—or have shared—his environment.

The physical characteristics which link man to animals, and the skills and social organizations he developed long before historic times, are the subject matter of the science of anthropology. The spiritual qualities which differentiate man from the brutes are the concern of philosophers and theologians, who now tend to accept the evidence of man's physical evolution from less highly developed animals, finding no necessary conflict with basic religious beliefs.

So in portraying the epic rise of man, the first step is to classify him in zoological terms. The scientists describe man as a member of the tremendously ancient GROUP of vertebrates, which includes all creatures with internal skeletons. Man is also a member of the large and variegated CLASS of mammals, which have warm blood and suckle their young; of the ORDER of primates, which are especially proficient in using their fingers and brains; of the FAMILY of Hominidae, comprising all manlike creatures that ever walked on their hind legs; and a member of the GENUS known as *Homo* (i.e., man).

Finally, modern man is a member—in fact the only member—of the SPECIES called *Homo sapiens* (thinking man), who is believed to have existed for at least 250,000 years. Other kinds and forerunners of man can be traced by their fossil remains, but all are long since extinct. The large-brained *Homo sapiens* is the sole survivor on the Hominidae family tree. All men today, regardless of color, size or achievement, belong to this single species.

Man is the dominant creature on earth largely because in his long evolutionary climb he has remained a "generalized" rather than a "specialized" animal. He has never developed, by natural selection, any such cumbersome features as the giraffe's exaggerated neck or the elephant's long nose. Man has retained, with wonderful improvements, the 10 fingers and toes of his amphibian ancestors—unlike, say, the horse, which specialized in speed and now runs on the magnified nails of only his middle toes. From the primates, man inherited grasping hands and powerful shoulders, which were developed by "brachiating" —swinging from branch to branch in trees. The lower primates also passed on to man the priceless faculty of binocular stereoscopic vision, enabling him to see the world in sharp focus and three dimensions.

What then are the specific traits which make *Homo sapiens* unique? Opinions differ, but most scientists hold that the prime physical asset of man—the initial endowment from which all his other good fortune sprang—was his erect posture. He was not the first, it is true, to use two limbs for locomotion. Some dinosaurs walked on their hind legs, but their forelimbs dwindled into feeble appendages. Man's living relations, the anthropoid apes, can stand and even take a few steps erect, but when they move fast they must also use their hands or knuckles for support. Only man, whose foot differs from that of all other animals in its marvelous supporting arch and the fused balancing pad at the base of the toes, walks serenely upright at all times. "Man stands alone," the anthropologist Weston LaBarre has observed, "because he alone stands."

With his hands left free to grasp things or to fight, some ancestral species of hominid found himself walking about in a world that offered rich rewards—in terms of food and other necessities for survival —for his unusual versatility. He responded, according to evolutionary principles, with a steady enlargement of brain tissue: he began to be intelligent. From a mere wielder of randomly acquired weapons, such as sticks and stones, he evolved into the world's only foresighted toolmaker. As *Homo sapiens*, in Old Stone Age times, he became not only an expert hunter but also a mystic and artist. He developed language and sought to transmit his knowledge by speech to later generations. And because he was so gregarious, out of his long experience he created culture, the very substance of human society.

GATHERING OF PRIMATES, representing 70 million years of evolution, is shown above. At lower left are a gibbon and its baby from Asia. The ring-tailed lemur in the tree at left is descended from one of the oldest known primates; it survives only on Madagascar. Behind the lemur are two New World monkeys; below them are two Proconsuls—an adult and a young one —extinct African apes who probably stood erect. The two creatures with clubs

PRIMATE FAMILY TREE

MAN is man because of his brain," says anthropologist William Howells, "and he got his brain by being a primate, and a descendant of primates." The first primate relatives of man were small but adventurous mammals—much like the ring-tailed lemur above—which began climbing and living in trees about 70 million years ago. Grasping and scampering among the branches, they developed great versatility in their fingers and toes. Because some lemurs depended more on sight than on smell, vision developed as the predominant sense, replacing smell, and became stereoscopic. Primates tended to sit up and look at the world; their heads became poised more vertically on their spines. Because primates could use their fingers to place food in their mouths, their jaws grew more capacious and box-like; they

became adapted to processing food rather than seizing it with the teeth.

There are great gaps in the fossil record connecting the most ancient primates with the emergence of man (*chart at right*). But experts generally agree that both man and his cousins, the anthropoid apes, are descended from a common ancestor which evolved about 30 million years ago. The remains of this creature have not yet been discovered, although Proconsul, a fossil ape from Africa that walked on feet and hands, is a possible candidate. It seems likely that in the late Oligocene or early Miocene periods, when tropical forests gave way to grasslands, some tree-dwelling primates came down on the ground to forage for their food. Those which thrived and learned to walk erect founded the line of hominids which led to man. Those which remained at least part of the time in trees began to evolve toward the present-day apes. During this process many species with vaguely human characteristics arose, flourished and became extinct. Other

are extinct Australopithecines; one threatens a baboon. At center two Java men (*Homo erectus*) cut a tree. The beetle-browed male at extreme right is a very early *Homo sapiens,* a Steinheim man. Behind him are two gorillas.

FAMILY TREE of the primates illustrates how the monkeys, great apes and hominids have been evolving along separate lines and at different periods. Any or all of the encircled primates could have been the ancestors of man.

species, such as Sivapithecus and Ramapithecus, had teeth similar to those of humans and may belong among the collateral ancestors of man. Oreopithecus, whose skeletons have been found in Italian coalbeds, had a remarkably human face but was definitely an ape. The most fearsome of these species was Gigantopithecus, known to us from his fossilized teeth, found in China; he is believed to have been about as large as a mountain gorilla.

What set evolving man apart was the increasing size of his brain. The extinct Australopithecines of Africa had upright bodies resembling man's and a brain capacity range of 450-700 cc., about that of gorillas. They could use simple stone tools. The range in brain capacity of the first species of man—*Homo erectus*—was 775-1,235 cc., making him superior to any ape. Earliest *Homo sapiens,* such as the Steinheim man in the painting above, had a probable brain capacity of 1,200 cc. Most people today range between 1,300 and 1,600 cc.

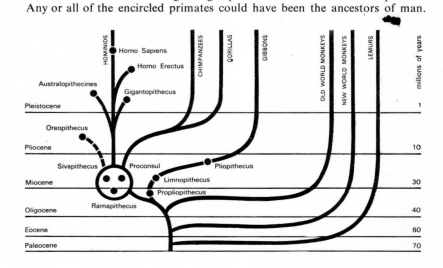

13

MAN'S WORLD IN ICE AGE TIMES is depicted on this map. It extended from the crown of Eurasia to the Cape of Good Hope, and from England across Siberia into the Americas. The white areas (*top*) show the ice at its greatest extent. Climate conditions in regions beyond the ice are shown in color according to the key at right. When the northern areas were sheeted in ice, heavy rains fell farther south, transforming deserts into game preserves and

FOUR TYPES OF ICE AGE MEN are shown above. At left is Peking man, a small-brained *Homo erectus* who lived around 360,000 years ago. His species became extinct with the rise of *Homo sapiens*. Next to him, hurling a spear, is Rhodesian man, who lived as recently as 25,000 years ago and may have been an ancestor of the African Negroes. His brain size was close to that of *Homo sapiens*. The two men to the right are both early types of *Homo*

14

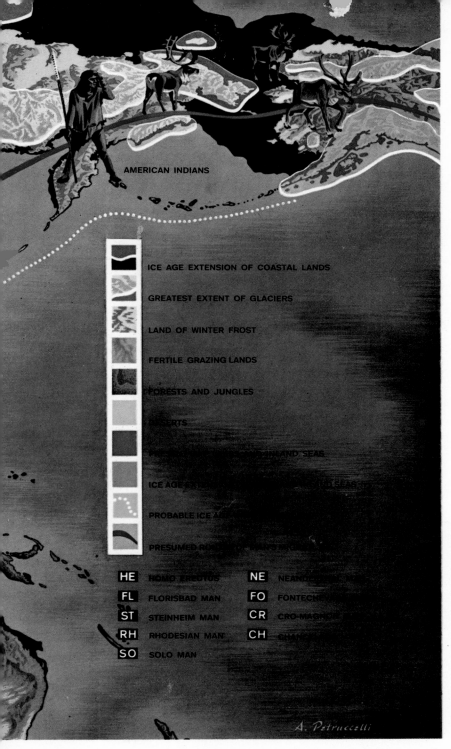

NEANDERTHAL MAN is shown here with the woolly rhinoceros he hunted, using a stone-tipped spear. He endured the ice age, flourishing in Europe and Asia while the last glacial period was at its peak. Although his brow was lower than modern man's, he was a crafty, inventive *Homo sapiens*.

The map legend reads:

ICE AGE EXTENSION OF COASTAL LANDS

GREATEST EXTENT OF GLACIERS

LAND OF WINTER FROST

FERTILE GRAZING LANDS

FORESTS AND JUNGLES

DESERTS

INLAND SEAS

ICE AGE

PROBABLE ICE

PRESUMED

HE	HOMO ERECTUS	NE	NEANDERTHAL
FL	FLORISBAD MAN	FO	FONTECHEVADE
ST	STEINHEIM MAN	CR	CRO-MAGNON
RH	RHODESIAN MAN	CH	
SO	SOLO MAN		

creating inland seas. The human figures and the letter symbols (*key at right above*) on the map indicate where remains of the principal kinds of ice age men have been found. The red bands suggest their migration routes.

sapiens. Florisbad man, to the extreme right, may have been ancestral to the Bushmen of Africa. Behind him is an extinct giraffe. Fontechevade man, to his left, shown skinning a hare, lived about 150,000 years ago.

THE ICE AGE

A VITAL factor in man's development was a great change in the weather which took place about 700,000 years ago, just as the genus *Homo* was emerging. During the previous 70 million years or more, while the mammals and primates were evolving, the earth's climate had been comfortably warm and stable. At the start of the geological era called Pleistocene, which corresponds with the Age of Man, something upset the balance. First there was a gradual cooling and some minor glaciations. Then followed three tremendous movements of ice sheets pushing south from the Arctic and down from the peaks of mountains. (The Antarctic, surrounded by water, did not increase its icecap greatly.)

As the glaciers advanced, coats of ice thousands of feet thick covered much of the Northern Hemisphere (*map at left*). But every 100,000 years or so, higher temperatures set in. During the so-called interglacial periods the ice slowly melted and the weather in what are now the temperate zones grew warmer than it is today. Man has so far survived three interglacial periods.

Thus what we call the ice age was not so much an era of unrelieved frigidity as it was one of long-range fluctuations from polar to tropical. The ever-changing climate eventually brought with it sharper distinctions between the seasons in most regions of the world, and constituted a constant challenge to survival. Blizzards and floods, numbing cold succeeded by searing droughts, became the accustomed lot of all forms of animal life. These conditions may have speeded up the adaptive processes by which man evolved.

Certainly they had a far-ranging effect on his migrating habits. By freezing vast quantities of snow and rain, the glaciers lowered ocean levels as much as 300 feet, creating natural land bridges that spanned the North Sea, the Dardanelles, the Persian Gulf and the Bering Strait. England became an extension of Europe, and Australia was tied to New Guinea. Driven by the changes in the weather, millions of animals crossed the new connections between the continents —and man the hunter followed. During the fourth glacial period, apparently, the men who became American Indians reached the New World by way of the Bering Strait land bridge from Asia.

The strenuous, weather-driven life of the ice age hunter has been the existence of man during 98 per cent of his career. Those who support the theory of "survival of the fittest" claim this proves that man's rise was the result of his strength and aggressiveness. Yet hundreds of species, many physically stronger than man, perished during the ice age. Most of the large mammals were probably killed off by hunters, while others flourished in areas where they had escaped man's prowess. The stamina and physical skills of man undoubtedly gave him an edge over many animals on the hunting grounds of Europe and Asia. But it was his brain, growing larger as it confronted new challenges, which brought man safely through the ice age.

ONE MAN DARES to pick up a burning stick in the path of a volcanic flow of hot coals and lava across an African landscape about 400,000 years ago. An act of savage courage like this might have initiated man's first scientific discovery: his ability to make use of fire. The band of men and women in this painting are of a type suggested by a reconstruction of a *Homo erectus* skull found in Africa and still under study by scientists. So far, the earliest

remains that can be definitely called those of *Homo sapiens* come from England and Germany. Several primate cousins of man have been found in Africa, but an earlier specimen of *Homo sapiens* is unlikely to be found there.

MOMENTS OF DECISION: THE MASTERY OF FIRE

IN the words of anthropologist Carleton Coon, "The use of fire is the only open-and-shut difference between man and all the other animals." Fire was man's first source of power that did not come from his own muscles. It warmed his cave and made existence possible in Europe and Asia during the last glacial period. It multiplied his feats as a hunter; discovering that all animals are deathly afraid of fire, prehistoric man used it in torches to stampede and bewilder his game. At some time in his career, early man began to use fire to cook his meat, which in many ways greatly improved his lot.

In Stone Age times the best source of fire was an erupting volcano or a forest fire. The painting at left envisions a scene which must have occurred many times in many different places. One adventurous human being, instead of fleeing from fire like the other animals and most of his companions, has picked up a brand. He will learn that it does not hurt him—if he keeps his fingers out of the flame. He will learn also that the flame can be kept alive if it is "fed" with wood and dry leaves. Nursing it solicitously, and no doubt revering it as a gift from the gods, he will transport the living fire to his shelter and keep it burning there indefinitely. One family will get fire from another, and thus it will spread from camp to camp, and even from continent to continent.

No one really knows where on the earth's surface or at what stage of early prehistory man first learned how to make use of fire. The oldest positive evidence of the existence of fire in connection with human remains, however, comes from the caves of Choukoutien in northern China, where ancient hearths indicate that Peking man, although he was somewhat handicapped by an undersized brain, knew enough to keep himself warm in his chilly northern habitat. The remains of Sinanthropus, or Peking man, were unearthed with other fossils by a number of anthropologists, including the noted Father Teilhard de Chardin, between 1927 and 1936. In 1930, according to the Abbé Breuil, dean of French prehistorians, Teilhard came to his office in Paris with a little stag's horn, obviously worked by early man, which had been found during the excavations in China. "I won't tell you where this comes from," he told the *abbé*, "but what do you make of it?" The *abbé's* appraisal was almost instantaneous: "It has been put in the fire when still fresh . . . it is an instrument fashioned by man . . . with a stone implement, the marks of which you can see on the shaft." "But," Teilhard exclaimed, "it comes from Choukoutien!" Abbé Breuil was adamant: "It doesn't matter where it comes from, I still maintain my diagnosis."

This evidence and Breuil's deduction confirmed Peking man's possession of fire. It is unlikely, however, that Sinanthropus, who lived some 360,000 years ago, could *make* fire. That is a comparatively recent accomplishment, and even now it is not understood everywhere. All primitive peoples existing in the world today are capable of using fire, but some still do not know how to make it.

The discovery of the useful art of cooking may have been closely bound up with early man's love of the rich marrow of large bones. When a raw bone is smashed with a stone, the marrow is still hard to get at, but when the bone is heated in an open fire, it splits easily. If it is boiled, the marrow is softened so that it can be sucked with ease or scraped off with the teeth. In the debris left by Neanderthal man, the long animal bones are split or broken, but there is no evidence that he boiled the bones to soften the marrow.

At some point in man's career, however, he began to cook. He must have soon discovered that cooking does more than release the marrow from bones. It also breaks down the tough fibers of meat and roots, makes them much easier to chew, and greatly reduces the time spent in eating. It was probably these basic discoveries that enabled prehistoric man to begin a truly human experience. Stopwatch studies of man's cousins, the gibbons, show that they spend half of their waking hours going through the process of eating, and the other half traveling back and forth between their feeding places and their roosts in trees. Wild gorillas, who subsist on coarse shoots of bamboo and other greenery, are busy eating and chewing during most of the daylight hours. Primitive man in the early Stone Age, no matter how strong his jaws or how large his teeth, must have had to go through much the same. But once he began to cook his food, he could do all the eating he required in a few hours and have the rest of the day free for hunting, toolmaking and other activities.

THE TOOLMAKER

ONE of the unique distinctions of man is his toolmaking ability. A chimpanzee or a monkey will pick up a natural object and use it as an improvised implement. But only man devises tools for his future needs. Through this ability he has augmented his strength to the awesome proportions of the nuclear bomb, increased his rate of locomotion to supersonic speeds and extended his range of travel into outer space. Thus equipped and empowered, man is apt to forget that during nine tenths of his existence his only tools were chipped stones and simple shafts of wood.

Just as the physical evolution of man is traced in terms of zoology, so his development as a thinking being is outlined by the stages of his toolmaking cultures. The first and by far the longest period of human progress is the Paleolithic or Old Stone Age, which began about 500,000 years ago and lasted until around 8000 B.C. It was succeeded by the brief Mesolithic Age, which in turn was followed by the Neolithic, characterized by polished stone tools (*see Chapter 3*). The vast span of the Old Stone Age is divided into three parts, the Lower, Middle and Upper Paleolithic, and—so far as Europe is concerned—into eight cultural subdivisions. The painting on these three pages depicts in sequence from left to right the growth of toolmaking in Europe during the Lower and Middle Paleolithic, which ended around 35,000 B.C. The remarkable fact it reveals is that man's technology during almost half a million years was limited to slow changes in the basic stone instruments shown below.

In the oldest, or Abbevillian, stage of culture, man made two kinds of tools: (1) core tools and (2) flake tools. The hand ax, which characterized the culture, was made from what anthropologists call a core of durable flint shaped toward a point by skillful pounding. (A rude Abbevillian hand ax is shown at the upper left in the photograph below.) The chips or flakes which came off the flint during this process were sometimes reshaped for use as scrapers, cutters and gougers.

In the succeeding Acheulian stage (from about 300,000 to about 100,000 B.C.), man greatly improved his hand tools by delicately flaking the face of his hand ax with a wooden baton, which produced a sharper, more symmetrical tool (*center and right, below*). In time he began to work flint cores purely for the purpose of manufacturing flakes, which he used as they were or inserted into wood or bone handles. Flake tools became the specialty of the Mousterian culture (roughly 100,000 to 35,000 B.C.) which coincided with the Middle Paleolithic and was dominated by Neanderthal man. He was the first hunter known to have attached flint points to his spears. As Europe's weather grew glacially cold he probably also wore furs prepared with a variety of flint scraping tools (*below, left*).

HAND AX

HAND AX

SCRAPER HAND AX SPEARHEAD

ABBEVILLIAN

Of the eight stages of Paleolithic man's toolmaking career in Europe, the three earliest are shown in this painting, which covers almost half a million years of human activity. In the Abbevillian stage—named, like most such

MOUSTERIAN

more carefully by chipping off flakes with a piece of wood. The *Homo sapiens* of this time may have worn rudimentary clothing, even though this was a warm period. During the last glacial advance, Neanderthal man (*right*), a full-brained *Homo sapiens,* spread the Mousterian flake culture in Asia and Africa as well as in Europe. He hunted with stone-tipped spears, warmed himself with fire and competed with bears for shelter in caves.

LOWER PERIGORDIAN

The last five cultural stages that brought Old Stone Age technology to its climax in Europe are pictured here in a painting that encompasses the 27,000 years of the Upper Paleolithic period. The setting is one of the many

AURIGNACIAN

open rock shelters, or mouths of caves, where men lived while ice covered much of Europe. In the Lower Perigordian, Combe Capelle man (*extreme left*) is seen hitting the edge of a core of flint with a stone hammer and wooden

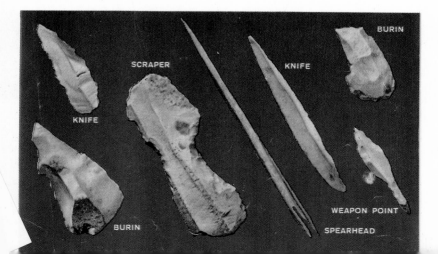

HIS SKILLS INCREASE

IT is believed that man may have journeyed south when the second and third glacial advances refrigerated Europe. But when the fourth glaciation set in, around 75,000 B.C., he remained in the north and developed new skills simply through the effort to keep warm.

The Upper Paleolithic period was marked by five distinct European cultures, illustrated in the painting above. The first big revolution in toolmaking was the invention of the flint blade. This

FOLD OUT: DO NOT TEAR

ACHEULIAN

anthropological terms, after the site where the initial discoveries of tools or human bones were made—the robust but small-brained *Homo erectus,* such as Heidelberg man (*left*), had only primitive stone tools, ate his game as he

killed it and, because the climate was warm, wore no clothes. At the height of the later Acheulian culture (*center*), about 250,000 B.C., when *Homo sapiens* had begun to multiply, he started to shape his flint tools

19

UPPER PERIGORDIAN

punch to strike off sharp blades—the beginning of the knife. A Combe Capelle woman uses a flintknife to cut thongs while another woman sits to scrape skin. In the Aurignacian, a Cro-Magnon toolmaker (*left foreground*) carves a spear point from an antler while the man bending over the fire in the background uses bone implements to straighten a wooden spear. A later Cro-Magnon of the Upper Perigordian culture skins a reindeer with his

came during the Lower Perigordian culture (35,000-28,000 B.C.), which also saw the emergence of Combe Capelle man, a modern-looking *Homo sapiens* with Mediterranean features. Combe Capelle man had special tools for dressing animal skins, and he probably laced his clothes together with thongs. In the Aurignacian culture (28,000-21,000 B.C.) the flint blade was modified into a beveled, chisel-like tool called the burin, which was used for splitting and shaping materials softer than stone. The burin was a crucial invention because it helped to create a whole new series of tools and weapons made from animal bone and horn. The mastermind of the

Aurignacian culture was Cro-Magnon man, a tall, strong-chinned *Homo sapiens* who resembled modern Irishmen and Norwegians. Cro-Magnon man also dominated the Upper Perigordian culture (21,000-18,000 B.C.), during which time he developed the first true straight-backed knife (shown with other Perigordian and Aurignacian implements in the photograph at left).

In the Solutrean stage (18,000-14,000 B.C.), descendants of Cro-Magnon and Combe Capelle men developed the art of pressure flaking—detaching flakes by pressing a flint instead of hitting it. This produced thin, leaf-shaped blades which made fine points for

SOLUTREAN

MAGDALENIAN

straight-backed knife. The Solutrean technique of pressure-flaking flint is practiced by a modified Cro-Magnon in the right foreground. At the far right a Magdalenian woman stitches handsome, ornamented leather clothing

with a bone needle, an invention of the Magdalenian culture. The Magdalenians (represented by Chancelade man) also wore pierced shells as jewelry. In the background a Magdalenian hunting party enjoys a Stone Age barbecue.

weapons. The final Paleolithic stage was the Magdalenian (14,000-8000 B.C.), during which a talented, high-cheekboned European people made the first needles with eyes, barbed spearheads and even a kind of saw (*right*), shown with Solutrean stonework.

Thus, by the end of the Old Stone Age, man had invented most of his fundamental tools. He still had only one form of power—his muscles—and he still knew nothing of agriculture. But he had learned to provide himself with shelter and warm clothing. With his finely wrought weapons and his aggressive intelligence he was well equipped to hunt the most powerful beasts on the face of the earth.

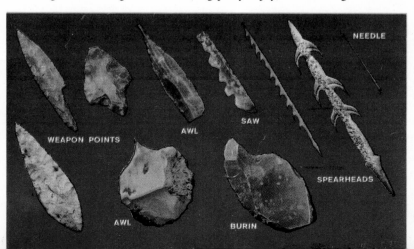

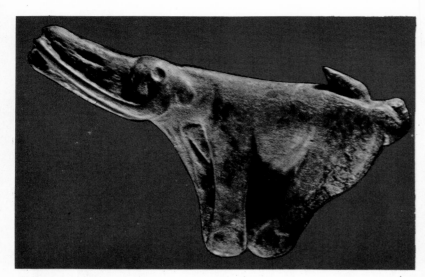

CARVING OF A MAMMOTH on a reindeer antler shaped for use as a spear thrower dates from the Upper Magdalenian culture. The trunk of the mammoth was on the shaft of the spear thrower, part of which remains intact.

HUNTER AND SCULPTOR

THROUGHOUT almost all of man's existence, hunting has been one of his main occupations as well as one of his chief pleasures. An appetite for meat distinguishes man from other large primates, such as gorillas, which subsist on bamboo shoots and fruit. Hunting has also had a considerable influence on man's physical evolution, and it has certainly shaped his character by the premium it places on quick thinking, endurance and courage.

The human economy of the Old Stone Age was based entirely on hunting, which not only gave man his food but provided raw materials, such as hide, sinew and bone, for his subsidiary industries. The early, small-brained *Homo erectus* probably had no better hunting equipment than stones, clubs and sticks with which to attack his prey. But sometime after *Homo sapiens* appeared during the Acheulian cultural stage, man invented a weapon that was to be his trusted companion for hundreds of thousands of years. This weapon began as a pointed stick, whittled with a hand ax and smoothed with a stone scraper—something that could be thrown or jabbed at a fleeing animal—in other words, a spear. Neanderthal man greatly improved the spear by attaching a sharp flint to its point. With this weapon he tracked down and trapped even the mighty mammoth, the largest land-dwelling animal that man has ever encountered.

CARVING OF A BISON from the Upper Magdalenian culture shows the head twisted back to fit the shape of an antler. The subject matter of Magdalenian sculpture included countless animal species, birds, fish and insects.

CLOSING IN FOR THE KILL (*right*) Neanderthal men surround a wounded mammoth. While two men hem it in with fire, another drives his spear into its belly, and others hack at its leg tendons or thrust at its open mouth.

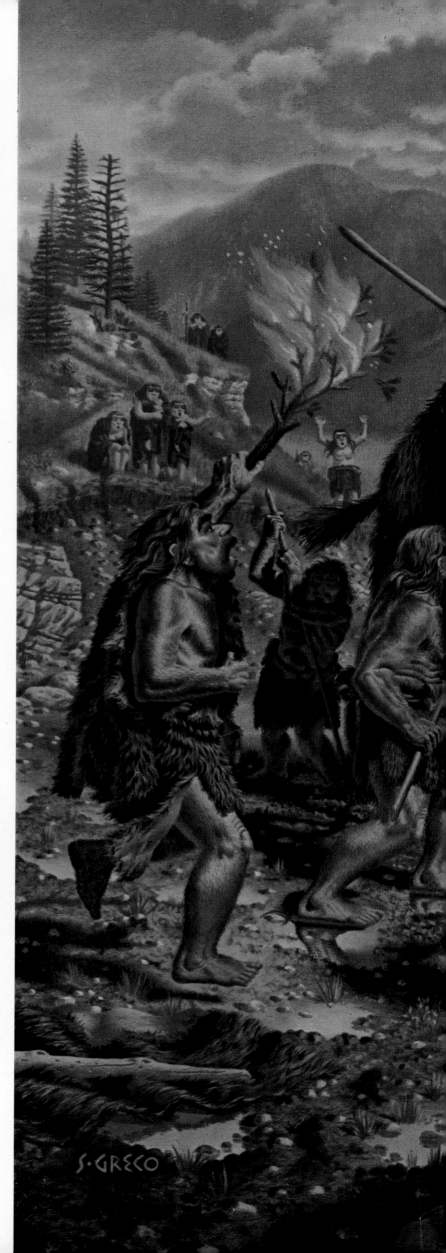

COOPERATIVE HUNTING

OUT of his urge to be a better hunter, prehistoric man evolved the art of government. The simple family and clanlike groups which he organized during the Old Stone Age were the direct ancestors of the complex nations and federations of nations with which he affiliates himself today.

The first step in this direction was taken when the males of several neighboring families overcame their mutual suspicions and formed a cooperative hunting band. The clever, well-built Cro-Magnons were among the first Stone Age people to create even larger communities; the remains of their semi-permanent settlements have been found in many parts of Europe.

Of these communities, one of the most interesting was a huge outdoor hunting station near Solutré in France, where the bones of an estimated 100,000 horses were found, along with those of other animals. Scientific study of this vast boneyard suggests that disciplined companies of Cro-Magnon hunters convened in the area, summer after summer, for organized "drives" on wild horses, conducted along the lines shown in the painting below. Since man had not yet learned that animals could be domesticated, the purpose of the Cro-Magnons

A STAMPEDE OF WILD HORSES has been engineered by Cro-Magnon hunters of the Aurignacian period in a European valley. Driving the horses up a slope to a cliff, the men keep them in line with bonfires and torches, jumping out from behind piles of boulders and urging them forward to the edge of a precipice, where the terrified animals leap to their death. At the bottom of the cliff other members of the party finish off the wounded

S·GRECO

was not to tame or ride the horses but to eat their flesh and make use of their skins. Similarly, during the winter, large-scale massacres of mammoths seem to have taken place in pits which were dug for the purpose by men in Russia and elsewhere. After the mammoths were eaten, their oily bones were used to stoke long-burning fires, and their tusks were employed as weights to hold down the skin roofs of crude dwellings dug out of the earth.

Such large accumulations of animal remains in any one spot can only mean that there must have been successive seasons of systematic hunts. And this in turn implies the existence of some teamwork and leadership—a distinct advance in the social organization of mankind.

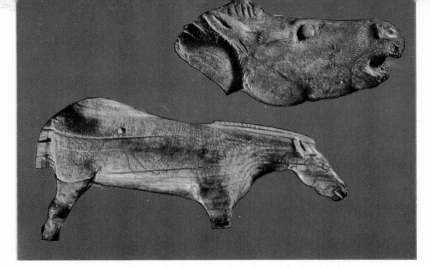

horses and begin to carve up the dead for food and skins. The wild horses of this glacial age were small, stocky creatures with shaggy hair, big hoofs and powerful jaws adapted to feeding on coarse grasses and dwarf plants.

PALEOLITHIC HORSES, of the type in the painting below, are magnificently rendered in two prehistoric carvings from France. The lower one, in ivory, may be part of a spear thrower; the upper was carved from an antler.

THE QUEST
FOR PRIMITIVE MAN

THE whole history of man's evolution, as far as it is known, has been traced in the remains of about 200 skulls and other small collections of bones that have been pieced together at scattered sites in Europe, Asia and Africa. The scientists who have studied these remains are the first to declare that their knowledge of early man is still highly imperfect and incomplete. As anthropologist William Howells points out, it is not easy to become a fossil. Countless hordes of human creatures have lived and died in the last half million years; but only a very few left their bones in limestone caves or in certain kinds of lake beds or gravel where they were impregnated with minerals and achieved a kind of immortality.

The search for these relics, and the interpretation of them, is a young and exciting science. It began in the summer of 1856 when a German schoolteacher, Johann Carl Fuhlrott, who was also an amateur geologist with an interest in fossils, was presented with some "cave bear" bones by quarrymen who had uncovered them in a cave in the Neanderthal valley, near Düsseldorf. Fuhlrott saw at once that among the Neanderthal finds was the top of a manlike skull with protruding bony ridges above the eyeholes, like those of living gorillas. The upper ends of the thighbones, although thicker and heavier than modern man's, were formed in a way which indicates that the creature must have walked upright. Finding among the quarry rubbish some more parts of arms, shoulders and ribs that were strikingly human, Fuhlrott decided that he had discovered a very primitive kind of man who had perhaps been washed into the cave at the time of the Biblical Flood. Leading German scientists disagreed.

In 1859, three years after the Neanderthal discovery, Charles Darwin of England published *The Origin of Species,* and the principle of evolution was on its way to becoming one of the great master keys of science. Opinion about Neanderthal man now swung in the other direction. For years he was considered an intermediate species between *Homo sapiens* and gorillas, or something very much like them. It is now known that this is impossible, for, as Darwin himself declared in 1871, man could not have evolved from the higher apes since all of them have been evolving as long as or longer than man.

The next significant find was in a French cave called Cro-Magnon, near the village of Les Eyzies. Explorations in caves of this sort over several decades had brought to light wall paintings and chipped stone tools which, a very few experts thought, must have been created by extremely ancient men. But no actual remains of such men were discovered until 1868, when Louis Lartet found five almost complete skeletons under deep piles of kitchen rubbish in the Cro-Magnon cave. The Cro-Magnon men had skulls very similar to those of modern Europeans, yet geological evidence showed they could not have been less than 30,000 years old. Other examples were soon uncovered in nearby caves, frequently surrounded by the trappings of deliberate and reverential burial such as shell jewelry and finely wrought tools. And below them, always at deeper levels, were often found the remains of the shorter, beetle-browed Neanderthal man.

WITH BRUSH AND PROBE, anthropologist Louis S. B. Leakey lays bare a fragment of bone in the Olduvai Gorge of Tanganyika. A number of human and prehuman remains have been uncovered in this African river gorge.

Now science had certain proof of two very different kinds of prehistoric man. Popular fancy seized on the notion that the Neanderthals and Cro-Magnons had battled for the mastery of Europe, with the "modern" Cro-Magnons winning out. In fact, it is now believed, the bulk of the Neanderthal population had died out or had been absorbed before the Cro-Magnons became very numerous. Nor is it likely that the Neanderthals were especially "brutish." They had brains as big as those of Cro-Magnon or later people, and are thus classed as full *Homo sapiens.* They made fine tools, lived in family groups and seem to have taken tender care of their toothless aged and of badly injured individuals. They certainly showed remarkable courage and stamina by maintaining themselves in European caves at the height of the fourth glacial period.

Man's third great discovery about himself came in far-off Java. Eugene Dubois, a teen-age student of anatomy in Amsterdam, was inspired by reading Darwin and others to hunt for the "missing link" between apes and man. He obtained an appointment as an army surgeon in the Dutch East Indies, where there were many apes, and began poking around in Sumatran caves. Hearing that a fossilized ape skull had been found in central Java, he transferred his search to that island. In 1891, on the banks of the Solo River, he found exactly what he had hoped for: a brain pan (a skull top with parts of the sides and back) that was too large for any known ape and too small for any living variety of man. Later on, he recovered a

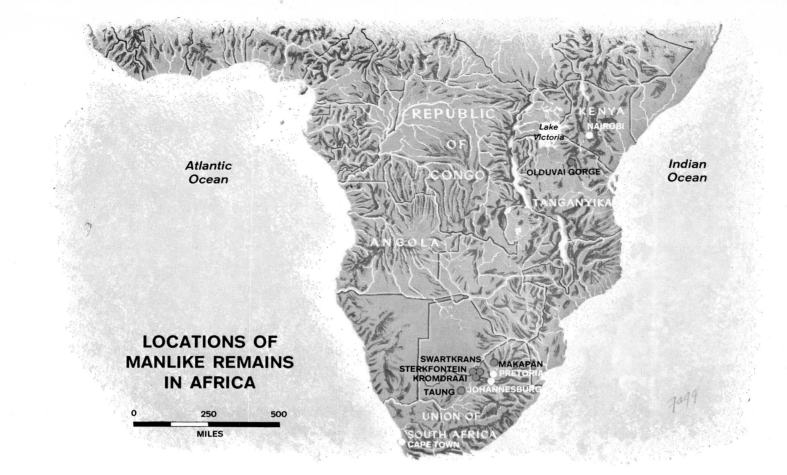

LOCATIONS OF MANLIKE REMAINS IN AFRICA

Atlantic Ocean

Indian Ocean

REPUBLIC OF CONGO

KENYA
NAIROBI
Lake Victoria
OLDUVAI GORGE
TANGANYIKA

ANGOLA

SWARTKRANS
STERKFONTEIN
KROMDRAAI
TAUNG
MAKAPAN
PRETORIA
JOHANNESBURG
UNION OF SOUTH AFRICA
CAPE TOWN

0   250   500
MILES

thighbone at the same place which showed beyond question that the creature had stood upright.

Dubois called his great discovery *Pithecanthropus erectus* (erect ape man). Evolutionists hailed it as an intermediate species which proved the descent of man from apes. But other scientists scorned it. Dubois himself changed his mind completely about the nature of his find. He hid the bones under the floor of his dining room at Haarlem, in the Netherlands, refusing others a chance to examine them, and wrote long articles to prove that his precious "ape man" was only a giant gibbon. Finally, in the 1920s, he allowed the fossils to be stored in the Leyden Museum, in a small safe locked inside a larger one. This left the status of Pithecanthropus very much up in the air. But in the 1930s, paleontologist G. H. R. von Koenigswald turned up parts of three similar skulls at different sites in Java, proving at least that Dubois' find was no isolated freak. By this time geological dating was able to establish the age of "Java man" as at least the middle Pleistocene, or about 500,000 B.C.

In China other experts had become fascinated by the fossilized "dragon teeth" that were sold in apothecary shops to be ground up for medicine. Some of them were undoubtedly human. Tracing the

teeth back to their source in the Choukoutien caves, not far from present-day Peking, they dug out the first skull of "Peking man" in 1929. Others were soon found. At the time of the Japanese invasion of China, fragments of bones and teeth belonging to 40 different prehistoric humans were stored at the Peking Union Medical College. On the very day of Pearl Harbor they were lost forever while being transferred from a railroad car to an American ship in the harbor of Chinwangtao. Fortunately, plaster casts had been made available for study; and in the last 20 years Communist Chinese searchers have found other examples.

Peking man, in the words of Dr. Howells, "is Java man's brainy brother." Both had beetling eyebrow ridges and thick thighbones. Basically, their skeletons were not too different from ours; the great distinction was in brain capacity. In the majority of cases, modern man's brain size ranges from 1,300 cc. to 1,600 cc. Java man had about 775 cc., and Peking man 1,235 cc. For these reasons, some scientists include both Java man and Peking man in the same genus (Homo) as modern man but assign them to a separate species (*Homo erectus*). All types of *Homo erectus* simply ceased to develop, not being versatile enough to overcome environmental difficulties. More recent discoveries such as a Swanscombe skull (1935 in England) and a Steinheim skull (1933 in Germany) suggest that the larger-brained *Homo sapiens* was already essentially developed while *Homo erectus* was still battling for existence.

Today the search for primitive man is centered largely in Africa. At Taung and Sterkkontein in the Transvaal, two South African anthropologists, Raymond Dart and Robert Broom, have recovered skulls and other bones of a remarkable creature with definite human tendencies, which Dart named Australopithecus or "southern ape." It was short—about four feet tall—but walked erect and according to Dart used splintered antelope bones as weapons and tools. Its brain size, smaller than Java man's, was larger in proportion to its size than any living ape's. Australopithecus has tentatively been placed in a separate genus as a "proto-human ape."

At Olduvai Gorge in Tanganyika—between Lake Victoria and Mount Kilimanjaro—Dr. Louis S. B. Leakey of England has been digging in what seems to be the richest store of human and prehuman remains ever discovered. Successive layers suggest for this site a continuous period of habitation extending over hundreds of thousands of years. In 1960 Dr. Leakey found the brain case of a man from the earliest period of hand-ax culture, about 400,000 B.C. Until then this "Chellean" man had been known only by the tools he made. In 1959 the same site produced the 600,000-year-old Zinjanthropus (nutcracker man), who is closely related to Dart's Australopithecus, with tremendously massive jaws and no brow at all. And early in 1961 Dr. Leakey reported the most sensational find of all: a child's skull, along with parts of its hands, one foot, collarbone and jaw, which are "considerably older" than Zinjanthropus, and may prove to be the earliest human bones that have been recovered from the earth.

EXHIBITING A FIND, Dr. Carleton S. Coon, anthropologist of the University of Pennsylvania, second from left above, works in a Syrian cave. This excavation in 1955 unearthed tools and animal bones over 40,000 years old.

IN A SACRED CAVERN in France, some 25,000 years ago, a Cro-Magnon shaman, or priestly practitioner, holds up a Stone Age talisman engraved with animal figures to insure successful hunting, while a group of youths watches with rapt attention. At his feet are two rounded female statuettes, probably meant to symbolize good living. On the walls are paintings of animals and human hands to suggest that man held power over the beasts.

THE DAWN OF RELIGION

Awed by the mysteries of life, man developed a belief in unseen powers and rites to honor the spirit world

MAN, according to one definition, is an animal that prays. His restless, inquiring brain has not been content to believe that his is the highest consciousness on earth or in the mysterious universe. Even during the Old Stone Age, when he was matching his flint-tipped spears against animal claws and fangs, man developed a form of religion, and he believed that his soul was immortal.

Evidence for this can be found today in great limestone caverns in Europe which Upper Paleolithic man converted into shrines. On the walls and ceilings of these caves are paintings of game animals, engraved and colored with surpassing skill and interspersed with symbols suggesting that the inspiration behind the paintings was a mixture of magic and reverence (*opposite*). In the floors of other caves are graves of Old Stone Age dead, interred with obvious ceremony and loving care. The human remains are often accompanied by valuable personal possessions and bones from large joints of meat—placed there, some experts believe, for use in a future world.

These discoveries indicate that man's capacity for faith awoke many thousands of years before the great religions of history. Studies of tribal hunting peoples in our own era show that the struggle for survival in the Stone Age was in itself an experience which promoted religious belief. Primitive man was dependent on the cycles of nature, but he did not understand its laws. As he studied the rising and setting sun or the nightly rotations of the stars, he could only imagine some powerful will behind such mighty phenomena. And he could only tremble in fear and wonder at the sudden disasters of nature—earthquakes, floods and lightning—which threatened his existence.

Ancient man must also have been aware of equally baffling occurrences within himself. What, for example, could he think of sleep? The difference between sleep and consciousness suggested something in him which transcended his body, which could go away and, in dreams, lead a wondrously active life of its own. Finally, there was death, which confronted man with the ultimate mystery. When

an individual died the vital aspects of his body—warmth, breath, movement—all vanished in an instant. Where did they go? Since the flesh disintegrated, the body must be only a temporary abode for the "something" which inhabited it in life.

So in the same way that early man interpreted the actions of nature as the work of supernatural powers, he seems to have concluded that in the body of every creature—animal or man—there existed an unseen agent, or spirit, which governed its behavior in life and moved on to another world at death.

The ability of early man to formulate such beliefs can be partly explained by his unique physiology. The evolutionary expansion of his higher brain centers gave man powers of memory, foresight and calculation far above those of other animals. He could conceive and shape abstract ideas with much of the ingenuity he displayed in inventing tools. Man's superior mental equipment also gave him a conscience—an awareness of his dilemma as an aggressive but reasoning animal, everlastingly torn between his own selfish desires and a sense of responsibility toward others with whom he lived.

The hunters of late Paleolithic times sought to solve this problem by establishing codes of belief and ethics—which were far more primitive than the creeds these codes foreshadowed but which were to evolve much later into religion as we know it today. In the dim cave-sanctuaries of prehistoric men, and also out in the open as at Stonehenge in England (*page 43*), are imposing physical remains which suggest the nature of their myths, taboos and ceremonies. Their leader in such matters was probably a kind of religious practitioner or medicine man who is called a "shaman" by anthropologists. The shaman is found today among most tribal hunting peoples, acting as a priest, healer, psychiatrist, foreteller of the future and teacher. He was the earliest professional man, and his profession laid great responsibility upon him, for it was he who spoke directly to the all-powerful spirits and conveyed their messages and wishes to man.

DEATH OF A HUNTER is depicted in this dramatic mural in the Lascaux cave in France. The wounded bison turns to look at its gushing entrails, but its horns are still directed at the dead man on the ground. The hunter's spear leans against the beast, and a pole surmounted by a bird (probably a totem) is near one of his hands. As usual in prehistoric art, the animal is painted with splendid realism, but the human figure is no more than a caricature.

TALISMAN with grossly exaggerated feminine features was found in Dordogne, France. It is considered to be a hunting symbol, intended to encourage fertility among the animals. The scarcity of game seems to have worried Stone Age hunters, who sometimes painted magic pictures of mating or pregnant animals.

MAGIC OF PICTURES

THE accomplishment of Upper Paleolithic man which is most vivid to us today is his astonishing artistic ability. His magnificent paintings of ice age animals, like the one shown above, have been found in more than 100 caves in France, Spain and Italy, preserved by darkness and constant humidity. Stone Age artists used flint chisels, or burins, to outline their pictures on the walls, ceilings and even the floors of caves. They filled in the outlines with natural pigments of red, yellow, black and brown. The limestone gradually absorbed the colors, and the constant humidity maintained their freshness through tens of thousands of years. Scientists have pointed out that most of these pictures have been found in caves which contain no traces of continuous human occupancy, such as tools or animal bones. They believe therefore that certain sacred caverns were reserved for religious rites in which the animal paintings performed a leading part. Sometimes the paintings depict bleeding wounds—realistically done in red ocher—or they are punctured by actual spear holes, as though men had pretended to kill them. (The same practice has been observed among American Indians.) By creating an image of the animal he was going to hunt, primitive man may have convinced himself that he held a mystic power over the animal's spirit, and thus felt surer of success. In the language of anthropology, this is "sympathetic magic."

The talented artists who created in such glowing perfection pictures of the bison, woolly mammoth and reindeer left few portraits of themselves. It is true that human beings sometimes appear in Upper Paleolithic art, but they are usually in caricature, or disguised by masks or the skins of animals. The reason for this is obvious, according to the anthropologist Johannes Maringer: Stone Age man had a mortal fear of becoming the victim of his own kind of "sympathetic magic."

A CAVERN WALL in Europe is decorated with lively animal portraits by skilled Magdalenian artists about 10,000 B.C. Their purpose, it is believed, was not merely to adorn the cave but to propitiate the spirits of animals and thus assure mastery over them in hunting. For coloring, these experts used mineral oxides and charcoal, with animal fat as a binder. They blew the pigment onto the stone walls through bone tubes, or molded "crayons" with it.

A PUBERTY CEREMONY, marking the emergence of four Stone Age boys into manhood, is shown in this painting. The boys are at the left, being led into the secret inner chamber of a cave sanctuary. All have been tested for courage and have been instructed by the shaman on their adult duties. As they enter, a group of young males performs a frenzied dance under the direction of the shaman, who is at the right, wearing reindeer dress and

RITES AND CEREMONIES

FROM works of art and symbols of worship found in ancient caves, anthropologists have reached some tentative conclusions about the rites of prehistoric man. They believe that his rituals—like those of later hunting tribes—probably fell into two main categories, known technically as "rites of passage" and "rites of intensification." The former celebrated changes in the lives of individuals, such as puberty, marriage and death. The latter sought to deal with community crises —famines, storms and epidemics—by strengthening or "intensifying" man's relations with powerful spirits.

No occasion inspired more elaborate and barbaric ceremonies than the mystery of puberty. For it was at this period of sexual awakening that the young male of the species entered into the high estate of man. To learn discipline and fortitude he was forced to undergo a physical loss, such as circumcision or the amputation of fingers. Only after he had suffered and had been taught the social and sexual responsibilities of the adult could he be initiated into manhood with solemn but joyous ceremony, as depicted in the painting at left.

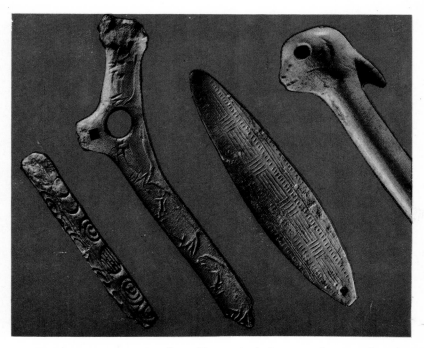

brandishing a wand and baton. The man squatting in the left foreground provides primitive music by whirling a churinga. Kneeling in front of the shaman is a man modeling a bison in clay as a symbol of virility and strength.

DECORATED IMPLEMENTS from France include part of a wand and a pierced baton, probably carried by shamans; a churinga, or magic noisemaker; and an animal-headed spear thrower. They may have been ritual objects.

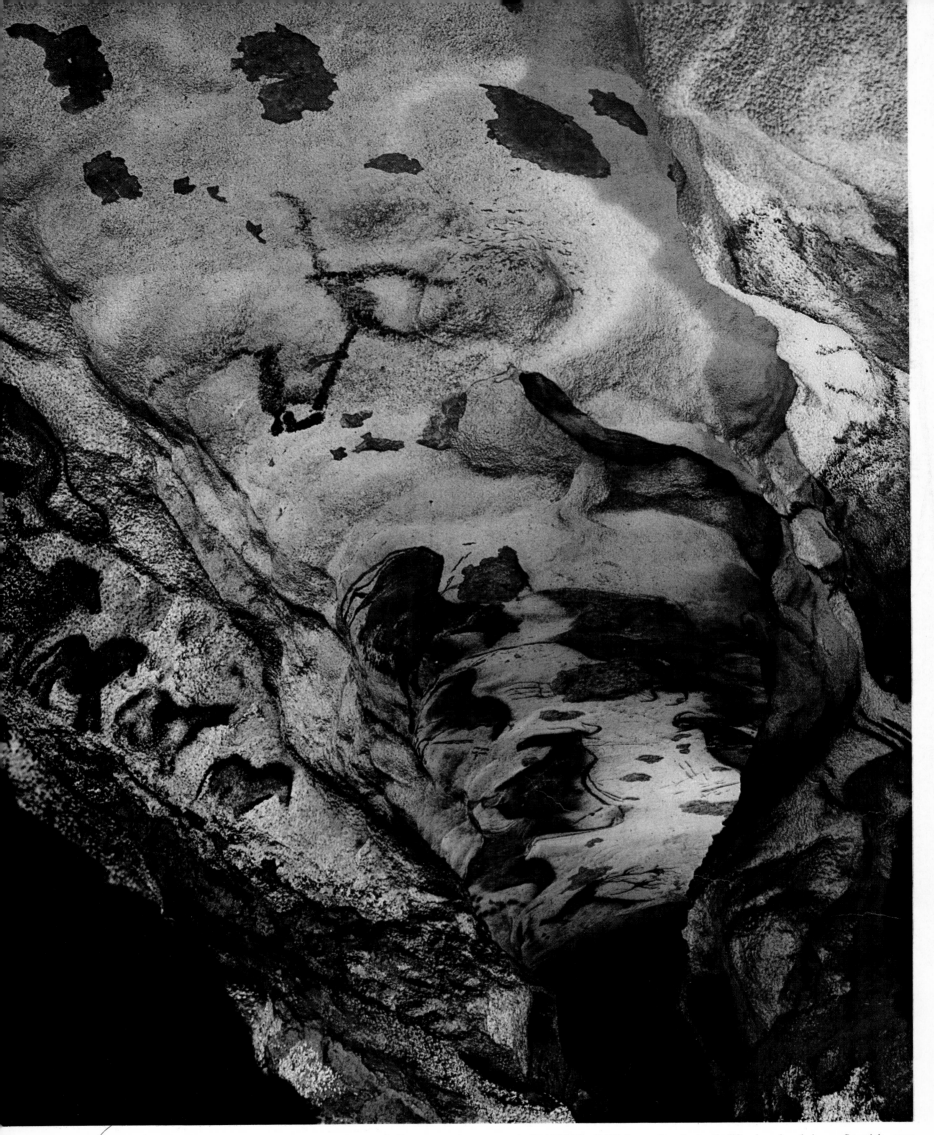

A HUGE HORNED BULL, outlined in black (*upper left*), stares down from the ceiling of the Lascaux cave above a troop of wild horses and other Stone Age game. This was a hunters' sanctuary for thousands of years.

A STARTLED DOE (*opposite, bottom*) lifts her head in a Spanish cave painting. Below her neck is seen a tiny bison. Ice age artists often mixed proportions; the image, not composition, was most important to them.

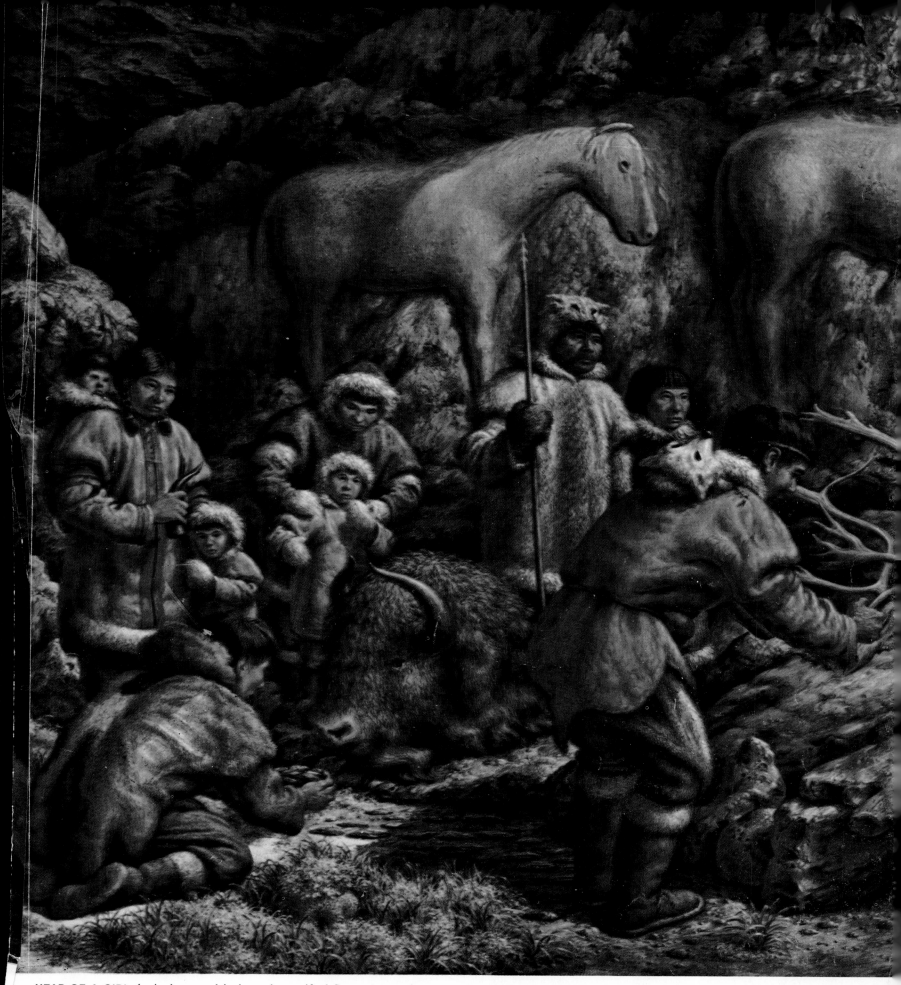

HEAD OF A GIRL, lovingly carved in ivory by a gifted Stone Age sculptor and found at Brassampouy in France, is shown below. It suggested the braided hair style and high cheekbones of the dead girl in the painting above.

A FUNERAL CEREMONY, conducted on a terrace in front of a rock shelter in France some 10,000 to 14,000 years ago, is shown in the painting on these three pages. Two members of a family have died and their local band

MAN AGAINST DEATH

BY far the oldest evidence of man's religious sentiments has to do with his treatment of his dead. Numerous and varied types of burials, beginning with the Mousterian culture, roughly 80,000 years ago, have been discovered in Stone Age caves in Europe, Palestine, the Crimea and Central Asia. These show that the Neanderthal hunters, once regarded because of their skull formations as little better than

FOLD OUT: DO NOT TEAR

the great cave bear had disappeared, but smaller brown bears were included in man's diet. The dancers wear skins and heads of bears in order to achieve a magical power over the spirits of animals. A shaman (*center*) plucks a one-stringed harp, and a hunter (*right*) thrusts his spear at the clay figure of a bear which is wrapped in skin and has a real bear's head. Similar ceremonial slayings of bears still occur among Arctic tribesmen and Japanese Ainus.

made the best kind of cold-weather garment. This animal, now extinct, was the *Ursus spelaeus,* or cave bear, which weighed over 1,000 pounds in maturity and was so prolific in the Austrian Alps that the bones of 50,000 cave bears have been found in a single cave.

The cave bear's unusually long teeth and claws would seem to have made it an extremely dangerous adversary. But its sluggish habits and awkward bulk actually appear to have rendered it an easy prey for man. Scientific studies even suggest that some sophisticated Stone Age men captured cave bears while they were young, filed down their ferocious teeth and confined them in rock pens until they were ready to be eaten. Man's joy at mastering such a useful animal seems to have inspired special religious rites designed to maintain and replenish his supply of cave bears. That at least is the interpretation given to ceremonial displays and burials of cave bear skulls and bones in certain Alpine caves. The niches and slabs of rock where the remains of bears were carefully preserved and arranged are—in the words of the anthropologist Johannes Maringer—"the oldest altars of sacrifice so far known." Even after the cave bear had been exterminated, cults of bear worship persisted and led to such complex observances as the late Stone Age ritual which is pictured above.

A BEAR HUNTERS' RITUAL, intended to improve man's food supply, incites these Stone Age Magdalenian spearmen, decorated with totemic markings, to a wild outburst of emotion. At this time, about 10,000 B.C.,

HUNTING CEREMONIES

AT the beginning of Europe's last glacial period, which extended over 75,000 years, cave-dwelling Paleolithic man was often desperately hungry. Because of the blizzards outside his caves, he was forced to hunt within them. And there, by a stroke of luck which was a turning point in man's career, he found just what he needed—a big, hibernating beast whose meat and fat were delicious and whose pelt

has gathered for the double burial. At left, one of the dead has already been interred under a mound of rocks on which a mourner is placing reindeer antlers. A bison's head—the totem of the clan—is on the ground beside the tomb. At center, the officiating shaman wears a bison mask and skin and holds a bison horn in his hand. At right, the second deceased, a girl, is being arranged in her grave, surrounded by shell ornaments. Her body is

brutes, were capable of tender affection and feelings of reverence. The Neanderthal dead were often buried in an attitude resembling sleep, and Neanderthal graves have been found covered with thin layers of charcoal, as though fires had been lit over them in order to warm the corpse. For protection against hyenas and other scavenging animals the graves were walled around with slabs of rock.

Under the hard conditions of Stone Age existence, most people died young. At least half the Neanderthal population perished in childhood, it is estimated, and less than 5 per cent lived past the age of 40. Skeletons show that arthritis and bone infections were common; doubtless epidemics and exposure were even more frequent causes of death. Among later Paleolithic men—whose total numbers are variously estimated at five to 10 million—only 10 per cent lived beyond 40, but less than one per cent could hope to pass 50.

Lacking any medical knowledge, primitive man turned to his shaman when afflicted with puzzling bodily ills. The shaman sought to placate or exorcise the evil spirits with incantations and magic spells. When death occurred, whole families and groups of families,

tightly bound to prevent her spirit from re-entering it and possibly molesting survivors. Two men brighten her corpse with red ocher, a favorite cosmetic, while another, at far right, brings up a boulder to help cover her grave.

WALL CARVING (*below*) is part of a longer frieze of eight horses on a cavern wall at Le Cap Blanc in France. One of the finest Stone Age animal sculptures, it was the model for the horse decorations in the painting above.

or clans, gathered to mourn and take part in elaborate funeral ceremonies, as shown in the painting above. No one knows what such rites were designed to accomplish. But analogies with living tribes suggest that when Stone Age men tied up a corpse, they wished to make sure that its wandering spirit would not reanimate the body and bring harm to the living. And when they laid in the grave weapons, food, jewelry and lumps of red ocher—the prized pigment which symbolized life in their religious paintings—it would seem that they sought to sustain and please the spirit in its new existence.

MINIATURE CHARIOT holding a pair of bronze disks representing the sun was found in a Danish field. A little more than two feet long and once plated with gold, the object is believed to have been a votive offering or sacrifice to a local sun god about 1400 B.C. This was a period when the late Stone Age tribesmen of northern Europe were just coming under the influence of the metalworking civilizations of the Mediterranean area.

MEMORIALS OF PIETY

TOWARD the end of the Paleolithic age the glaciers receded and the men who survived in Europe emerged from their caves. Before civilization reached them, their religious rites for several thousand years were often conducted in tremendous open-air sanctuaries enclosed by pillars and slabs of rock known as "megaliths"—*i.e.,* great stones. The most famous megalithic center today is Stonehenge in England. But hundreds of similar structures exist in Scandinavia, Ireland, France, Portugal, Spain, Italy and Malta (*right*). At one site in Brittany the sacred enclosure is two and a half miles long and includes 2,935 "menhirs," or upright stones. Perhaps man has never designed more impressive places for worship than these vast outdoor tabernacles with the whole sky for a ceiling and the rays of the rising or setting sun casting shadows among their avenues of stone.

If the original megalithic peoples beautified their temples with paintings or symbols—which might have explained the nature of their ceremonies—the evidence has been destroyed by time. Scholars generally agree, however, that megalithic religion faced two ways: into the grave and toward the sun. The basic form of its architecture—two upright stones topped by a slab—resembles a tomb, and some of the monuments were actually built as tombs. But the gigantic scope of the larger examples suggests they were used for the worship of ancestors, who were beginning to achieve the status of gods.

Students have also noted that rows of megaliths are often arranged to line up with the path of the sun. At Stonehenge (*opposite page*), for example, viewers near the central altar could see a great stone arch that framed the setting sun at the exact moment of its winter solstice—the moment when, according to myth, the sun god dies and is reborn. Other sacred idols and objects indicate that in this transitional period man was at last shedding the traces of his long stay in gloomy caves, and was gladly lifting his eyes toward the sun.

TEMPLE DOORWAY at Mnajdra (*opposite*), on the island of Malta, is flanked by two large "altar" stones. The islanders built these structures without metal tools. They used round stone balls as rollers to move the megaliths.

STONEHENGE SANCTUARY broods over Salisbury Plain in England (*above*), a monument to the religious fervor of prehistoric man. The pillars were shaped at distant quarries and brought to the site on rafts or sledges.

THE GREAT
CAVE DISCOVERIES

ABBE OF THE CAVES, Henri Breuil, 84, has been a leading authority on Paleolithic art. He began exploring caves while still in his teens. He became a priest in 1900 and continued charting sites and interpreting Stone Age art.

THE Upper Paleolithic school of religious, magic-evoking art sprang up roughly 30,000 years ago, flourished for the incredible span of nearly 20,000 years, then vanished from the sight of man for over 10,000 more. Its recent rediscovery, attended both by lucky accident and by bitter controversy, has given the world a wonderful new insight into the minds of western man's ancestors of 300 and more generations ago.

The so-called "portable expressions" of early man's art—small sculptures, crude wands, animal or human figures scratched on ivory, antler and stone—were first dug up or picked up from the floors of European caves around the middle of the 19th Century. Scientists were skeptical about the age of such relics until a momentous find made in 1864 by Edouard Lartet, a tireless French digger. Poking about in the cave of La Magdeleine in the Vézère River valley of southwestern France, Lartet found a fragment of mammoth tusk engraved with the figure of a mammoth. Since the artist had worked on a fresh tusk and not a fossilized one, and obviously had had first-hand knowledge of the glacial-era animal he drew, there could be no doubt that this was a piece of Paleolithic art.

Discoveries of this sort accumulated as the green valley of the Vézère and the nearby Dordogne became the world's richest center for relics of Old Stone Age creativity. (One town in the region, Les Eyzies, is called "the Upper Paleolithic capital of the world.") The fantastic scope of this Stone Age creativity, however, remained unsuspected for years. It was in Spain that the first clue was provided to the vast outpouring of Paleolithic art—paintings and rock engravings—that had been preserved underground in limestone vaults from western Europe to Siberia and down to the Mediterranean. The discovery came about in this fashion:

In the summer of 1879, a well-to-do Cantabrian named Marcelino de Sautuola took his young daughter Maria for a stroll to a cave near his summer place at Altamira. Don Marcelino was an amateur archaeologist and had done some digging near the cave. Its entrance had been found some years before by a hunter whose dog had scrambled into the cave's small aperture, which had been hidden for thousands of years by a rockfall. Now Maria wandered into the cave, noticed strange figures on its ceiling and called out, *"Papa, mira! Toros pintados!"* (Papa, look! Painted bulls!) Her father ran in, looked up at the walls and saw, not bulls, but the vigorous likenesses of great bison painted on the rough rock surface. In other corridors, he found scores of painted or engraved animal silhouettes.

Don Marcelino and the local scholars he called in to share his exciting find were sure that the figures were the work of prehistoric artists. The age and origin of the figures were warmly debated by the scientific world for a time, but few came to see for themselves. One who did, in 1895, was the French prehistorian, Emile Rivière. Amazed and perplexed by what he saw, he went back to his own district of Dordogne for a new search of the caverns there. In one, La Mouthe, whose long-blocked entrance had just been opened, he

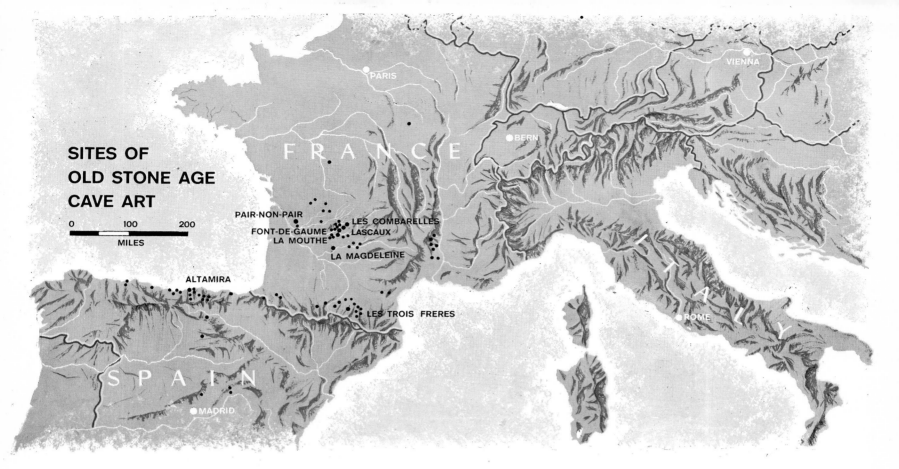

cleared a great corridor of paintings and engravings that had been deeply chiseled in the rock with a flint. Before long, in the neighboring caves of Pair-non-Pair, Les Combarelles and Font-de-Gaume, still more Stone Age engravings and paintings were revealed in the light of archaeologists' torches. By now many men joined in the hunt, including a French priest, Abbé Henri Breuil, who was to spend more than half a century at it, examining some 50 caves and hundreds of rock shelters, and becoming the greatest and best known cataloguer in the field.

The all-important ritual and magic symbolism of cave art in all its forms began to be evident to prehistorians when the caves of Tuc d'Audoubert and Les Trois Frères, in the French department of Ariège, were explored just before the first World War. Count Henri Bégouen, owner of a little estate near which the caves were located, began a systematic search of the meandering grottoes in 1912. With his three sons he made arduous trips underground that led across black rivers, around pools of unknown depth and past stalactites hanging like giant icicles from the ceilings. In some pinched passages the count stuck fast and his sons had to push and pull him through. On one expedition, tired and half inclined to turn back, the three brothers and a friend finally reached the innermost recesses of the Tuc d'Audoubert cave, where their torches picked out engraved representations of bison, wild horses and reindeer. Some of the animals were depicted with arrows and boomerangs flying around them. On another trip, deep in the Trois Frères cave, they found an impressive show of mammoths, woolly rhinoceroses and bison. Nearby was a wounded cave bear, blood streaming from its jaws. Another painting depicted a man dressed in the hide of a beast, playing a flutelike pipe to bewitch two reindeer.

The remoteness of the galleries, reachable only with great physical exertion, could mean just one thing: ancient men could not conceivably have lived in these places, but must have made their way to them only for special religious occasions. Here in the bowels of the earth, by the light of limestone oil lamps, the Stone Age artists certainly had not been creating decoration for self-expression.

And if their work could not have served a merely artistic purpose, it must have served a mystic one, as an essential part of rites directed at insuring man's mastery over the spirits of beasts.

The richest storehouse of this art so far opened up is in the cave of Lascaux, just outside Montignac-sur-Vézère on the road to Les Eyzies. The cave was found on the morning of September 12, 1940, by five teen-age French boys who were out for a day of rabbit hunting on Lascaux hill. Their dog, Robot, dropped from sight down a hole which had been opened up some years before when a storm had uprooted and felled a tall fir tree. Widening the hole with their knives and sticks, the boys squeezed in after the dog. They slid 25 feet down the hole to the floor of an enormous chamber. The light of the matches they struck did not illuminate the chamber fully but revealed, on the walls beside them, the outlines of massive bulls.

Word of their adventure spread through the cave-conscious valleys, where every schoolboy knows the Lower Perigordian from the Aurignacian. In a few days, Abbé Breuil, who was working in the area, came to look. He reported that inside Lascaux hill was "the Versailles of the prehistoric."

THE teenagers had entered the main hall, where Abbé Breuil found an enormous fresco of bulls, the largest about 17 feet long. They were painted in black outline over earlier paintings done in dark red ochre. Among them was a puzzling intruder: the body was that of a rhinoceros, but the head belonged to a pantheolops, or Tibetan antelope. In other galleries the *abbé* noted a dazzling variety of animals, among them more bulls and cows, 60 horses, a lovely frieze of stags' heads, engravings of six feline animals and a splendid pair of dark brown bison, standing tail to tail. At the bottom of a pit in the right-hand gallery was one of the most remarkable and memorable scenes in all Paleolithic art—the wounded bison transfixed with a spear and glaring at a dead or dying hunter— which is reproduced on page 32.

Most of the work of photographing, tracing and classifying the treasures of Lascaux had to await the end of the war, and is still going on. Although it is difficult to date this kind of art—Lascaux reflects the styles and techniques of many artisans who worked over a stretch of thousands of years—it is generally regarded as more spontaneous, dynamic and "primitive"—and therefore earlier in origin—than the skillful and deliberately composed polychromatic art at Altamira and Font-de-Gaume.

Every year more caves are opened, surrendering secrets held for a hundred centuries and more. In 1960 the Italian art historian Paolo Graziosi, recapitulating the first century of Paleolithic rediscovery, listed 97 sites where "stationary" art (etchings, carvings and paintings on cave and rock-shelter walls, and a few clay models standing against walls) had been found. Portable or "mobiliary" art (carvings, etchings and paintings that a man could carry about) had been collected in 110 places. By far the greatest number of both kinds of sites were in France, followed by Spain, Germany and Italy. But outside the Franco-Cantabrian center of their art world, the Stone Age painters and sculptors are known to have worked as far west as England and as far east as Lake Baikal in Siberia. Their output of portable art had been uninterrupted from the Lower Perigordian through the Aurignacian, Solutrean and Magdalenian cultural stages. Their cave painting evidently had been interrupted during the Solutrean in favor of sculpture at the mouths of caves. Then it had resumed, to reach an artistic climax in the latest Magdalenian period in the expertly rendered polychrome figures of Font-de-Gaume and Altamira and the delicate engravings of Les Trois Frères.

Europe in those times was beginning to grow considerably warmer; its whole ecology was shifting; and man was getting ready to emerge from his caves and leave the magic of his cave art behind him.

HARVESTING THE SEA'S BOUNTY, along with the harvesting of wild crops, was one of man's great victories in his fight against hunger. Here early Danes empty salmon from their fish trap, made of birch with rods of sycamore. Their boat is of wood and skins. A row of stakes across the mouth of a stream forces the fish into funneled traps. In the background, clansmen have gathered to welcome a fishing boat returning from the sea.

THE GROWTH OF SOCIETY

In a warm post-glacial Europe, man organized his food supply and started to live in established communities

THROUGH the vast span of the Old Stone Age, man survived three glacial advances that buried much of Europe and Asia under masses of ice. Then, mysteriously, about 20,000 years ago, the glaciers began a slow withdrawal that is still going on today. The landscape began to change—trees took root in the warming earth, the melting ice created lakes and rivers, and men began to abandon their caves to live a more abundant life in the open.

Scientists divide the era that followed the Paleolithic or Old Stone Age and preceded the era of civilization into two cultures: the Mesolithic or Middle Stone Age, and the Neolithic or New Stone Age. The Mesolithic began in Europe about 8000 B.C., later than in Africa and Asia. It was marked by tremendous improvements in man's hunting and food-gathering techniques. The big animals of ice age times were either killed off by the hunters, or traveled north with the ice and became extinct there. But their places were more than filled by the teeming creatures of woods and waters: red deer, wild pig and every kind of fish and fowl.

Mesolithic man had to use cunning to hunt his new, swift prey: it could not be taken by force alone. On land he hunted with bow and arrow, which allowed him to stalk and kill unseen. He studied the migrations of fish, made and baited traps which caught them in quantity, and dried the surplus for future use. He established the first year-round settlements, usually on or near waters with a constant supply of fish and bivalves. He learned, in his successful battle against hunger, to store other foods—seeds, nuts, fruits and berries—which appeared seasonally in certain localities.

In the next period, the Neolithic, he discovered the secret of agriculture in the relationship of seed to plant, and he began to domesticate farm animals. These two achievements were the most decisive in human prehistory. By finally stabilizing his food supply, man won the leisure to engage in religion, politics, wars, business, science and the arts—in short, to create civilization. This fateful moment in the rise of man is known as the Neolithic revolution. "New stone," which is the original meaning of the word "Neolithic," refers to the polished stone implements in use at the time (many modern anthropologists consider the term inadequate but it remains in general use). One result of the revolution was an expansion of the human population. Villages grew up which were firmly based on the daily tasks of farming. Some turned into trading towns, and later some towns became cities. The process of growth was fabulously rapid when viewed in the long perspective of man's existence on earth. Only 3,500 years after Neolithic farmers began sowing seeds and reaping their own harvests, the first urban civilization dawned in the valleys of the Tigris and Euphrates, a region that is often called Mesopotamia.

The Neolithic revolution found some of the answers to man's basic needs. Our food still comes from fields and flocks; our clothes are largely made from the wool and vegetable fibers that Neolithic women learned to spin and weave. We still build houses from Neolithic materials—wood, stone and clay—and our table utensils are mostly pottery, which was a Neolithic invention. We still enjoy wine and beer, which are Neolithic products.

Along with such lasting contributions, the Neolithic period also gave birth to problems that still plague man. By altering his natural environment, by tilling and exploiting the earth's surface and cutting the forests, man set in motion processes of erosion that have wasted the soil and created deserts and wastelands. By confining animals and calling them his own, he awakened the envy of his fellow men who had fewer or none. And even though the land itself was community property in Neolithic times, the farmer's love of land was then instilled in man, and it has created conflicts between nations ever since. In its article on man, the first edition of the Columbia Encyclopedia, published just before World War II, said that "man has not mastered a social organization more ambitious than that of the New Stone Age; his attempts are the subject matter of history."

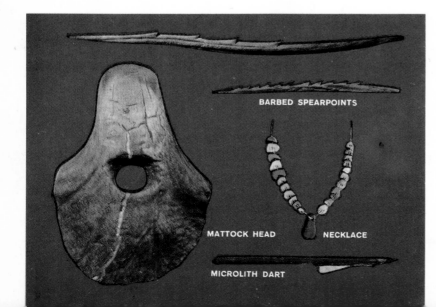

BARBED SPEARPOINTS

MATTOCK HEAD   NECKLACE

MICROLITH DART

A PRIMITIVE FACTORY, set up every autumn beside an English lake, turns out quantities of assorted Mesolithic tools and weapons of flint and horn. This painting of the period around 7500 B.C. shows a craftsman (*far left*)

MESOLITHIC INDUSTRY

AS men spread out across the land, clustering in forest clearings and beside bodies of water, they began to combine their skills in new, cooperative enterprises. To produce the special implements they needed in their changed environment, they used a wide range of materials and employed assembly-line techniques.

The earliest known example of a "factory" designed for large-scale production was uncovered by archaeologist Grahame Clark beneath a drained field at Star Carr, Yorkshire, in England (*painting above*). Here Mesolithic man constructed a stage, 230 yards square,

are then hung out to dry in the wind by the man at left. At the upper left, young women bring reeds from the marsh to repair the thatched roofs of the huts. Inside one of the huts a woman is laying down bark for flooring. In the right foreground, a skilled craftsman fashions a fish net from cords of twisted plant fibers. Near him, dogs wait for scraps of fish, and a boy cracks hazelnuts. In the background, two woodsmen fell trees with hafted stone axes.

tools to make the boats and gear required for successful fishing. Around 6000-5000 B.C., great areas of what are now the Baltic and North Seas consisted of fresh-water estuaries alive with fish in silver shoals and wildfowl overhead. Among these marshes and nearby forests lived a tall, broad-chested people (*painting above*) whose prosperous culture gave rise to waterside communities. Ingenious craftsmen, they perfected some of man's most useful inventions: the fishhook, fish nets and traps, the three-pronged fishing spear or trident, and the feathered fowling arrow to bring down flying game. With their hafted stone axes (*photograph at left*) they built huts of branch and bark, and hollowed out canoes for long journeys at sea. They hunted seals and even whales with harpoons whose barbed and detachable heads were secured to strong lines of vegetable fiber.

With some food to spare, man in this period acquired his first tame animal, the dog (*above*), which had probably skulked and scavenged on the outskirts of Paleolithic encampments but was admitted as a valued partner in Mesolithic society. Subsisting happily on surplus scraps of fish, the dog justified his keep by protecting human settlements at night, by tracking and overtaking game, and by retrieving wounded birds from open water and tangled marshes.

attaching tiny flint barbs to spears with pitch from heated rolls of birch bark. An old woman tends the fire and a girl brings more bark rolls. Another woman (*left*), with a mattock over one shoulder, carries a basket of

mosses used for steaming antlers. In the background, a man strips bark from a tree, on which chunks of venison hang. In the center, two hunters, one wearing his antler camouflage and holding a bow, return with a slain deer

at the shore of a now vanished lake, and on it set up an assembly line for the manufacture of tools and weapons. The platform was built of birch and brush, piled layer upon layer in the marshy ooze and made solid with stones and clay. It was surrounded on three sides by water, where craftsmen could soak the antlers of red deer and moose to soften them for cutting and chiseling. From the antlers they fashioned spear points, daggers, skin scrapers and mattocks, as well as headdresses used for camouflage by hunters stalking deer (*photograph at right*). Here too they manufactured microliths, a Mesolithic invention consisting of small triangular pieces of flint used as barbs on arrows and spears. The implements made at Star Carr reflected man's altered way of life in the temperate post-glacial

climate. In the earliest stage of the Mesolithic, fast-growing woods of birch and willow spread across the plains of Europe and reached to the water's edge. Marsh plants thrived in the brimming lakes, and dense shrubs wove an underbrush.

Man now devised the mattock (*photograph at left*), a blade of antler with a wooden handle, for digging through tangled roots to extract edible bulbs. He used the hafted stone ax and adz for cutting trees and shaping wood. His watercraft included circular coracles, birch-bark and dugout canoes, and rafts. To transport heavy loads on land he invented the sled, and in the winter he hunted on skis. No one knows for certain where and when the bow and arrow originated—perhaps in northern Africa in late Paleolithic times. In the

and a captured fawn. The sight diverts two workmen (*far right*) from their task of making spearheads out of water-softened antlers. In the foreground, a woman and a man unload more antlers from a skin-covered coracle.

Mesolithic they spread throughout Europe, and remained the most efficient hand weapons of man until the perfection of the rifle over 9,000 years later.

The people who worked at Star Carr were probably descended from pure Paleolithic stocks. Their settlement must have included a number of families living in deerskin tents and sharing their tools and food on a communal basis. They were doubtless related by blood, forming what anthropologists call a kinship unit, which obeyed a common leader. Although the growth of society into fixed communities was still in the future, the evidence from Star Carr suggests that even at this early date, men had exchanged some of their wild freedom for the benefits of living in a larger group.

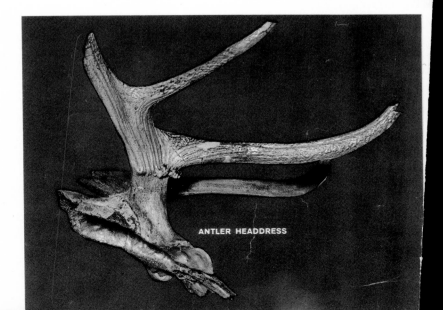

ANTLER HEADDRESS

CARROLL JONES

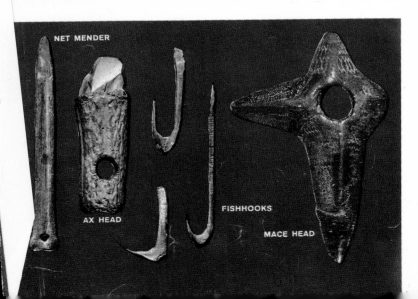

NET MENDER

AX HEAD

FISHHOOKS

MACE HEAD

A MESOLITHIC COMMUNITY near the seacoast of northern Europe prepares food and works with building materials. The time is late summer or early autumn, some 7,000 years ago. In the center, women clean pike, which

FISHING AND FOWLING

FISH was man's first staple food. Even in Mesolithic forests he sometimes could not obtain enough game, but the waters never failed him. Fish, caught in great numbers while swimming in schools or basking in the shoals, could be dried and stored for future use, and surplus supplies, soaked and dried, could be used in trade, thus furthering the exchange of goods and ideas that helped to build society. But none of this was possible until men had acquired efficient

FOLD OUT: DO NOT TEAR

A FLIGHT OF GEESE presents an easy target for Mesolithic bowmen in a northern European marsh. Some of the arrows are tipped with flint; others have blunt wooden heads to stun the birds without mutilating them. The bows are of water-softened ash and the strings of animal sinew. Stone axes and possibly fire were used to hollow the canoes out of single logs. The plentiful wild fowl of the time included ducks, swans, grouse and herons.

POTTERY TRAY shows ridging designed to remove husks from grain. The Neolithic invention of pottery was helpful in agriculture. It provided tight containers for sealing and storing grain and oil over long periods of time.

CLAY SICKLE is one of the implements used by Neolithic farmers. Where flint was plentiful, sickles were often made with blades of flint (*painting opposite*). Whether of fire-baked clay or of flint, sickles were basic to agriculture.

KERNELS OF BARLEY, enlarged in this photograph, are upwards of 8,000 years old. They were carbonized by village fires at Jarmo in northern Iraq. The small branch of the grain at left suggests that it was cultivated barley.

MAN THE PLANTER
AND REAPER OF GRAIN

THE transition from Mesolithic food-collecting to Neolithic husbandry was the longest step toward a stable society mankind had ever taken. Its beginnings are not recorded in history, for man had not yet learned to write. But there is reason to believe that the two decisive developments—the cultivation of plants and the domestication of animals—occurred first in the Old World, somewhere among the low, sun-drenched hills that stretch eastward from Asia Minor through northern Iraq and Iran toward the steppes of southern Asia. The best evidence suggests that man began farming between 6000 and 7000 B.C., and efforts to determine a more exact date are now being made by the carbon 14 process. Agriculture began to change the face of Europe before 3000 B.C. and was soon discovered in America. It also arose independently in the rice lands of the Far East.

It was certainly no coincidence that man first converted his sweat into bread in the same general region which, it is said, sheltered the Biblical Garden of Eden. The climate of this part of the world in the early Neolithic was warm and dry, as it is today. But the landscape was more verdant. As yet unravaged by man, it rolled toward the mountains and seas, an open, fertile parkland studded with trees and natural meadows of wild wheat and barley. Here was an ideal amphitheater for the agricultural revolution. The basic crops were present in the wild state, and so were the basic animals—sheep, goats, cattle and pigs. There were no dense woods to clear away. The rainfall was adequate for grain.

The actual methods by which plants and animals were deliberately made to serve human needs can be stated only in terms of conjecture. It seems likely that woman was the real pioneer. Among hunting peoples today, womenfolk gather the foods—fruits, nuts, roots and seeds—which supplement their diet of game. Even in Paleolithic times, women had learned to remove the hulls and soften the kernels of wild cereals by pounding them in mortar-shaped stones. This was the earliest form of milling. Some anthropologists suggest that before true farming began, stone knives were used to cut away useless growth which interfered with the grains. This was the start of cultivation.

Perhaps the greatest discovery of all was made in a Neolithic garbage pile. Discarded seeds would sprout luxuriantly when thrown among other vegetable remains, which acted as fertilizers. Next came the experiment of dropping or sowing seeds in the soil, and watching to see what the next season brought forth. In time, rough fields of grain, sprinkled with weeds and wildflowers, as depicted in the painting on the opposite page, wove patterns of plenty across the Middle Eastern highlands.

Into these man-made meadows wandered herds of grazing animals, accustomed for centuries to foraging there. From time to time an infant lamb or kid was captured and brought to the village as a playmate for children. Certain zoologists believe that the keeping of pets was the initial stage in domesticating sociable animals like sheep and goats, and that women, with their maternal instincts, protected the first tiny prisoners and probably nursed them to maturity. How the bigger and stronger beasts—cattle, camels and horses—were reconciled to captivity is still an enigma.

After man had mastered the basic secret of agriculture, it spread swiftly. Its most famous ancient testing ground was the region known as the Fertile Crescent, bending north from Egypt through Palestine and Syria and turning south again through the valley of the Tigris and Euphrates. Much of this is desert today, but its virgin Neolithic soil was wonderfully productive. Here man may have tended his first orchards of dates, figs and olives. Here he probably began to cultivate the grape for wine and brew beer from grains. The selective breeding of plants and seeds, and their transformation into better varieties, also began in this period. No people has ever flourished mightily without abundant sources of grain. "Civilization," says historian Morris de Camp Crawford, "is, as it were, a second flowering of barley, wheat, rice and Indian corn." Evidence points to the northern fringes of the Fertile Crescent as the place where emmer, a wild small-kerneled wheat with a thick hull and a spiky "beard," was developed into the superior types that still give us white flour and bread, and that would not exist without the intervention of man. From Iran the improved "bread wheats" spread into Europe. Because barley produces more bushels per acre than wheat and will grow on poorer land, it became the cheap staple food for the first urban warehouses.

PRODUCING THEIR OWN FOOD, a Neolithic man and woman glean wheat and barley on a spring morning in Mesopotamia about 5000 B.C. Equipped only with crude sickles, Neolithic farmers cut their primitive grain high on the stalk, avoiding the scattering of the loosely attached seed. The tall grain in this painting is wild barley, the shorter stalks are domesticated wheat and barley. In the background stand the mud houses of the permanent village.

NEOLITHIC CATTLE DRIVE is recorded above in a 6,000-year-old painting discovered on a surface of rock deep in the Sahara desert. This was a fertile region in prehistoric times. Herdsmen surround the animals, which belong to two species; one, with outspread lyre-shaped horns, suggests the Texas long-horn. The artist has vividly reproduced the loping gait of the cattle, the agile movements of the herders and the stiff body of a slaughtered ox (*upper right*).

TAMING WILD BEASTS

NO one knows how the formidable auroch—the wild, horned ancestor of modern cattle—was tamed by Neolithic man. Some experts suggest that the beasts grew fat on the stubble of early grain plots and discarded husks, and thus became increasingly dependent on man's farming activity. Others believe that stock herding arose from hunting, and especially from the capture of young animals, which were driven off to rock-enclosed valleys or desert oases where escape was impossible. However this may be, Neolithic societies usually consisted of "mixed" farmers who grew grain and also had domestic animals. The specialization by which whole tribes became herdsmen, giving rise to powerful nomadic nations, occurred much later.

The animals tamed by the first farmers (*painting above*) provided a constant meat supply that largely replenished itself. But the animals also enlarged human economy in a great many other ways. By selective breeding, the wild cow was converted into a docile dairy. Sheep and goats, whose fleece gradually improved during captivity, provided clothing materials. Animal dung was always a valuable fertilizer. And at a time when all land was still community property, the wealth of an individual was measured by his herds and flocks.

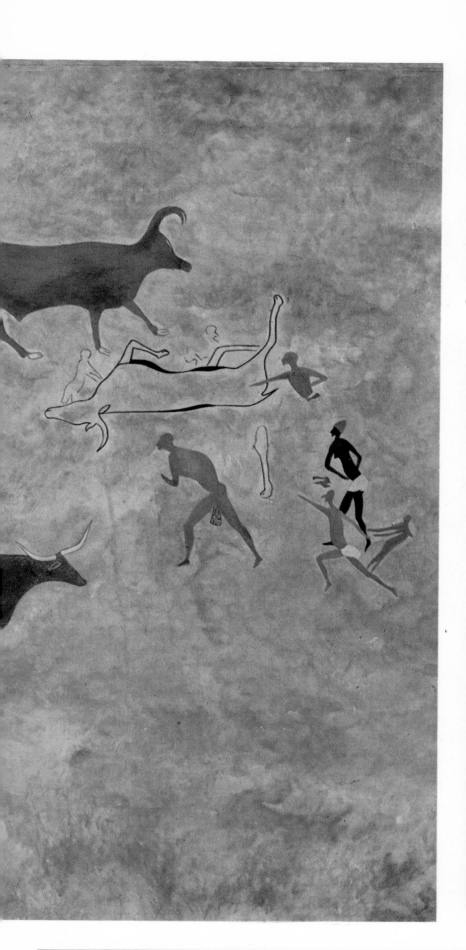

SEATED WOMAN figure with "bun" hairdo and the lines of a traditional mother goddess comes from Hacilar, a Neolithic town site in Turkey.

A SKULL with clay overlay to form a human likeness (*below*) is from Jericho, where evidences of early farming and domestication were found.

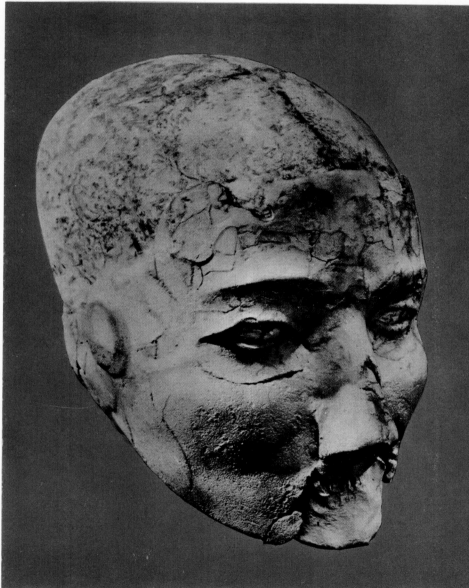

FIGURINES in unbaked clay (*left*), from Jarmo, a Neolithic village in Iraq, are either religious symbols or toys. An English critic once described them as "curiously resembling a pack of Thurber's dogs at full cry."

FRAGMENT OF A NEOLITHIC JAR is decorated with a woman's face (*below*) which has short black tribal markings on both cheeks. Similar markings, probably considered a beauty aid, may be seen in the painting above.

NEOLITHIC VILLAGERS busy themselves in front of pressed-mud houses somewhere in Mesopotamia about 4500 B.C. At the left, under a shelter hung with bladders of cheese, a woman chastises squabbling children,

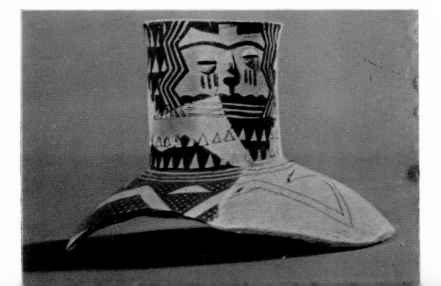

THE FIRST VILLAGES

MOST men are born with an urge to wander, a feeling that dates from Paleolithic times. But most men are also endowed with a feeling for home, an allegiance to a spot of earth. These sentiments are an inheritance from Neolithic society, the first to afford the luxury of permanent habitations. From the steady habits of farming and stock raising, and the security of surplus food, there evolved in early Neolithic times an enduring social invention: the village, which was simply a cluster of houses within walking distance of fields and pastures. The architecture of the Neolithic villages varied according to local

yoked oxen pull a plow—a Neolithic invention—along a rich strip of soil watered by an irrigation ditch. At the river's edge, traders unloading a sailboat begin to transport their goods to town on sledges drawn by cattle. The

town itself—based on the actual plan of Eridu in Iraq—stands on high ground (*left background*). Once a farming village itself, the town has become a market center for surrounding villages and boasts a population of about

above depicts such a town about 4000 B.C. It is based on findings at Eridu, in southern Iraq, where archaeologists have uncovered layers of continuous habitation, rising from village to town to a Sumerian city—a remarkably full archaeological profile of man's progression from farming to urban civilization.

Perhaps it was because of the challenge he faced that man made rapid advances in this last phase of his prehistory. To protect his new fields from inundation and drought, he devised the first systems of flood control and irrigation. Since the rivers annually deposited silt along their banks, which built up into natural dikes or levees, it is believed that Neolithic engineers reinforced these bulwarks by

adding soil at the most exposed places. In times of drought, they pierced the dikes and dug ditches to carry water to crops. Thus the men of late Neolithic times added stronger strands to the tightening web of human society. Engineering enterprises required the work of many hands and the planning of many brains. One village could not fight floods alone, nor water its own fields exclusively. The welfare of each village along the banks was linked to that of its neighbors; villages began to make alliances, and to form the prototypes of nations.

To the needs of his complex society, Neolithic man responded with fresh outbursts of creativity. He invented the plow, and thus began the mechanization of agriculture. He trained cattle to pull plows and

another grinds flour in a mortar stone, a third (*with bracelets*) spins wool, and a fourth (*in wool headdress*) molds a pottery jar. In the center background a girl feeds gruel to a crouching old man, one woman plucks wool from a sheep and an older woman milks a goat. A gray-bearded elder with the look of a patriarch surveys the scene. In the foreground a baby is being suckled and two boys are having a tug of war over a leather sling. The men

conditions. In the open landscape of Mesopotamia—as shown in the painting above—the first houses were made of pressed mud, hardened under the blazing sun, and roofed with loose branches and a thin layer of clay which allowed the air to circulate. In forested Europe, where the Neolithic age was reached much later, tight houses were built around a framework of poles that was filled in with wattle and daub (a woven mixture of wooden rods and clay) and topped by a peaked roof that would shed the rain and snow. In Russia and central Asia, village houses were—and still are—constructed of turf and woven grass. The economic advances made possible by the Neolithic village quickly resulted in a higher standard of living. The new prosperity swelled the population and prolonged the average span

of life. As hunters, few human beings could have lived beyond the age of 40. Now much older men and women survived and were useful to the community, performing such sedentary tasks as milking and weaving, and nourished by the soft, boiled foods which were made possible by pottery. Children in Paleolithic times had been only extra mouths to feed—now they could tend to animals and do light farming chores. And the women, of course, found their work never-ending as they milled grain, baked bread and fashioned their own household utensils of pottery.

Because farmers are deeply concerned with the weather, the village rain priests and wind priests, rather than hunting shamans, began to dominate religious practice. Each village was likely to have its

and dogs at the right have just returned from a hunting trip with an antelope. At the extreme right a woman prepares a round loaf of bread for baking in an oven shaped like a beehive. Cattle graze in the nearby fields.

FERTILITY FIGURES, torsos in baked pottery (*below*) have realisti[c] tribal markings on breasts and thighs. Only three inches high, they we[re] found at Tepe Gawra, site of a middle Neolithic town in northern Ira[q.]

own local spirit or god, who was expected to aid the inhabitants in times of adversity or war. Happily, the Neolithic way of life appears to have been conducive to peace. Village dwellers not only cooperated with each other, but villages cooperated with other villages. Trade seems to have proceeded smoothly between those who had extra wheat, for example, and those who had building clay to spare. There is archaeological evidence to show that some Neolithic villages existed for centuries, fulfilling the needs of their settled folk and accumulating primitive wealth without suffering the destruction of war. This is not to say that Neolithic villages were ever entirely self-sufficient, or free from the aggressive passions of man. But perhaps they came closer to that ideal than any later community.

[SK]IRTS OF A NEOLITHIC TOWN begin to stir with morning activity [as the sun ri]ses over the Euphrates River on a clear autumn day some 6,000 [years ago. In] the foreground, workmen are putting the final touches on a sailboat, calking it with asphalt and lashing its gunwales with reeds. At left, a woman cuts rushes for thatch and floor matting while a man who has climbed a palm tree drops fronds for fuel to his wife below. In the center,

[B]URGEONING TOWN

[A]fter he invented agriculture, Neolithic man contin-[ued to] prosper in the pleasant highland villages of Meso-[potamia. Beca]use of population pressures and other reasons, he [be]gan to colonize the plains of the Tigris and [Euphrates. It m]ay have been the date palm that attracted him [to the gr]eater fertility of the alluvial soil built up by [the rivers. In his n]ew environment, man confronted alarming [problems. The Eu]phrates plain presented, as it does even today, a combination of land so dry that nothing would grow on it without irrigation and land so wet that it could not be tilled without considerable drainage. Each year the rivers were given to unpredictable flooding, alternating with drought and scorching heat. Altogether, the region was one of the hottest, most unfriendly and most unreliable places on earth. It also turned out to be the "cradle of civilization."

The fact that man solved these difficulties—and even turned them to his advantage—is one of the great triumphs of human courage and ingenuity. For it was in this setting that the early Neolithic village became the late Neolithic town, precursor of the city. The painting

A MODEL SAILBOAT, perhaps a child's toy, is an exact replica of a real Neolithic sailboat. It is 10 inches long, with a socket for a mast and sail. It was found at Eridu, the town re-created in the painting on these pages.

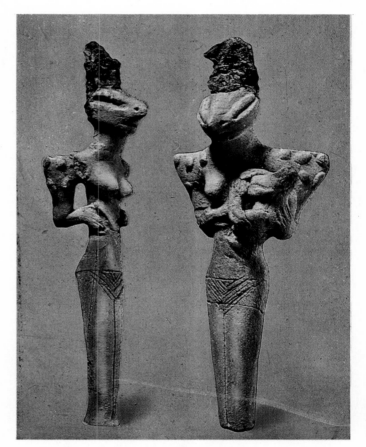

COIFFURED WOMEN are of the late Neolithic. Although the faces appear to be religious masks, the clay bodies are modeled with much more realism than earlier caricatures of females.

2,000. Although it has some seemingly pretentious houses of brick, most are simple arched structures of reeds and clay, open at both ends to give maximum ventilation. Dominating one end of the town is a lofty temple.

sledges, inaugurating a revolution in power. He probably invented the sailboat, turning the broad rivers into highways. With better means of transport came a great surge of commerce and trade. Soon the banks of the Euphrates and Tigris were dotted with towns where farmers and herdsmen bartered with each other, and exchanged their produce for foreign wealth: lapis lazuli from Persia, alabaster from Egypt, shell jewelry from the Red Sea.

As civilization drew near, the town builders completed its necessary foundations: settled communities where human beings could work in organized security, and improved transport and communication that extended the range of their interests throughout their world.

ARTISTIC VASE from Tepe Gawra, Iraq, whose bowl-shaped surface is decorated with one of the earliest known landscape paintings, shows mountains, domestic animals and a river that is believed to be the Euphrates.

63

UNCOVERING
THE NEOLITHIC

THE agricultural revolution brought about by early Neolithic men and women stands as the most important event in the early history of man. Until cereal plants and animals were domesticated around 10,000 years ago, civilization was impossible; afterward the growth of society was inevitable. It follows that no field of inquiry is more absorbing to many archaeologists than the agricultural revolution. Each year, at widely scattered sites, teams of diggers unearth, interpret and compare notes on new evidence that bears significantly on the story.

All this intense scientific interest is fairly new. For a number of reasons, most of the prime Neolithic sites of the Middle East were unexplored until recent years. The Neolithic villagers left behind

COPYING PAINTINGS, artists reproduce work executed on rock shelters by Sahara herdsmen of 4000 B.C., before the region became a desert. The site of the art is at Tassili-n-Ajjer, a plateau 900 miles south of Algiers.

them no pyramid tombs or colossal temples; they left nothing more than mounds of rubble. Hundreds of these mounds, called *tells* in Arabic-speaking areas, dotted the landscape of the Fertile Crescent, undisturbed for the most part by all the civilizations that later thrived and died in the region.

The most intense and systematic investigations of the Neolithic began after the Second World War. There had been much theorizing about the areas where tiny human communities might have crossed the threshold from food collecting to food producing, but there had been little planned digging. One place to look for signs of the first such transition was on the hilly flanks of the Fertile Crescent. There, wild wheat and barley—and wild sheep, goats and cattle—were to be found together in a single environment.

STARTING in 1948, Robert J. Braidwood of the University of Chicago led a number of expeditions into the hills of Kurdistan in Iraq and Iran. The parties included geologists, botanists and zoologists. Over several seasons at Jarmo, in the grassy uplands of northern Iraq, they uncovered a year-round settlement of about 25 mud-walled houses. It was a typical *tell* in that its inhabitants, never more than 150, kept rebuilding right on top of the crumbled huts of their ancestors; this had created about a dozen distinct levels of occupancy over a period of perhaps 300 years. The site yielded carbonized grains of two types of domestic wheat as well as wild and cultivated barley. The villagers evidently had domesticated goats, dogs and possibly sheep, but they still hunted wild animals and collected nuts, acorns and other wild foods. Since they had not yet learned to make pottery, they used stone vessels and chipped flint tools (including sickle blades). The later occupants began to make pottery and left small clay figurines of animals and goddesses.

In 1959 the Chicagoans began exploring new sites 120 miles to the southeast, near Kermanshah in Iran. At the small mound of Tepe Sarab they found more advanced pottery than at Jarmo, but no mud-walled houses; the people had lived in shallow pits. Both at Jarmo and at the Kermanshah sites, the searchers found signs of commerce with other prehistoric areas. There were decorative shells from the Persian Gulf and tools made of obsidian, a volcanic glass, the nearest source for which was hundreds of miles away in what is now Turkey. The dates of these settlements Braidwood estimated by carbon 14 tests at around 8,000 years ago.

Since 1952, teams led by Kathleen M. Kenyon, director of the British School of Archaeology in Jerusalem, have been digging into the huge *tell* of ancient Jericho. Nineteen levels down, at bedrock, their trenches exposed a remarkable Neolithic town. Its residents were estimated at 3,000. Not yet having learned how to bake pottery, like the early citizens of Jarmo they used polished limestone dishes and bowls. Their houses were well planned and roomy, some opening on courtyards, and the floors and walls were surfaced with a highly burnished plaster. Grain was one of their staple foods; they cut it with

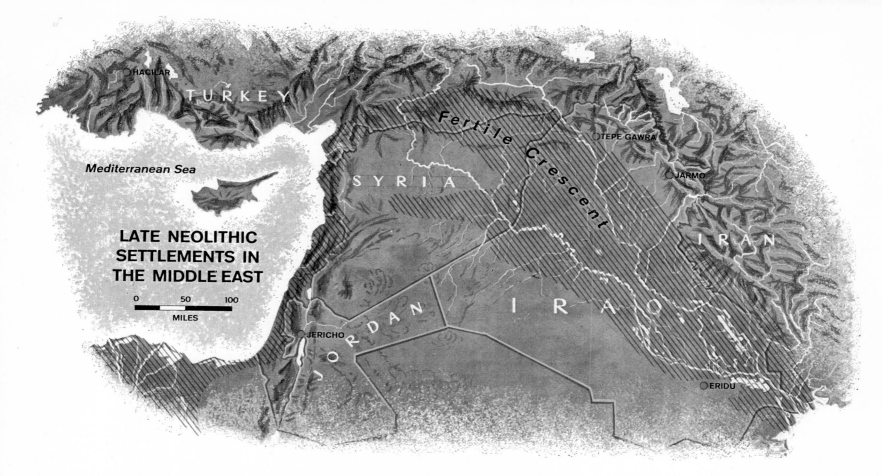

LATE NEOLITHIC
SETTLEMENTS IN
THE MIDDLE EAST

0   50   100
MILES

Mediterranean Sea

fine-edged sickle blades which acquired a high gloss from the silica in the grain stalks. They knew about irrigation, engaged in trade, supported various kinds of artisans, and they fortified Jericho—several millenniums before the building of the walls that were to fall to Joshua—with sturdy ramparts and a tower 25 feet thick. They apparently had accomplished the Neolithic revolution, and gone on to well-established urban life, at about 8000 to 7000 B.C.

Perhaps the most surprising Neolithic finds of all have been made at an unlikely spot well to the northwest of the Fertile Crescent. In 1956 at Hacilar, on the Anatolian plateau of southwestern Turkey, British archaeologist James Mellaart was shown a mound where enterprising peasants were busily digging up painted pots for sale in the Istanbul Bazaar. The next year Mellaart took an expedition from the British Institute of Archaeology at Ankara to the site, and digging has gone on ever since. Twenty building levels have been reached. The early Neolithic people who lived on the lowest of these had no pottery, but carefully made hearths, ovens and clay bins indicate that they already practiced farming. Like the pre-pottery people of Jericho, they had what appears to have been an ancestor cult involving the veneration of skulls, as shown on page 57.

Late Neolithic people, who had apparently come to Hacilar from somewhere else, built very well on top of the housing rubble left by their predecessors. Piecing together the evidence, archaeologists have determined that the houses had windows and double doors, three-foot-thick walls, and in some cases a second story reached by a stone staircase. The housewives wore jewelry and rouge, and the men played a game like jacks—using the knucklebones of cattle—that is still played in Turkey today. One building was a potter's workshop that turned out beautifully painted jars and bowls.

Mellaart's most astonishing artistic find was a group of clay statuettes of the "mother goddess" like the one reproduced on page 57, which showed her at various ages and in different postures. While parts of her anatomy were exaggerated, all the statuettes were carved in a naturalistic fashion that was highly sophisticated for the time.

But the real importance of Hacilar is that the digging there upset some favorite theories about the Neolithic. Until the 1950s it was assumed that Anatolia had not been settled until about 3000 B.C. Mellaart estimated that Hacilar's early Neolithic levels went back to about 7500 B.C.—and he found much evidence that the site was contemporary with pre-pottery levels both at Jarmo and at Jericho.

The problem of dating Neolithic finds has been a frustrating one for the diggers. Until a decade ago, they depended on systems of identifying pottery sequences and upon meticulous study of stratification and the composition of the soil around each object found. Then the method known as carbon 14 dating became available. It is based on the fact that every living thing, plant or animal, absorbs radioactivity throughout its life, and at death starts to lose it at a constant, measurable rate. The amount of carbon 14 it retains at any later time, as measured by Geiger counters, thus indicates its age

—as old as 30,000 years—plus or minus a margin for deviation. The difficulty with it is that such testable archaeological samples as charcoal and charred bones are not always "pure," as carbon 14 from two or more sources may be disintegrating in them. As a result the spread of dates in many Neolithic sites is so great that the best age estimates are still open to question.

A vast amount of digging and dating must be done before the time spread of the Neolithic becomes more exact, but the pattern of the agricultural revolution is becoming increasingly clear. Once it succeeded in the Middle East, its lessons spread up into Europe and down into Africa. It occurred spontaneously, much later, in Asia and the Americas, and elsewhere by cultural diffusion or by borrowing.

THE WALLS OF JERICHO are exposed by a shaft sunk at a corner of the 70-foot-deep mound covering what scholars believe is one of the world's oldest towns. The lowest layer reached here dates back to about 6000 B.C.

A MILITARY CHARIOT, carrying a driver and a soldier supporting a wounded man, lumbers past prisoners of war toward the gates of a Sumerian city. The yoked animals are onagers, a kind of Asiatic wild ass. The wheels, a Sumerian invention, are bound with leather tires and fixed rigidly to the axles. A later development was more efficient wheels that turned freely on the axle. In the distance at right a second city rises above green irrigated fields.

4

THE COMING OF CIVILIZATION

In the cities of ancient Sumer, man first learned to write, use metals, make war and to think about his role on earth

SOME 5,000 years ago, in a desert plain scorched by the sun and nourished by two great rivers, the long progression described in the previous chapters brought man at last to the stage of development that we call civilization. The huge span of time called prehistory had ended. History now began.

What is history and what is civilization? The essential element in history is writing, from which the thoughts and events of the past may be read rather than merely deduced from archaeological relics. Civilization is much harder to define. It did not burst upon the world, as is widely supposed, in a sudden and miraculous surge upward from savagery and barbarism, from darkness into light. Instead it evolved naturally and gradually from the life, means and skills of the settled communities described in the previous chapter. Among the components of a civilized society are: the pursuit of knowledge and the arts, a high level of political organization, a complex social and economic order, true specialization in crafts and skills, and submission of the individual to the impersonal requirements of the state. Usually but not invariably, the ability to write and thus to record and convey information is an ingredient. Most if not all of these elements depend upon the margin of security and leisure that comes only with the evolution of the village into the town and the town into the city. "The transition to civilization," Professor Thorkild Jacobsen has observed, "appears thus not as a break. Rather it is a quickening of the pulse, a fever almost, of cultural creativity. In that feverish crisis a style comes into being, a characteristic, new, total design for living."

Man's creative fever first struck in the area loosely known as the Middle East. Here, without question, the spark of civilization was kindled. Within the thousand years between 3500 and 2500 B.C., the first true cities on earth grew along and near the fertile banks of the Tigris and Euphrates Rivers, in the valley of the River Nile and on the flood plain of the Indus River. Of these primary centers of civilization, the earliest by several centuries were the cities along the Tigris and Euphrates. These were the cities of Sumer, the Old Testament's "land of Shinar." It lay at the head of the Persian Gulf in the southern portion of what used to be known as Mesopotamia and is now a part of Iraq.

A formative period, from 4500 to 2900 B.C., witnessed the great transition from simpler societies to civilization. Then came the full flowering of Sumer's civilization during the Early Dynastic period, down to 2400 B.C., and finally its gradual extinction in a tumultuous period of wars, expansion and decline, followed by a brief revival before the end. From the standpoint of science and invention, the formative period was one of the most fruitful phases of human history prior to the age of Galileo and Newton. Out of it came the wheel, the first use of metal in quantity and the world's first known writing. From this followed arithmetic and geometry, the idea of money, an unprecedented abundance of representational art and a monumental architecture.

At the beginning of the Early Dynastic period, Sumer was a land of separate, self-sufficient and politically autonomous city-states: holy Nippur, wealthy Ur, prideful Lagash and many others, including Uruk, Khafajah and Kish. At each site a walled and fortified city, dominated by one or more monumental temples, rose high above the flat plain and the irrigated farmlands which supplied the cities. Conflicts over land and water rights arose between city-states, and Sumer thus initiated full-scale war along with other attributes of civilization. Warfare led to the discovery that man could be domesticated—i.e., slavery. Despite its evils, war vastly stimulated man's technology. Early metallurgy, for instance, grew largely out of the demand for weapons, and the war chariot furthered the perfection of the wheel. Within Sumer's fortified and warring cities, nourished by urban life, man developed the prime elements of human culture: science and art, and the exercise of reflective thought.

THE TEMPLE OVAL at Khafajah looms above the surrounding city. The outer wall defines the sacred area, two acres in all. The inner wall encloses the temple proper, whose highest point stands about 40 feet above the city streets.

CITY AND TEMPLE

THE temples of Sumer rose above the flat plain, climbing tier on tier to the sanctuaries that crowned their parapets. As centuries passed, their walls grew ever higher, culminating at last in the colossal neo-Babylonian ziggurat of Nebuchadnezzar, the Biblical Tower of Babel. Some scholars have seen in the soaring architecture of the Sumerians a desire to worship their gods in "high places." To these city dwellers, in their unrelieved landscape, mountains represented the concentrated strength of the earth, the source of rain, the home of the dead and the active theater of the world's supernatural powers. In their high temples the Sumerians perhaps felt they could best communicate with their gods. And it was crucial to communicate with them, for the Sumerians believed that man was created to serve the gods and remained dependent on them always. The gods were not always benign deities, but capricious and often terrible. Sumerian civilization was characterized by a deep sense of man's helplessness in a cosmos governed by unpredictable forces. "Mere man—his days are numbered," reads a Sumerian poem, "whatever he may do, he is but wind." Their insecurity stemmed from the violence of their environment. Sumerian literature is filled with verses like this:

> The rampant flood which no man can oppose,
> Which shakes the heavens and causes earth to tremble . . .
> And drowns the harvest in its time of ripeness.

In Egypt, by contrast, a kinder environment produced a civilization noted for its unity and serene stability.

Since the welfare of the Sumerian city depended utterly on the good will of the gods, the temples played a vital role in city life. Over and above their religious function (*right*), they also served as focal centers for the city's social and economic activity. Because the gods were believed to own the cities and claim all the inhabitants as their chattels, the temples were regarded as the earthly homes of the deities to whom they were consecrated. Within them there were workshops for bakers, brewers, weavers, smiths and clerks. There was also a home for the high priest who administered the community in behalf of the city god. The temple superintended the network of irrigation canals which sustained the life of the city. It also owned a large proportion of the outlying fields, which were tilled and harvested for the god by all healthy adults. For this labor the temple provided equipment, and in return distributed surplus products to the population on feast days and in times of famine.

But there was still considerable scope for individual initiative. Part of the land was privately owned, and part could be rented. Everyday civic affairs were originally settled by a general assembly and a council of elders. In time of war or other emergency, an individual could be elected to temporary kingship, an institution which gradually became permanent. But in essence the Sumerian city was the private estate of its god. Religious and secular life, temple and city, were indivisible.

A PROCESSION OF PRIESTS is watched by a gathering of Sumerians in the courtyard of the Temple Oval on a bright spring morning. Approaching the steep stairs to the sanctuary, the priests, customarily naked in such

ceremonies, bear gifts of food and drink for Inanna, the goddess of love and war, whose symbolic marriage to the lord of the city is re-enacted annually to mark the new year. In this painting the procession is headed by a single priest, followed by the ruler of the city, garbed in a long red robe. At the top of the stairs (*center*), before the entrance to the inner shrine, a temple priestess represents Inanna, while the ruler of the city acts out the role of Dumuzi, her

foreground, a workman bringing in a bundle of finished spears passes three seated metalworkers. One metalworker is removing bronze spearheads from a clay mold, the second is opening a mold to remove a bronze axhead and

a third is enchasing a design on a silver vessel. The group in right foreground transacts a sale of copper and silver ingots. A temple aide holds a balance; another adds stone weights to the weighing pan at left while a young trader

hammered or cast into useful shapes. Then came the far more important discovery that tin and copper fused together produced a tough, hard alloy—bronze. The Sumerians imported both the metals and the techniques of working them from the mountain regions of Turkey and Iran. But it was in Sumer that the techniques were first perfected and made the basis of a great business in metallurgy.

The growth of technology had profound effects. With the development of specialized skills, society became more complex, and its horizons expanded as long-distance trade was evolved to obtain the materials needed by the craftsmen and to market their products. By land and sea, the Sumerians imported metal, wood, lapis lazuli, carnelian and other stones, and exported such finished items as textiles, jewelry and weapons. This expanding trade and the consequent social complexities furthered—indeed required—the invention of

arithmetic and the perfection of writing. Before 3000 B.C., Sumer's temple accountants had developed systems of numerical notation based both on tens (the decimal system) and on sixties (the sexagesimal system). Our way of telling time and our division of the circle into 360 degrees stem from the Sumerian sexagesimal system. The inventive Sumerians also evolved precise systems of weights and measures, and could reckon by volume, length and area.

This knowledge originated in the temples, but its use spread far beyond them. A highly commercial people, the Sumerians were the world's first businessmen, the first capitalists in our sense of the word. Private traders operated under strict government—meaning temple—supervision and according to detailed laws. But Sumer's entrepreneurs remained remarkably free and, much as in our own society, infused the economy with its vital energy. In trade with

A SUMERIAN BOAT is shown in an impression from a finely carved early Sumerian cylinder seal, probably representing a mythological scene. In their small boats, the Sumerians traded actively throughout the Persian Gulf.

A GOLD TUMBLER, fluted and decorated with herringbone and zigzag patterns, displays the skill of Sumerian artisans. It was found with other sumptuous items in the tomb of Queen Shub-ad in the Royal Cemetery at Ur.

RLIEST KNOWN WRITING is inscribed on Sumerian tablets like tablet at left, almost 5,000 years old, bears numerals and is prob- ing entry. The other records the sizes of two pieces of land.

THE TEMPLE WORKSHOPS around the courtyard at Khafajah are alive with craftsmen's labors. At far left, one stone carver is sculpturing a religious statue, a second is boring the interior of a stone vessel. In left

CRAFTS AND BUSINESS

THE inventions that made the heyday of Sumer one of the most brilliant epochs in history were the product of numerous craftsmen. Many of them toiled in the complex of rooms surrounding the courtyard of the Temple Oval at Khafajah. It was in the temple that the economic life of the city, as of other Sumerian cities, was concentrated. Private artisans and businessmen also played a great part in the commercial life of Sumer, but the temples were the main centers.

Of all the skills that evolved in Sumer, two were crucial for future ages: the invention of writing and the art of metallurgy. The transition from stone to metal began with the discovery, at the end of the Neolithic period, that various metals could be melted out of ore and

mythological husband, an actual Sumerian ruler who was deified after his
death. The union of Dumuzi and Inanna in the ceremony depicted above
symbolized the identity of Sumerian rulers with their gods. In some versions
of the ritual, the union was actually reconsummated by the living r[...]
the priestess in the privacy of the shrine. The busy life of the te[...]
munity goes on at the right while the climax of the cerem[...]

places silver ingots on the pan at right. Above them an older trader discusses the deal with a bald-headed temple administrator while a bearded scribe takes notes. At far right, a potter fashions a clay utensil on a wheel.

places as far away as Egypt, India and Anatolia, they ran big risks and earned high profits. An exchange of letters between two merchants in different cities, in which one asks the other to collect a debt from a third, reveals how sternly Sumerian businessmen regarded business debts: "Catch Warad-ilishu and make him weigh out the silver with interest more or less; from this sum take fourteen shekels and send me the balance." Although coined money appeared later (a shekel was a unit of weight, not a coin), the *idea* of money was first grasped and used by the Sumerians: barley, copper, silver and gold came to have fixed values in relationship to each other and to all sorts of goods. With the simultaneous invention of credit, these values were expressed in writing without the older, cumbersome barter of specific goods. All this not only furthered but necessitated the development of the greatest Sumerian invention of all—writing.

INLAID PANEL reveals early artists' acute sense of animal forms. The fox and lion (*second from top*) offer food and libations to a god or ruler.

MEMORIAL STATUE depicts Dudu the Scribe, who dedicated this portrait of himself to the city god. He lived in Sumerian Lagash in 2500 B.C.

DEITY OF VEGETATION, the god Abu is attended by his consort. The two were found beneath a temple sanctuary at Eshnunna. The stylized, almost geometrical lines and staring eyes characterize much Sumerian sculpture.

IN ALL THINGS, GODS

TO the Sumerians the will of the gods was exhibited throughout the universe. They believed that the world had been created and was governed by an assembly of gods with human forms and faces. Religion had thus become anthropomorphic—man saw the gods in his own image. There were universal gods and local or "city" gods. High priests and rulers were their earthly servants and deputies, powerful only as the gods gave them power.

The greatest gods in the Sumerian pantheon were four who personified the forces of nature most important in that region. Paramount among them was Anu, god of the all-encircling sky. The Sumerians wrote of him, "O father of the gods, thy command, the very foundation of heaven and earth, what god could spurn it?" Beside him stood Enlil, god of the storm, executor of the gods' decrees. The third great deity was the earth goddess—variously named Ki (earth) or Nintu (the lady who gives birth)—who represented the passive reproductive forces of the cosmos. Her masculine counterpart was Enki, lord of the active creative forces of the world and of the life-giving waters. Statues of these deities and others stood in the temple sanctuaries. Since they were regarded as human, thrice-daily offerings of food, beer and wine were presented to them by temple priests in rituals like that depicted in the painting at left.

IN A TEMPLE SANCTUARY (*left*) two priests bring offerings of food and wine to the city goddess, enshrined in an arched recess. The figures at the far left are "reverence statues," standing in perpetual adoration of the deity.

A DINNER PARTY held in a Sumerian home some 4,500 years ago is serenaded by a harpist (*left*). The refreshments include fish; wine, drunk from fluted cups; and beer, sucked from a jug through a drinking tube.

A COURT FEAST after a victory is shown in part of the so-called "Royal Standard" of Ur. A musician with a lyre entertains seated captains of the royal host while, below, captured bullock and asses are led to the palace.

A NOBLE LADY, carved in translucent stone with head of gold, stands in a prayerful attitude. She was found in 1960 at Nippur. More delicately made than most Sumerian statues, she may be praying to the goddess Inanna.

PROSPEROUS SUMER

THE evidence from which we derive our impressions of Sumer—the remains of temples and cities, statuary and reliefs, cuneiform records—gives different scholars somewhat different notions of how Sumerian society was organized. Archaeologist Henri Frankfort discerned "a fact unparalleled in the ancient world, namely, that in principle all members of the community were equal." Sir Leonard Woolley, who uncovered the wonders of Ur, pointed out that as time went on, Sumer actually developed an upper class of government officials, priests and professional warriors; a mixed "burgher class" of merchants, schoolmasters, laborers, farmers and artisans; and a chattel class of slaves. Certainly there were rich and poor, masters and servants, and a commercial middle class that in its relative prosperity and spirit of enterprise came close to its modern equivalents.

The host at the party depicted above—the furnishings of his home indicate that he was more prosperous than the average citizen —could have been a well-to-do importer, a local tradesman with a small farm outside the city, a scribe whose writing skill was much in demand or a tax collector who had made his money by extortion. The house of sun-dried brick had no windows opening on the narrow street outside but did have an inner, brick-paved court on which the kitchen, living rooms and bedrooms opened. The furniture—backless chairs, light tables and stands made of wood or reed wickerwork —seemed ample to the host and his guests. And their dinner would have seemed ample to anybody: an appetizer of garlic in sour cream, barley soup, Tigris salmon, roast pig or lamb, unleavened bread, dates and pomegranates, goat cheese, and plenty of beer and wine. A guest of honor might have left, happy and tipsy, with a present: a new red robe or a gold ring for himself, his wife or his concubine.

GOLD AND SILVER STATUETTE, found in the Great Death Pit at Ur, represents a ram nibbling at leaves. The head and legs are of gold, the body is silver on wood, the fleece is rendered in carved shell and lapis lazuli.

ART, WEALTH, DEATH

THE golden objects pictured here came from the graves of kings and courtiers at splendid Ur, and they demonstrate a high order of Sumerian art dating back to 2500 B.C. But they also confirm the importance of wealth as a basic element in civilization. The Sumerians learned early to use and enjoy their wealth. A mythical god-king of Uruk called upon the rival city of Aratta to acknowledge its submission by sending him rich gifts of gold, silver and semiprecious lapis lazuli. Much later, rich merchants and traders decked their wives in gold. A professional scribe could support a wastrel son in ruinous luxury and complain to him: "Perverse one with whom I am furious . . . night and day you waste in pleasures." The great temples represented massive investments not only in monumental masonry but in the swarms of priests, managers, artisans and servants who could be sustained only by the "social surplus" of a highly productive economy.

Fantastic evidence of the abundant life in Sumer was provided by Sir Leonard Woolley's discovery and excavation of the famous Royal Cemetery at Ur. Along with their profusion of gold and silver ornaments and jewelry, the royal graves disclosed that soldiers, cart drivers, gentlemen and ladies of the court went gracefully and voluntarily to death with their monarchs, probably by taking poison on the spot. In one grave alone, now called the Great Death Pit, 74 skeletons were found. As to why, we have no record. The bones are silent.

BULL'S HEAD (*right*) decorates a royal harp from a grave. Harps and lyres found at Ur were often made in the form of bulls. The head of the bull above is rendered in lapis lazuli and gold hammered on a wooden core.

RICH HEADDRESS consists of a long gold hair ribbon with beaded wreaths, gold pendants, heavy earrings and a golden comb with seven rosettes. It was worn by Queen Shub-ad on her deathbed in the Royal Cemetery at Ur.

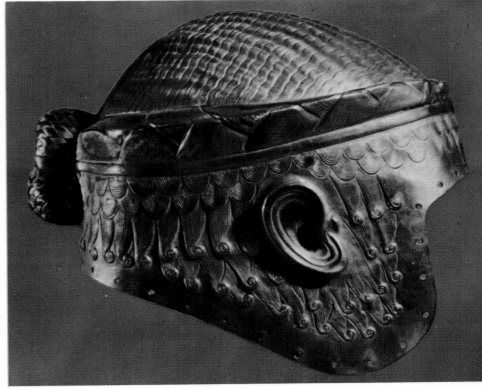

GOLDEN HELMET from a rich citizen's grave shows the knotted hairdo that Sumerians wore in battle. It was hammered from a single sheet of gold and then enchased. A quilted lining was once attached to the holes at bottom.

LEGACIES OF SUMER: WRITING, MYTHS AND LAW

THROUGH the veil of time the people of ancient Sumer are seen as shadows on a crumbled wall—now vividly alive in an account of a schoolboy's troubles and triumphs 4,000 years ago, now murky in fragmentary records dimly etched in clay. One record from around 2000 B.C. has a schoolboy tell what he did at school on a particular day: "I recited my tablet, ate my lunch, prepared my [new] tablet, wrote it, finished it"—and we see the earnest boy, shaping and smoothing his tablets of clay, copying on them his lessons for the day from a master tablet. In the same account, the boy has a bad day at school, is repeatedly flogged, and in desperation asks his father to invite the teacher home for a meal. Thus wined,

dined and given "a new garment" and "a ring on his hand," the teacher proclaims that the boy will "reach the pinnacle of the scribal art" and has already "become a man of learning." Professor Samuel Noah Kramer of the University of Pennsylvania, who pieced together and translated the fragments of this account, calls it "the first case of 'apple-polishing.'"

The very name of Sumer had been in oblivion for more than 2,000 years when the ruins of its cities were first discovered in 1854. Since then, scholars like Professor Kramer have amassed an amazing body of fact and reasoned surmise about the land and its people.

Recovered Sumerian clay tablets reveal how men first learned to

SUMERIAN TEMPLE OF INANNA is uncovered by American excavators in the religious center of Nippur. The Sumerians considered Nippur the abode of Enlil, god of the storm. The temple shown here, dating from about 2600 B.C., is one of seven built on the site between 3500 B.C. and 200 A.D. It had a double sanctuary, an entry porch and kitchens. Many ritual objects and statues were unearthed here by excavations that were first begun in 1958.

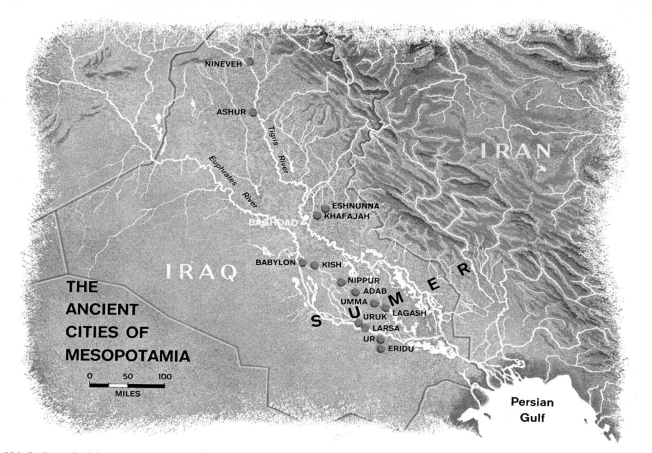

THE
ANCIENT
CITIES OF
MESOPOTAMIA

0   50   100
MILES

write. Around 3500 B.C., primitive scribes were still using sharpened reeds and scratched pictures of human heads, birds, fish, trees and spears on rough tablets. These pictographs were gradually refined. Eventually they were flexible enough to be used to make lists and even tally numbers of things for records.

As trade grew with the rise of villages and towns, the need for business records stimulated progress in writing. Over the years the pictographic symbols lost their identification with actual things and evolved toward a system of abstract syllable signs, capable of conveying ideas in words. The final stages of this process took nearly a thousand years. During this period the temple scribes reduced the old pictographs to a system of simple, wedge-shaped marks impressed in soft clay by the edge of a cut reed. Known as cuneiform (meaning "wedge-shaped"), the system was adopted by the later Assyrians, Babylonians and Persians. The Egyptians used a different system, but many scholars now agree that it was Sumer that gave the rest of the ancient world the idea of writing.

At least a thousand years before the Hebrews wrote down the Old Testament and Homer recorded the *Iliad* and *Odyssey,* the Sumerians had already created a rich and varied literature of their own. Their myths, hymns, lamentations and accounts of contemporary events show them to have been a lively people who were at once imaginative and intensely earthly. Rather stocky and dark, they probably lacked the physical grace and elegance of the Egyptians. But they cared about grace and beauty.

Many episodes and concepts of the Old Testament resemble Sumerian myths. The concepts of heaven and hell ("the great above" and "the great below") often appear in Sumerian mythology. The Garden of Eden could have been Dilmun, the Sumerians' paradise, and a story very much like that of Noah and his Ark figures in the Babylonian *Epic of Gilgamesh,* which seems to be derived from the Sumerian tale of Ziusudra. Ziusudra was a pious king who was warned by the gods that they proposed to "destroy the seed of mankind" by flood, whereupon the king prepared a "huge boat" and rode out a great inundation that "swept over the land" for seven days and seven nights instead of the Biblical 40.

The Sumerians were assiduous lawmakers and litigators. Their trade was conducted under laws and regulations that for sheer complexity would do credit to a modern bureaucracy. Their early assemblies appear to have served both as legislatures and as courts, somewhat as the first British Parliaments did. Among the odd quirks of Sumerian law were the laws governing slavery. Slaves could own land, conduct business, buy their freedom and appeal to the authorities against sale to an undesirable purchaser. Yet they also could be branded and flogged by their owners and were often mistreated. To satisfy his creditors, a man in debt could sell his wife and children into slavery for three years. There is no record of a wife's selling her husband.

Some scholars believe that Sumerian society in its first urban phase was a society of equals, where every man was expected to work

for his living and all were equal before the law. But by 2400 B.C., civilization had produced a plague of great and petty tyrants, corrupt officials and greedy plutocrats. A city king of Lagash made a name for himself by decreeing an end to official extortion, the abuse of the poor by the rich and confiscatory taxation. But the reign of this king, Urukagina, lasted only 10 years, and in one of the petty wars that led to the end of Sumer, Lagash fell under the hard hand of a king from nearby Umma.

Such was often the fate of the cities of Sumer. For around a thousand years they warred with each other, and each city came briefly under the sway of one city and then another. No ruler succeeded in unifying the land until the 24th Century B.C., when the first great conqueror appeared. He was Sargon of Akkad, king of an area just north of Sumer between the Tigris and the Euphrates, inhabited by a Semitic people. Sargon conquered the Sumerian cities, mastered the plain down to the Persian Gulf and turned to foreign conquest. His empire, the first known in history, soon embraced Elam, northeast of the Persian Gulf, and perhaps parts of Asia Minor. It may even have stretched to the Lebanon of today, on the Mediterranean. Alternately expanding and shrinking under Sargon's descendants, the Sargonid empire finally collapsed around 2200 B.C.

"Who was king, who was not king?" a later chronicler remarked of the confused and turbulent period that followed. About 2100 B.C., King Ur-Nammu of Ur, styling himself "King of Sumer and Akkad," established a united kingdom that lasted, under progressive Sumerian monarchs, for a century. Ur-Nammu built great temples at Eridu, at holy Nippur, and at Lagash, Adab and Larsa. At Ur itself he raised a vast ziggurat, or temple, that towered 80 feet above the plain and was 200 feet long and 140 feet wide. This was the period of Sumer's renaissance, remembered by the Jews, who centuries later were proud to claim Ur of the Chaldees as Abraham's birthplace. But when the Ur-Nammu dynasty died out, Sumer began to die with it. In one of the finest elegies of all time, a great anonymous poet sang of Ur and of Sumer:

> *O thou city of high walls, thy land has perished.*
> *O my city, like an innocent ewe thy lamb has been torn away*
>   *from thee;*
> *O Ur, like an innocent goat thy kid has perished. . . .*
> *The judgment of the land perished. The people mourn.*

Ur and its kingdom fell under the onslaughts of Elamites and Amorites around 2025 B.C. About 1792 B.C., both Sumer and Akkad were incorporated into the Old Babylonian Kingdom. Hammurabi, the first great king of storied Babylon, has won an imperishable place in history with his Code of Laws, inscribed on a column of diorite, which reflects laws and usages going back to older Sumerian times. In the next six centuries the region lapsed into quiescence, but toward the close of this period the mighty Assyrian empire arose in upper Mesopotamia and by conquest engulfed all of the Babylonian kingdom.

LIFE ALONG THE RIVER is depicted in an artist's reconstruction of the busy waterfront area of Monhenjo-daro, one of the two capital cities of the earliest civilization in ancient India. Before the gateway, garbed in yellow, stands one of the city's dignitaries. To his left, near a typical streetside shop, is a dancing girl out for a quick airing. The people of the Indus valley appear to have been highly skilled organizers of communities and government.

COMMUNITIES OF THE INDUS

The remains of the world's third great civilization reveal a genius for big-city planning unrivaled in ancient times

WHY people in certain areas of the ancient world—and not in others—first accomplished the progression from primitive societies to urban civilization remains a fascinating mystery. The first civilizations in the world arose along or near three great river systems: the Tigris-Euphrates in what is now Iraq, the Nile in Egypt and the Indus in modern Pakistan and India. This suggests that at a given stage of human development, men plus fertile river valleys equaled civilization.

Certainly the three great valleys—in potential at least—were immensely fertile. But each presented challenges of flood, drought and stubborn soil that would have taxed the courage and ability of any people less advanced than those who inhabited this area during the fourth and third millenniums B.C. Some modern historians, including Arnold Toynbee, reason that it was the human response to challenges of this kind which brought the first civilizations into being.

The problem posed by each river was fundamentally the same, though differing in degree. The Nile has always been regarded by the Egyptians as the source of all good things; nevertheless, the ancient Egyptians had to wrestle with it continuously, diking it in times of flood or tapping its precious waters in times of drought. The Tigris and Euphrates were also both friendly and hostile, harmful and challenging. Swamps had to be drained and fields irrigated, and the erratic rivers often afflicted both the countryside and the cities with troublesome floods.

The Indus was at times a baleful stream. It rose and fell annually, like the Nile, in response to the accumulation and melting of the snows in the high mountains whence it came. Now and again, overfed by sudden storms, it would burst over its banks, imperiling fields, villages and cities within its reach. When not in raging flood, the Indus was a beneficent stream. Running through countryside which varied from barren sands to thickly wooded scrub and lush marshland, it provided easy transport from the hinterland to the sea, thus furthering the development of urban trading communities. Even so, the early peoples along the Indus and its tributaries must have had to meet sharper challenges than did their contemporaries in either Sumer or Egypt.

Of all the mysteries of civilized man's emergence, that of the Indus valley is the most complete. By 2300 B.C., two cities, which were to become twin centers of the Indus civilization, had grown up on the river banks—first Mohenjo-daro on the lower Indus, and later the city of Harappa, 400 miles to the northeast on the tributary river Ravi. These cities, dominating a cultural area of nearly 500,000 square miles, were designed with wide streets, rectangular blocks and efficient drainage in accordance with a well-organized plan. Indeed, evidence from the ruins points to a degree of control and planning under some central civic authority unprecedented in the history of early civilizations.

The inhabitants of the Indus valley could write, but we cannot decipher what little of their writing has been found. No temples have been uncovered, no richly furnished tombs like those of Sumer and Egypt. We have learned what we know of the Indus civilization solely from the physical remains of the towns and cities and from the artifacts that have so far been excavated. These reveal a well-ordered but somewhat static society whose people could afford many of the amenities of life: substantial houses, some with bathrooms; gracefully shaped pottery; simple but practical household tools of copper and bronze; and semiprecious personal jewelry. The Indus civilization preserved its essential features with little change for about a thousand years. Then slow decay, combined with cataclysmic flooding and invasions—possibly by the Asians generally called "Aryans"—eventually brought about the downfall of its main centers. Unlike Sumer and Egypt, the Indus civilization, so far as scholars are able to tell, had very little discernible impact on western civilization, although it had some influence on the later Hindu people of India.

RITUAL BATH, the ruins of which are shown below, may have served for religious functions similar to Hindu practices of today. In the citadel area, it was 40 by 24 feet, and eight feet deep, with dressing rooms off three sides.

CITADEL AREA of Mohenjo-daro, raised on a platform and surrounded by a wall, occupies the foreground of the painting above. The massive state-controlled granary is shown at the left; the open, rectangular building behind

CITY AND CITADEL

THE painting on these pages shows Mohenjo-daro as it might have looked some 300 years after its founding, at the high point of its development. The ruins of Mohenjo-daro and Harappa indicate that these twin cities grew according to a central plan that had been conceived at their foundation—much as Washington, D.C., to this day follows the conception of George Washington's French planner, Pierre L'Enfant. Cities like these could have been built and sustained only by a very prosperous and resourceful people. Cotton and wheat were grown in the fertile fields near Mohenjo-daro, and the surplus wealth accumulated from this produce served both to support the inhabitants of the city and to promote a lively trade.

Each city at its peak covered an area of six or seven miles and could house some 20,000 to 50,000 people, a very large urban population for that period. The wide main streets bordered rectangular city blocks that measured about 400 yards in length and 200 yards in width, far

it surrounds the open-air ritual bath. The large fortlike building in the center of the painting could have been a seminary for priests and scribes. The city proper, laid out in rectangular blocks, extends beyond the citadel.

RUINS OF THE GRANARY (*below*) represent the remains of the region's economic center. Here farmers delivered wheat, unloading it from their bullock carts in the recessed area behind the built-up well shaft at the left.

larger than a typical block in modern Manhattan. The centers of urban and presumably national life were the raised citadels, surrounded by massive walls, that dominated Mohenjo-daro and Harappa. The one at Mohenjo-daro, which appears in the foreground of the painting above, consisted of a monumental platform of dried mud brick, faced and reinforced with burnt brick, 40 to 50 feet high and approximately 400 by 200 feet at the base. Upon this platform, which afforded ample protection against the recurrent floods of the Indus River, were erected a tremendous storehouse for grain (*left*), a brick-walled public bath (*behind it*) and buildings that scholars believe to have been an assembly hall and perhaps a school.

The general appearance of the citadels suggests that they served a dual purpose as both religious meeting places and administrative centers. This conjecture ties in with the theory, supported by the striking evidence of a uniformity in weights, measures and building methods throughout the area, that the Indus cities and the whole region were ruled through a highly centralized bureaucratic government, undoubtedly a theocracy with a priest-king as the head bureaucrat.

FOUNDATIONS of a four-room house are revealed after excavation. The remains of a long hall are seen at the right. The rooms of the house appear large here, but were actually small. The white patches are salt deposits.

BRONZE TOOLS AND WEAPONS of the Indus civilization (*opposite*) include a sword (*right*), goad (*top, center*), spearhead (*left*), razor (*left of sword*), daggers, knives, fishhooks, arrowheads, an axhead and a hammerhead.

TOY CART, found in the ruins, is complete with a driver and oxen. Some 1,300 years after the Indus civilization vanished, an object like this inspired a famous Indian play in which a thief hides jewels in a boy's toy cart.

MASTER ARTISANS

THE Sumerians built mostly in sun-dried brick of clay and mud, the Egyptians in stone. But the people of the Indus valley used baked brick of two standard sizes (11 by 5.5 by 2.5 and 9.2 by 4.5 by 2.2), molded in large quantities and hardened in kilns. Clay was also fashioned into less functional but delightful objects like the child's toy shown above. Indus masons used mortar, followed precise specifications and at a late stage occasionally added bitumen from Baluchistan to their stock of materials. How well the Indus bricks and the structures they made possible have survived is shown here in photographs of Mohenjo-daro as its excavated portions look today.

In and around the cities, intermittent floods left silt deposits that gradually raised the ground level. By stages the builders erected new structures and additions upon the solid foundations of the old. The massive citadels were erected at the start on high brick bases, perhaps partly for protection from floods and partly as a reverential salute to the Indus gods. The drainage and sewage systems found under the streets and in some houses were extraordinary achievements for their time, indicating a remarkably high level of public and private sanitation. The wealthier residents lived in substantial brick houses, which usually had no windows on the streets but opened upon inner courtyards. The poorer people lived in smaller brick cottages, and these, like the bigger houses, stood wall to wall in solid rows.

A HOUSEHOLD WELL, seen from a building that is thought to have been the ruler's palace, was left standing by excavators. It had been built up to the city's topmost level. A covered drain runs down the center of the street.

EXCAVATED ALLEY shows the results of digging through 2,500 years of accumulated soil. The slits at right were rubbish chutes, demonstrating the high state of Indus sanitation. The chutes emptied into bins on the street.

MEASURING DEVICES, uniform throughout the area, attest the accuracy of Indus artisans. The balance is of bronze. The broken ivory scale is accurately incised in a decimal system.

JARS FOR COSMETICS, which could also serve as vases, are made of pottery. The black eyebrow paint kept in such jars was used by men and women. Indus pottery was often crude.

BRONZE DANCER, four and a half inches high (*right*), is among the best examples of Indus art. The flat nose and thick lips suggest that the model came from the Baluchistan hills.

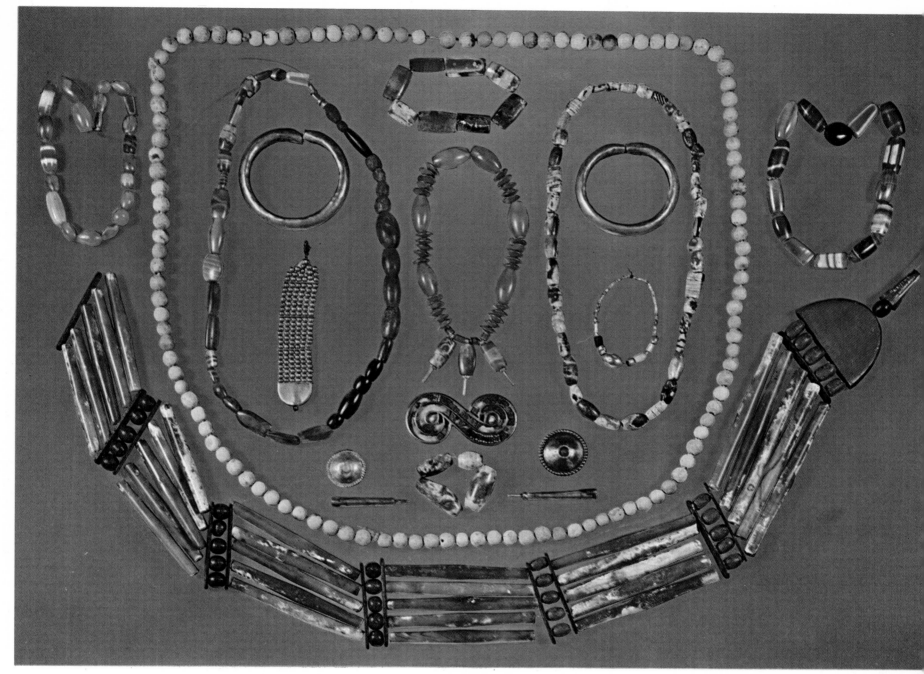

INDUS JEWELRY (*above*) includes beads of carnelian, which was very popular, as were agate and jadeite. Jewelry was worn by both men and women, although only women sported bead girdles, earrings and head ornaments.

PLAYTHINGS for young and old (*below*) include dice marked like those of today (but with the sides in different order), marbles, a maze and stone balls. The perforated clay sphere at right and the clay roller at left are rattles.

WEALTH AND LEISURE

IN the absence of deciphered written records, the artifacts and figurines of the kind illustrated here and on the following pages tell much of what is known about the Indus way of life. They demonstrate, among other things, that the Indus artisans and merchants enjoyed a lucrative market for goods ranging from cosmetics and costume jewelry to gamblers' dice and children's rattles. The artisans who satisfied this varied demand worked in copper, bronze, semiprecious stones, gold, silver and, of course, clay. Although they sometimes attained real artistry—the bronze figure of the dancing girl shown on the opposite page is an example—most of their products were obviously designed for people who cared more for utility than beauty.

Weights and measures were uniform throughout the Indus region. Polished stone weights were graduated upward by the doubling of successive units from 1 to 64 (from 1 to 2 to 4, etc.). The higher ranges rose in a decimal system. For measurement, the Indus artisans used a linear scale based on intervals of 1.32 inches with a standard "foot" of 13.2 inches. The uniform standards of weight and length used throughout the area again suggest to many scholars that the region was under strong central rule. Sir Mortimer Wheeler, the British specialist in Indus lore, deduces from this and similar evidence that the civilization at its height may have constituted "the vastest political experiment before the advent of the Roman Empire."

A RAM ON WHEELS is typical of hundreds of children's toys found at Mohenjo-daro and elsewhere. Other animals favored for toys were bullocks, birds and fish. Most were roughly made, but some were quite sophisticated.

A FLYING DOVE has a hole in its base so that it can be set on a wooden pin. The bird figures discovered at Mohenjo-daro may have been either toys or votive offerings. Doves figured in ancient worship of the mother goddess.

A WAGGLING TOY is a cow or bullock whose head moves with the pull of a string. Many others like it have been found, so they must have been popular. A profusion of toys is evidence of a prosperous and secure society.

A SACRED BULL (*above*) is shaped in terra cotta with the care and precision that mark most Indus renderings of animals. Human figures, as usual in primitive societies, were seldom made with as much skill as animal images.

FOR FUN, WITH LOVE

OUT of the dimness that enshrouds the Indus past, some of the objects found in excavated ruins cast a revealing glow on the people who made and used them. Such are the figures of animals shown here. Only artisans who loved animals and lived closely with them could have fashioned these objects with such loving care, and only people who shared that love would have cherished them. The manufacture of figurines, particularly items designed as toys, was a major Indus industry. The large number found suggests that they were manufactured for export. Many of the clay toys had mountings for wheels and holes for drawstrings. Some have been found in underground brick drains, suggesting that children played with their toys and sometimes lost them just as children do today. Both at Chanhu-daro, a town about 80 miles south of Mohenjo-daro, and at the southern port city of Lothal, the remains of large-scale shops and kilns for burnt-clay products have been found.

Not all the figures made by the Indus artisans were designed for play. Some, like the handsome bull shown above, probably had a religious significance: ritual dancers leaping over bulls, an important practice in Minoan Crete (as shown in Chapter 8), also appear on some Indus seals.

Typically, the animals are fashioned with the greatest care, and the human figures often seem deliberately clumsy. Some of the figurines, like the munching squirrels at the upper right, were clearly made and highly valued as ornaments. The makers and owners of these objects, like all ancient peoples, lived in a world largely dominated by fearsome spirits and threatened by natural forces that appeared to be demonic. But their world and their lives had a lighter side: happy, laughing children played with toy rams, and grown-ups found pleasure in owning objects imbued with a kindly grace.

MUNCHING SQUIRRELS, probably eating walnuts, are miniatures in faïence. The smaller is just an inch high. Squirrels are still common in the uplands and Himalayan foothills in the northern part of the Indian subcontinent.

A SIGHTLESS MONKEY of faïence, or glazed clay (*below*), has lost the inlay that marked its eyes. Monkeys were common in the Indus area, with such other wildlife as squirrels, parrots, deer, crocodiles, mongooses and tortoises.

A FANCIFUL CREATURE is a caricature of a bearded human face on an animal body, possibly that of a puppy or cat. Remains of cats found in the Indus valley ruins indicate that they must have resembled today's alley cats.

A PET RAM in faïence, complete except for the inlaid eyes, still bears traces of its original brown glaze. Indus sheep, probably long-tailed and domesticated from wild urial stock, were evidently bred for both meat and wool.

CRUDE FIGURINES probably represent a worshiper (*second from right*) and mother goddesses, who figured importantly in the Indus and other old religions. The goddess at the extreme left carries receptacles on her head, possibly for incense. The adornment of the figure at the far right may suggest the costuming of wealthy Indus women. Since no temples have been identified, religious worship may have been largely a household rite.

RITUALS AND WRITING

THREE important elements of the Indus civilization are illustrated on these pages—its undeciphered script (*left*), its mother-goddess cult (*above*) and its efficient bureaucracy (the portrait opposite may be that of a top bureaucrat). The famous seals at left are at once the most enigmatic and most intriguing of all the Indus remnants so far unearthed. They, with a few engraved copper plates and occasional potsherds, bear the only known examples of Indus writing, which nobody has yet been able to decipher. It seems to have employed more than 250 symbols and about 400 characters, and is essentially a pictographic script. Numerals may have been employed, though no firm evidence for this exists. Indus seals from Mesopotamia first revealed that the Indus civilization had developed by 2300 B.C., the estimated date of the ruins where they were found. These seals, and others of the same type, discovered on the Persian Gulf island of Bahrain—probably called Dilmun in ancient times—are the principal evidence that a sea-borne trade linked the Indus cities with Sumer and its neighboring states. The discovery of other artifacts at sites along the vast Iranian plateau indicates that overland travelers and traders also established contacts between the Indus region and the older civilizations to the west.

The seals, which may have been used either as personal identification or in religious rituals, were carved on steatite, a soft soapstone. Many of them must have had a religious connotation. The most frequent figure on the seals is the so-called unicorn, undoubtedly a urus, or long-horned ox, portrayed in profile and thus appearing to have only one horn. This beast was a familiar object of worship throughout much of the ancient world. But probably the most significant religious symbols may be the pipal, or fig tree, which is still sacred today to Buddhists as well as to Hindus, and a three-headed figure, which was almost certainly an Indus idol. Many scholars perceive in the several forms of this figure the forerunner of Siva, one of the supreme deities of Hinduism.

Hundreds of grotesque terra cotta figurines like those shown above have been found in the ruins of the Indus cities. Many of them are assumed to represent Indus conceptions of the mother goddess who embodied ancient peoples' notions of creation and of man's mysterious subjection to beings and forces beyond his understanding.

INDUS SEALS with pictographs (*left, top to bottom*) show a bull, a rhinoceros and an elephant, which supplied ivory to Indus craftsmen. At right (*from top*) are a tree spirit and worshipers, the sacred pipal tree and a god.

THE REGAL AIR AND RICH DRESS of the magnificent stone figure opposite, found at Mohenjo-daro, indicate that it may represent either a local Indus god or one of the priest-kings who may have ruled the entire Indus region.

LIFE AND DEATH
OF THE INDUS CITIES

KNOWLEDGE of the Indus culture is still fragmentary and incomplete, and further excavations may yet reveal new and unsuspected aspects of this third great civilization of the world. As far as is known, the civilization had its beginnings when village tribesmen from the rugged hills and uplands of what is now Baluchistan moved across the deserts to the banks of the Indus between 4,000 and 5,000 years ago. Within half a century these early settlers of the valley had learned to dike and drain the fertile lowlands and thus to maintain permanent farms and villages against the recurrent Indus floods. Toward the end of this period, other villagers and farmers from the Iranian plateau, west of the Indus, migrated into the valley. They brought with them, it is thought, some knowledge of the cities and civilizations of ancient Sumer, whose traders and travelers may have visited and occasionally settled in the Iranian villages. Perhaps Sumerians, or Iranians familiar with the ways of Sumer, stimulated the growth of the Indus villages into rudimentary towns and the simultaneous development around them of farming and trading communities which had many of the facilities and characteristics of small rural states.

Sometime before 2500 B.C., all of the elements of early civilization were present in the Indus valley except one—real cities. Priests in the

villages and emerging towns could perhaps already write in pictographs, which gradually became ideographs or whole words. The priests, as natural rulers, probably accustomed the populace to increasing degrees of central authority and communal management. Artisans were already making copper tools and shaping pottery on the wheel, an invention which may have been brought across the Iranian plateau from Sumer. Wheeled carts drawn by oxen and water buffaloes, and boats and rafts on the Indus and its tributaries, provided the transport necessary for a widening trade. The coppersmiths and potters, using fire in their work, discovered that burnt-clay brick could withstand the floods and rains as sun-dried mud never could. The valley countryside abounded with scrub trees, and additional logs for the kilns could be floated down the Indus from the timbered highlands to the north and east.

The river, although it was terrible when rampaging in flood, supported a growing boat traffic and opened the way to and from the coasts of the Arabian Sea in the south. As port towns developed west and southeast of the mouth of the Indus, trading vessels from the Persian Gulf brought more and more of the goods and techniques of Sumer to the coast and up the Indus into the valley.

From all this, around 2600 B.C. there emerged the miracle of Mohenjo-daro. The residents of the area elected to build beside the river a town such as their world had never seen. Over the next two or three centuries the town grew into the city whose remains the archaeologists of today are still exploring. The riches, political strength and technical skill that made the town and then the city possible also enabled its people and rulers to extend their authority and influence northeast and south of Mohenjo-daro. On the tributary Ravi, 400 miles to the northeast, the city Harappa grew up to share the dominance of an area which by 2000 B.C. had spread far beyond the Indus valley proper.

Of the many lesser communities that were included within the Indus valley civilization, the port city of Lothal, southeast of the mouth of the Indus near the Arabian Sea, is perhaps the most interesting. Lothal enjoyed the advantage of a sheltered harbor, into which two rivers flowed, with easy access to the rich fields of cotton and wheat in the interior. At the height of its prosperity, between 2500 and 1500 B.C., Lothal was a flourishing center for agriculture as well as overseas trade. It boasted a number of local industries, including the manufacture of beads and shell bangles and the working of copper. Its massive dockyard of burnt brick, measuring about 710 by 120 feet, was the largest such structure built by the people of the Indus valley. Through a gap in its eastern embankment, ships were sluiced into the dockyard at high tide through an inlet 23 feet wide. Where the inlet cut through the side of the dockyard, a low wall retained enough water within the docks at low tide to enable the ships to be moved about. A loading platform 800 feet long ran along the western embankment of the dockyard. The city of Lothal itself, not far from the sea, was, like Mohenjo-daro and Harappa, carefully planned in

EXPERT ON THE INDUS is Britain's Sir Mortimer Wheeler, who has conducted extensive excavations in India and Pakistan. He is also known for his television broadcasts, his books and his wartime exploits as a brigadier.

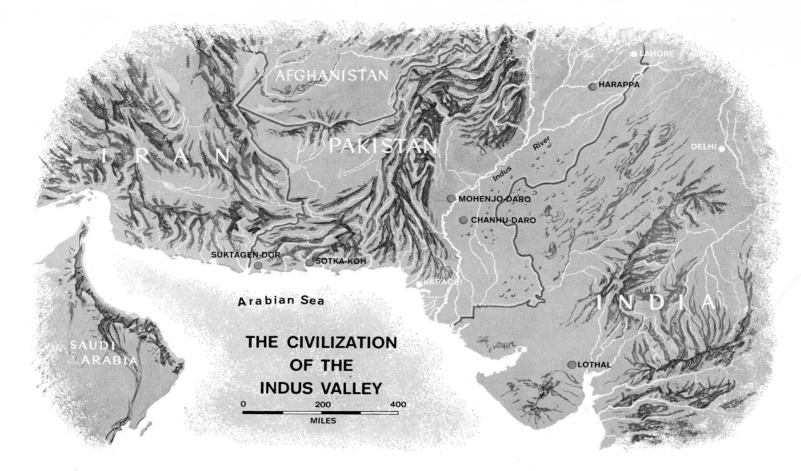

THE CIVILIZATION OF THE INDUS VALLEY

0   200   400
MILES

six rectangular blocks, with a fine drainage system and a bazaar section lined with shops.

The Indus civilization stretched along the coast of the Arabian Sea from a point north of modern Bombay to well beyond the site of Karachi. Inland it reached over 700 miles to the northeast and 300 miles to the west. How this culturally unified expanse of more than half a million square miles was administered is not known. Some scholars like to believe that the whole region was centrally ruled, with the aspects of an early empire. But the Indus region could have been what Sumer was during much of its existence—a complex of autonomous city-states with common standards and customs. Perhaps they enjoyed cultural unity without permanent political unity of the kind that is known to have prevailed at the time only in ancient Egypt.

It is known that a static and sterile quality pervaded Indus society. Over 10 centuries or more, the towns and cities changed only in the sense that they grew somewhat larger and that they were raised ever higher to avoid the floods. The standards of art, housing and communal life seemed to remain from generation to generation as they had been from the time of Mohenjo-daro's founding. Whatever the systems of religion and government presumably centered in the major citadels may have been, they seemed to persist without the invigorating infusion of new ideas and ways. What is remarkable is not that the Indus civilization finally passed from the earth, but that it lasted as long as it did.

The manner of its passing suggests that the Indus centers at their peak were in some measure independent of each other. Certainly they did not die together. The death that eventually claimed them all seems to have come upon them from the north and to have struck last in the coastal south, where such cities as Lothal survived Harappa and Mohenjo-daro by several centuries.

Both attrition from within and invasion from without contributed to the civilization's demise. Any static society is bound to wither sooner or later, and the Indus cities presumably died in part of sheer inanition. The theory that excessive cutting of forests to supply fuel for the voracious brick kilns led to disastrous soil erosion, perhaps aggravated by a gradual change from a relatively wet to a very dry climate, is now questioned by scholars who hold that the area's climate and topography were then just about as they are today.

However this may have been, a human event of infinitely greater proportions had much to do with the final passing of the Indus culture. This event was the arrival in the upper reaches of the Indus area of the varied, dimly understood nomads who are usually known as Aryans. From the Iranian plateau and parts of what is now southeastern Europe, these adventurers spread in successive and probably quite different waves over a vast area extending from today's India and Pakistan all the way to the eastern Mediterranean. Some of them actually called themselves Aryans: Darius the Persian, a conqueror whose power spread to the Indus area in the Sixth Century B.C., had his gravestone grandiloquently inscribed in letters that may be

translated: "A Persian, son of a Persian, an Aryan of Aryan descent."

The "Aryan" predecessors of Darius appeared in the northern Indus area now known as the Punjab at least 10 centuries before he lived. They either overran such cities as Harappa or took them over by slow infiltration from the surrounding countryside. Bones uncovered at Mohenjo-daro—the skeletons of people who obviously were attacked and slain without warning—attest that this center of Indus culture was overwhelmed in the end by military assault. The newcomers apparently had no taste for city life and left the major centers in empty ruins for a time. In due course, however, degenerated communities occupied some part of the derelict sites as may be discerned from the shoddy construction of later houses. Only in the coastlands of the south did the Indus civilization merge with later cultures, which, in the first millennium B.C., gradually linked up with what we know as Indian history.

A thousand years after the Indus civilization had withered at the core, the Persian Cyrus, who conquered Babylon, and one of his successors, Darius, extended their empire to and far beyond the Indus. Along with India, which by then had absorbed it, the Indus region was part of the Persian Empire that Alexander of Macedon conquered or traversed in the Fourth Century B.C. The Greeks who marched with him and chronicled his exploits marveled at the mighty Indian rivers, the sight of "wool" growing on trees (it was, of course, cotton) and the sweet sugar cane. But such impressions were the extent of the subcontinent's early impact upon western thought and civilization.

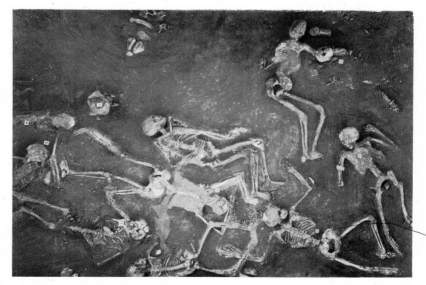

SPRAWLING SKELETONS of men, women and children, victims of a massacre by invaders, tell the story of Mohenjo-daro's end. The bones, some showing sword or ax cuts, were uncovered in the topmost level of the city.

THE DIVINITY OF THE KING, one of the great creative and unifying ideas of Egyptian civilization, is celebrated in a symbolic ritual that emphasizes the god-king's role as mediator between the people and his fellow gods.

Delegates from distant provinces are prostrating themselves before the god-king, who has just had his feet washed with Nile water by two courtiers. In the foreground, priests and standard-bearers move on to the next ceremony.

A NATION UNDER GOD-KINGS

In the valley of the Nile, the self-confident Egyptians evolved a united state with rulers believed to be divine

SHORT, slight, strong-boned and swarthy, the Egyptians appeared on the stage of history about 3100 B.C. as a product of the Afro-Asian melting pot. At least some of them may have reached Egypt as migrants in search of water when the once verdant Sahara region to the west began to dry up. Like the peoples of the Indus and the Tigris and Euphrates, they encountered a hard land. The banks of the Nile were swampy papyrus jungles bordered by desert, demanding a cooperative effort of clearing, draining and irrigation.

But the jungled valley of the Nile also offered two enormous boons: a potential of sustained superabundance, and the security of comparative isolation. With beneficent regularity, the Nile each summer overflowed its banks to deposit a rich black silt from which the Egyptians obtained two or even three harvests a year. And the valley was guarded on the east and west by desert, on the south by the Nile's cataracts, on the north by a Mediterranean upon which few men of 5,000 years ago dared venture far from shore. Thus the settlers along the Nile enjoyed many years of freedom from foreign attack, years in which they could build a society of their own.

But environment, as in Sumer and in the Indus region, can provide only problems and opportunities. Man needed ideas and leadership. The Sumerians seem to have supplied some of the ideas—notably writing—that helped bring Egyptian civilization to birth. But the two fundamental ideas which produced the enduring civilization of the Nile were the Egyptians' own.

The first was the idea of union. The Nile valley north of the cataracts is a natural economic, political and social unit. But until about 3100 B.C. it was a region of feuding tribes and villages, broadly divided between Upper (southern) and Lower (northern) districts. Tradition preserves only the name—Menes—of the southern king who at that time brought the beginnings of national order and prosperity by effecting a union which still survives. The second and related idea was the divinity of the king. In a time when no man doubted the total power of the gods, the existence of a visible god devoted to guiding the nation was both a profound unifying influence and a source of tremendous confidence.

After some 400 scantily recorded years of formative and fruitful union, Egypt emerged about 2700 B.C. with a fully organized central government, high technological skills, a flexible written language, a distinctive national style of art and architecture, and the world's first calendar of 365 days. This was the beginning of the creative half millennium of Egyptian life known as the Old Kingdom, which set the pattern for succeeding epochs.

In this early period of exuberant fertility, the Egyptians perfected their historic innovations in art and architecture, made the world's first scientific medical diagnoses, manufactured the world's first paper (out of papyrus reeds) and invented ink to go with it. Though these achievements were less inventive than the earlier innovations of the Sumerians, they were products of a happier and more durable civilization. It lasted for some 3,000 years, through the three major epochs known as the Old, Middle and New Kingdoms, and under more than 30 ruling families, from the First Dynasty to the last, founded by Ptolemy in 323 B.C.

The written records, art and artifacts preserved by the desert air, in the pyramids and other tombs left by Old Kingdom Egyptians, show them to have been a people buoyant with the conviction that they had been chosen by divine providence for a great national destiny. They were energetic, resourceful, pragmatic, individualistic, lovers of bigness, and self-confident to the point of bumptiousness. Success in the form of wealth and status, which they expected to carry intact into the next life, was their highest goal. These qualities, which helped bring them world power and an enduring place in history, were also to lead to their worst troubles and eventual downfall. Nevertheless, they made the people of the Old Kingdom the first in history to achieve what a man of today might recognize as the good life.

A **HIPPOPOTAMUS HUNT** on the Nile (*below*) is depicted in a Fifth Dynasty tomb. Hunters use spears and harpoons to attack their prey, one of which is fighting a crocodile. The vertical lines represent papyrus plants.

A **ROYAL SHIP** which has been on a pleasure cruise down the Nile is shown putting about to head upstream to Memphis. While the king and his consort watch from the companionway and the captain shouts directions

THE GIFT OF THE NILE

ANYONE who sees Egypt," wrote Herodotus in about 440 B.C., ". . . must perceive that it is an acquired country, the gift of the river." Rudyard Kipling echoed him by calling Egypt ". . . a longish strip of market garden."

Egypt is essentially a narrow green trench cut by the Nile through the red sands of a virtually rainless desert. Today, as in ancient times, the vast majority of its people cluster on a tiny fraction of its land. Through irrigation, ancient Egyptians extended the fertile strip to a width of two to 20 miles in Upper Egypt, broadening it to 120 miles at the Mediterranean delta. The Nile did more than sustain ancient

from the forecastle, a tender helps the vessel swing to port. The design of the sail shown here is copied from fragmentary reliefs of a 2500 B.C. royal ship. At right are three Nile River craft: a sailboat and (*in foreground*) two skiffs, the nearer one made of sycamore, the other of papyrus. To sail upstream the boatmen took the prevailing wind from the Mediterranean; heading downstream they folded their sails and rode with the current.

Egypt with its silt-laden floods. It was also a great national unifier, the main highway of communication and trade. Vessels of many sizes (*above*) plied it constantly. The Nile was also Egypt's playground. Its papyrus swamps, the clearing and draining of which probably took thousands of years, teemed with wildlife. Lovers of both nature and pleasure, Egyptians fished and hunted zestfully (*opposite*).

Fed by melting snows from the highlands of Abyssinia and equatorial Africa, the Nile began its yearly rise in late July and crested in October. To time their agricultural operations, the Egyptians carefully noted the beginning of each annual rise, and found over a half century that the average period between rises was 365 days. Thus came the world's first solar calendar, which the Egyptians divided into three four-month seasons of 120 days each, plus five days. But the Nile

was neither so regular nor so mild as to encourage lethargy. Over the ages the river cut deep into the Egyptian plateau, so that much of its bordering land lay well above it. Irrigation required a constant labor of lifting and carrying water, as well as of cleaning and repairing catch basins and canals. And a rise of only a few inches in the normal flood crest brought destruction of property, while a subnormal crest meant waterless fields and famine. Joseph's Biblical dream of seven fat and seven lean years had a real foundation. Such alternations of prosperity and disaster were not frequent, and the people of the Old Kingdom, with their god-king and sense of special election, believed that any national setback could be only temporary. Even so, though they were profoundly grateful to their great benefactor the Nile, they remained alert, watchful, industrious and foresighted.

A SCRIBE of the Fifth Dynasty is depicted in the statue below. Boys who went to school to learn the difficult hieroglyphic writing and cursive hieratic were assured of good jobs as government officials or estate stewards.

A COURT OF JUSTICE is shown in this painting in session outside the whitewashed walls of Memphis, capital of Egypt's Old Kingdom. Bailiffs are bringing tax-delinquent village chiefs before the judge on the dais at

THE LAW AND "MA'AT"

THE capital of the Old Kingdom was Memphis, near present-day Cairo. Here, according to tradition, King Menes established his government and fortified it with the whitewashed ramparts that gave the city its Egyptian name, "The White Walls." Here tax and census records were filed, and courts dealt with such offenders as the tax delinquents shown above and in the ancient bas-relief opposite.

In theory, ancient Egypt was a totalitarian state. The god-king owned the nation, allowing some private ownership of land but exacting a lion's share of its produce as a tax for the royal treasury. There was no written code of law; the law was the king's will. But in practice there was considerable freedom in Egyptian life. Of necessity, the king delegated many duties of government to ordinary mortals. Legal procedures became established. Thus there arose the world's first centralized bureaucracy, which descended from the king through ministers and governors down to mayors and subsuperintendents of scribes. Provincial governors and other officials grew increasingly independent. Despite unchanging dogmas, the Old Kingdom's secure prosperity and freedom from fear of foreign attack encouraged tolerance of individualism and change. The life of the

the left. He is flanked by scribes who are ready with such equipment of their scholarly profession as reed pens, writing boards, ink cakes and pots of water. At the far right, a previously convicted prisoner is being flogged.

peasant was probably little different from that of ordinary Egyptians today. But there was never a rigid caste system. Burgeoning trade and government required men of talent, and such men could rise, through ability and energy, above the class in which they were born.

But perhaps the greatest leaven of potential tyranny was the concept of *ma'at*—an anticipation of the idea of natural moral law, or "higher law," which was long afterward to become a dominant theme in Anglo-Saxon thought. *Ma'at* combined the concepts of divine order, justice, harmony, goodness and truth; the king and all his officials were supposed to govern in accordance with it.

Despite the beginnings the Egyptians had made in science—in medicine, anatomy, mathematics and astronomy—they continued to believe firmly in the arbitrary powers of the gods, and did not seek any other explanation of natural phenomena. They were not bothered by logical inconsistencies. Perhaps because they believed themselves especially favored by the gods—perhaps because of the Nile's unfailing yearly overflow and the unfailing rise and fall of the sun in Egypt's normally cloudless sky—they perceived a rational order in the universe. This order they applied to human affairs in the practice of *ma'at*. The philosopher-statesman Ptah-hotep set forth one of its practical applications: "Be kindly as thou listenest to what the petitioner has to say. . . . A good hearing is soothing to the heart."

CHIEF READER-PRIEST Ka'aper resembles a modern politician. The Arab diggers who found this 2500 B.C. wooden statue in 1860 said Ka'aper was a double of their village sheikh, indicating the survival of an ancient strain.

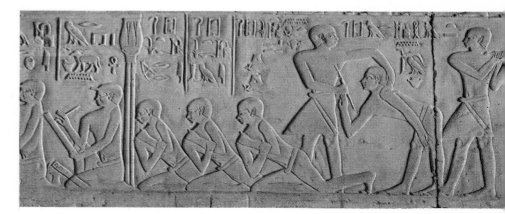

A TRIAL OF TAX DELINQUENTS is shown in this bas-relief from an early Sixth Dynasty tomb. The defendants are village headmen who have not collected taxes properly. The hieroglyphs describe them as local scribes.

AT A QUARRY in the cliffs above the Nile, craftsmen cut and dress blocks of white limestone for a royal pyramid-tomb. In center foreground, the quarry overseer consults a scribe. Surveyors (*left background*) measure the cliff face for new cuttings, while other quarrymen work to free partially detached blocks. The finished block at left is being checked with a plumb line and try square. In left foreground, coppersmiths make chisels by heating,

MASTERS OF STONE

THE supreme artistic innovation of the ancient Egyptians was their use of stone in architecture. The first people to build extensively in stone, they employed it with awesome prodigality.

Their incentives were twofold. One was the abundance of white limestone, red and gray granite, black and green diorite, and alabaster in white, peach and rose. The other was their belief in immortality. The Egyptians built their earthly homes of brick and wood. But their tombs, their homes for eternity, they wrought of lasting stone. Egyptian architecture required feats of engineering which have been

the marvel of the world ever since. In the Old Kingdom, the era of pyramid-building, builders had no iron tools to quarry stones and no wheels or pulleys to transport and hoist the massive blocks, which weighed up to 45 tons. They quarried soft rock such as limestone with copper chisels and saws. They worked hard granite by pounding it with even harder balls of diorite. Having no draft animals, they moved their huge blocks and columns into place by manpower, with no equipment save sledges, ramps, rollers and ropes.

To build the royal monuments, all able-bodied commoners were subject to conscription for a few months' work each year. (Later they were joined by foreign labor, including Hebrews.) Contrary to legend, the workers were not brutalized by whiplashing overseers. Indeed,

pounding and rubbing. At right, a work gang eases a block down a steep ramp, to be dragged away by a sledge on rollers. In the valley, blocks are loaded on barges, which wait for the Nile flood to put them afloat.

THE GREAT SPHINX at Gizeh (*below*) rises 66 feet and is 189 feet long. It was hewn from rock in the 26th Century B.C., during the reign of King Khaf-Re. The Great Pyramid is at right, the Pyramid of Khaf-Re at left.

they received free food, clothes and housing. One scholar has even suggested that, in slack times, the building of the pyramids may have been a form of unemployment relief.

In the later centuries of the Middle and New Kingdoms, Egyptian building was often careless and shoddy. But the men of the Old Kingdom, armed with mathematics of their own devising, had built with pride and precision. The Great Pyramid of Khufu (Cheops) at Gizeh (*right*) no longer gleams white in the desert. More than a thousand years ago Egypt's Arab conquerors stripped away its white limestone facing. But the magnificent workmanship remains. The blocks, averaging two and a half tons each, of the Great Pyramid's 6.25 million tons of stone were laid with joints no bigger than one fiftieth of an inch.

KING KHAF-RE, ruler at about 2550 B.C., who may also have been the model for the face of the Great Sphinx, is portrayed as majestic and serene in this diorite statue. Old Kingdom art was solid, massive and motionless.

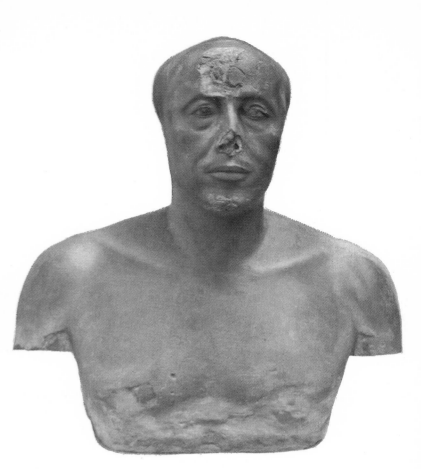

PRINCE ANKH-HAF, Khaf-Re's prime minister and superintendent of royal building, is shown with a lifelike realism that gives this painted bust of stucco-covered limestone a unique place among Old Kingdom sculptures.

ART FOR ETERNITY

ART and literature flourished in the Old Kingdom. They were closely related to religion, which in turn was centered primarily on the afterlife. Members of a god-centered society and living close to a bountiful nature, the Egyptians possessed that joyful serenity which comes only to those who feel themselves in harmony with the universe. Even their materialism was religious; prosperous Egyptians never doubted that the gods intended them to enjoy the good things of this world. If they seem to have been obsessed with death, it was because they enjoyed life to the full and believed that life in the next world —which they called the west because the sun "died" there each day— would be more of the same, but better.

Thus it was reasonable that they should store up for future use, in their eternal homes, the things that had given them sustenance and pleasure on earth: food, clothing, furniture, jewelry, works of art, writings which included records of their own virtues and achievements—plus reminders of their human companions, courtiers and servants. It is to this practice, and to the preservation of these things in the dry air of the desert, that we owe most of our knowledge of ancient Egypt.

The mastery of the Old Kingdom's artists is revealed by their ability to convey their beliefs in line and form. Beginning with the first pyramid (*lower left*), the tombs of the kings embodied a sense of eternity, and the gods, including god-kings such as Khaf-Re (*upper left*), were shown meditating with timeless serenity. Except in a few royal tombs of the First Dynasty, where servants were apparently executed and sometimes interred with the tools of their various trades, no evidence has been found that attendants were actually compelled to die with their master or mistress. Instead they were represented by statues or wall carvings and paintings. Each royal tomb also possessed an adjoining mortuary temple (*opposite*), where priests could serve and glorify the departed monarch. The Old Kingdom zest for life showed itself in tomb scenes depicting not only the pleasures of an abundant harvest, of the hunt, and of feasts and games, but also such touches of broad humor as an ape tripping up a servant, or a bustling dwarf beside a pompous nobleman.

THE FIRST PYRAMID (*left*) is called the Step Pyramid of Sakkarah. The first stone building, it was built for King Djoser about 2650 B.C. His minister, Im-hotep, may have been the genius who founded Egypt's architecture.

IN A TEMPLE attached to a royal pyramid, artists adorn the walls for the glorification of their king. In the foreground are the chief architect (*left*) and the chief artist, directing draftsmen, sculptors and painters. Palm columns, hewn from single blocks of red granite, form a cloister around an open court. The hieroglyphic inscription above the columns reads in part: "Lord of diadems, King of Upper and Lower Egypt . . . Sahu-Re, living forever."

AN ARISTOCRATIC FAMILY of the Old Kingdom enjoys the tranquil beauty of its country estate. A daughter dangles her toes in a lotus-strewn pool, while gardeners tend lush beds of banana, marguerites and other plants.

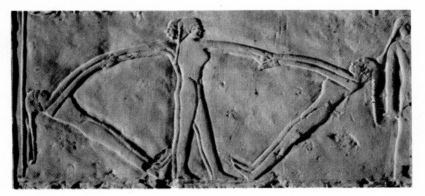

YOUNG GIRLS dance with each other (*below*) in a tomb bas-relief of about 2300 B.C. The Egyptians, who loved children, believed in a happy, uninhibited youth, and frequently showed youngsters at play in their tomb paintings.

A GOOD LIFE AT HOME

AROUND Memphis and other centers of ancient Egypt, many a prosperous, nature-loving Egyptian sought refuge in the pleasures of country living. Sun worshipers and nature lovers, they dressed scantily, and developed on their rural retreats vineyards, orchards and gardens geometrically balanced in accordance with the sense of symmetry found in Egyptian art. To enjoy the prevailing cool wind from the Mediterranean, and avoid occasional hot winds from the desert, they built their houses facing north. The windows were high, the

Only daughters are present; the sons are away at school. Behind the airy brick-and-wood house, the servants are making wine by a process shown in the 24th Century B.C. bas-relief below. The dogs are Egyptian greyhounds.

MAKING WINE, serfs wring out the last drops from a sack of pulp in a press (*below*). Grapes were trampled by foot in a stone vat, then transferred to sacks to be pressed. The juice fermented in flat-bottomed vessels.

rooms airy, the front doors shaded by porticoes with wooden pillars topped by floral capitals representing the palm, papyrus or lotus. Perhaps because of the traditional dignity of the Egyptian queen, who was considered the wife, the mother and often the daughter of gods, ordinary women enjoyed a rarely matched place of honor in Egyptian society. Though the upper-class Egyptian was permitted concubines, the bond between a husband and his wife was normally close, affectionate and durable. In the decoration of his tomb, the Egyptian always included portraits of his wife, her arm around him, sharing the pleasures of the past and the future. Wrote the sage Ptah-hotep: "If thou be wise, marry. Love thy wife sincerely. Make glad her heart all thy life. She is a profitable field for her lord."

THE OLD WAYS CHANGE

ABOUT 2160 B.C., the Old Kingdom collapsed, ushering in more than a century of anarchy and civil war. There were many reasons for the collapse. One scholar blames "the excesses of unrelieved materialism." In a society which measured success only by wealth and status, self-seeking gradually eliminated any devotion to the common good. Over the centuries, the nobles in outlying provinces grew increasingly independent and powerful, the king correspondingly weaker. The monarchs themselves often failed in their duty to the nation. The immense diversion of labor and wealth entailed in building and furnishing the pyramids weakened the national economy. Foreign trade declined. In the end, peace and order departed from the land.

To the staggering discovery that their way of life was not eternal, some Egyptians reacted with despair and suicide. But among others there arose history's first stirring of social conscience. Old Kingdom aristocrats had presumably regarded their peasantry as beasts of burden. Now pioneer reformers anticipated the Hebrews and Greeks by more than a thousand years with concepts of individual human worth and social justice. There was a new emphasis on the rights of the ruled and the responsibilities of the ruler. Special stress was placed on the right of everyone to speak out. One "eloquent peasant" spoke to a chief steward in words that are still preserved: "If falsehood walk about, it goes astray. . . . As for him who grows rich thereby, he has no children, he has no heirs upon earth. . . . Now *ma'at* lasts unto eternity; it goes down into the necropolis with him who does it. When he is buried and interred, his name is not wiped out upon earth, he is remembered for goodness. That is a principle of the word of god."

Another extraordinary document has the supreme creator-god declare: "I made the four winds that every man might breathe thereof like his fellow in his time. . . . I made the great inundation that the poor man might have rights therein like the great man. . . . I made every man like his fellow. I did not command that they do evil; it was their hearts that violated what I had said."

One lasting effect of the reform was what has been called the "democratization of the hereafter." Originally the Egyptians appeared to believe that only members of the royal family and their chosen companions were expected to enjoy eternal life. Gradually nobles and high officials joined them. Now this privilege was claimed for all "good men," and prosperous middle-class families began to make modest imitations of royal burials. It was asserted that the tribunal of the gods would judge the dead not by their wealth, prestige and rich offerings, but by the righteousness of their lives. "More acceptable is the character of one upright of heart than the ox of the evildoer."

A MIDDLE-CLASS FAMILY enjoys eternal happiness (*below*). This Middle Kingdom tomb bas-relief shows a man seated between his wife and friend. At the right, beside a pile of foodstuffs stored for the hereafter, stands his sister.

A NOBLE COUPLE of the Old Kingdom, Prince Ra-hotep and his wife Nefret are portrayed for their tomb in painted limestone images with rock crystal eyes. These lifelike statues startled the excavators who found them in 1871.

OLD KINGDOM AMUSEMENT is pictured above. The pigtails of the dancing girls are weighted to give a swinging motion to the dance. The lady watching in the right foreground wears a high-fashion formal wig and eye shadow.

NEW KINGDOM PAINTING of the 18th Dynasty (*below*) depicts musicians and dancing girls in a naturalistic style that broke with the old formalism. The musicians' heads are topped by cones of perfume, which drip as they play.

A GREAT WOMAN AND THE BIRTH OF EMPIRE

ABOUT 2050 B.C. the rulers of Thebes reunited Egypt by conquest, and established what is known as the Middle Kingdom. Under a succession of strong, conscientious kings, active in promoting public works, the nation prospered. But the reform movement did not long survive the return of prosperity. Nor did the Middle Kingdom itself last long. The new rulers never won full control of the provinces and their feudal princes, and in time internal strains exposed Egypt to another great shock. This was the humiliation of the first conquest by foreign invaders.

The invaders, who came and conquered about 1700 B.C., were Asiatic tribesmen called Hyksos or shepherd kings. Introducing such novel military equipment as the horse and the chariot, they remained for some one hundred years but were never able to rule all Egypt. In time the Egyptians adopted their armament, drove them out of the country and began the period known as the New Kingdom.

Only now did Egypt's rulers begin to acquire the title "pharaoh," a word meaning "great house" and long used solely in reference to the king's palace. One of the great pharaohs of the 18th Dynasty was Queen Hat-shepsut, Egypt's first woman ruler. By a custom designed to prevent dilution of the royal and hence presumably divine blood, and because the royal succession was conveyed through the female line, prospective pharaohs often married their sisters. Hat-shepsut seized the throne on the death of her husband-brother, Thut-mose II, and rightfully took credit for Egypt's recovery from the barbarian occupation: "I have restored that which had been ruined." A vigorous monarch, she sponsored vast public works, sent commercial expeditions afar, and had built for herself one of the most beautiful temples of all time (*left*).

But the Egyptians were never to be the same again; the old complacency and isolationism were gone. Their long conviction of superiority gave way to a fear of foreign powers. One result was that the country's tolerant, life-loving spirit was replaced by a demand for conformity. The strict rule of pharaohs and an increasingly powerful priesthood required Egyptians to submerge their lusty individualism and close ranks in silent obedience for the national security.

A second result was the world's first great organized empire. Not content with driving out the Hyksos, the Theban founders of the 18th Dynasty set out to conquer bordering lands. The process was consummated by Egypt's greatest military genius, Pharaoh Thut-mose III, a stepson-nephew of Queen Hat-shepsut, who had long bitterly resented her presence on the throne he considered his. After her death he overthrew the statues in her temple and marched off to war against a coalition of city-kings from Palestine, Syria and Lebanon. Thereafter for 20 years he led an army into Asia almost every spring. His conquests brought Egypt to the peak of imperial power.

HAT-SHEPSUT was history's first great woman. Here she wears the pharaoh's ceremonial headdress.

THUT-MOSE III is remembered as the great conqueror. He succeeded his stepmother-aunt on the throne.

TEMPLE OF HAT-SHEPSUT nestles below the cliffs near Thebes (*left*). Built by an architect named Sen-Mut, it is a graceful departure from massiveness. The colonnades rise in three tiers to a sanctuary of solid rock.

EGYPT'S MANY GODS

FOR all their preoccupation with eternity, the Egyptians never evolved a coherent system of religious thought. Gods rose and fell as political dominance shifted, their names changing and their identities merging as one deity absorbed the attributes of another. For Egyptian philosophy was myth-making, not logical or speculative; the Egyptian mentality was such that it could embrace irreconcilable concepts and regard them as complementary rather than opposed.

In the beginning, like other early peoples, the Egyptians saw their gods in nature—in wind and water, in trees and animals, and in the sky. As society coalesced into villages and townships, local deities rose to local dominion. In the small delta town of Behdet, for example, people worshiped a god named Horus who appeared in the form of a falcon. In another part of the delta a legendary king named Osiris was originally deified as a god of vegetation. The town of Heliopolis became the center of a cult dedicated to the god Atum, later called Re. With the passing centuries, the competing gods, claiming ever-wider allegiance, impinged on one another's domains. By the time of the Old Kingdom, the major gods had become members of a divine family known as the Ennead, or The Nine. According to this cosmogony, the creator Atum rose from the waters of chaos and on a primeval hillock engendered the first two additional gods, Shu, god

THE GODDESS ISIS holds her son Horus on her knee in a statuette of post-empire times. The wife of Osiris, ruler of the kingdom of the dead, she was revered by Egyptians as the prototype of the ever-faithful consort.

THE SKY GODDESS NUT is depicted on a painted papyrus (*above*) as spanning the earth. Her star-spangled body is supported by the upraised arms of Shu, god of the air. Her husband Geb, god of the earth, reclines below.

THE GOD RE-HARAKHTE, an incarnation of the sun god Re, is shown in this wall painting with a falcon's head, symbol of Horus, topped by a solar disk, symbol of Re. Behind him sits Hat-Hor, goddess of love and joy.

of air, and Tefnut, goddess of moisture. From their union came Geb, god of the earth, and Nut, goddess of the sky (*below*). And these in turn bore four offspring, Osiris (*above*) and his consort Isis (*left*), and Seth and his consort Nephthys.

This legend was the starting point for endless elaborations. As in the Bible story of Cain and Abel, a jealous brother, Seth, committed murder: he killed Osiris. Isis found her husband's body and miraculously restored it to life. Osiris became king of the region of the dead and Isis bore their child, Horus. The legend had an important application to divine kingship. Each pharaoh was the son of Osiris and the living incarnation of Horus. An equally important doctrine held that each pharaoh was the son of Re, who perished each evening at sundown and was reborn at dawn. Both stories involve resurrection, and the Egyptians liked and believed in both.

Of all the gods, the one who ultimately attained greatest power was Amon-Re. From prehistoric times the people of Thebes had worshiped their local god, Amon, god of the invisible wind. But like all Egyptians they had also acknowledged the sun god, Re. When Thebes became capital of the empire, the composite Amon-Re emerged as king of the gods, a universal deity uniting the cosmic forces of sun and air and endowing Egyptian rule with a divine sanction that transcended all boundaries on earth. Enriched by various tributes, the priesthood of Amon-Re became the world's wealthiest organization, with his high priest rivaling the pharaoh in power.

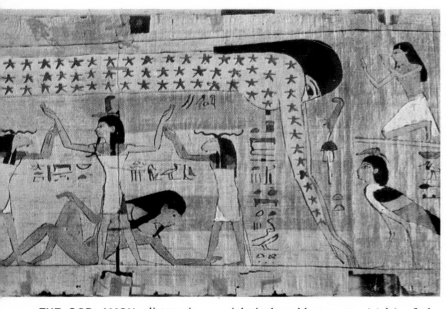

THE GOD AMON glistens in an eight-inch gold statuette (*right*) of the 22nd Dynasty. Regarded as the most powerful of Egyptian gods, he is shown holding the scimitar, symbol of conquest, and the hieroglyph for "life."

PROPHET OF ONE GOD

THE most extraordinary character in Egyptian history was a mis-shapen pharaoh born about 1400 B.C. and given the dynastic name Amen-hotep IV. Dreamer, esthete, iconoclast and intellectual genius, he became the first man known in history to make the inspired leap from belief in many gods to the concept of one god. He identified Aton, hitherto considered the visible disk of the sun and Re's resting place, as the source of life in the universe, dispenser of light and love and joy not only to Egypt but to all the world. Changing his name from Amen-hotep (Amon Is Satisfied) to Akh-en-Aton (He Who Is Serviceable to Aton), he abandoned Thebes to build a new capital, which he called Akhet-Aton (The Place of the Effective Glory of the Aton). Here he erected a great temple and many smaller chapels, all without statues and open to the sun.

In his new capital, Akh-en-Aton lived serenely with his beautiful queen Nefert-iti (*below*) and their six daughters, despite the tumult that was created by his attempt to overthrow the old gods throughout the land. While the empire crumbled, he wrote poems to Aton and fostered art. Also a rebel against the static, stylized tradition of Egyptian art, he encouraged the depiction of people, things, and even himself (*right*) as the artist saw them. He also dispelled some of the awesome mystery of the divine kingship by allowing informal portraits of himself and his family eating, kissing, playing.

Akh-en-Aton's religious revolution ended in failure. His message, chiefly intellectual, did not reach the people but it roused fierce opposition among the powerful priesthoods. But, though the date of the Biblical Exodus from Egypt is uncertain, his great idea may conceivably have influenced Moses, the foundling of the Egyptian bulrushes, whose name is a variant of the Egyptian word for "child."

NEFERT-ITI, Akh-en-Aton's queen, is pictured in this famous bust. The legend that she was also Akh-en-Aton's sister is now questioned by scholars. She participated loyally in her husband's struggle against polytheism.

AKH-EN-ATON is shown here as he allowed a sculptor to depict his narrow shoulders and swollen abdomen and hips. The artistic naturalism he encouraged is called "Amarna style," after the modern name of his capital.

115

COLOSSI OF AMEN-HOTEP III tower above the flooding Nile River. Carved from single blocks of quartzite standing as high as a six-story building, they commemorate the great Egyptian king who was the father of Akh-en-Aton.

HEAD OF RAMSES II (*opposite*) lies on the ground amid the ruins of a temple constructed by the pharaoh around 1280 B.C. for the glory of the god Amon and himself. The head, of black granite, is about 12 feet high.

THE GIGANTIC RUINS
OF A DYING EMPIRE

THE TEMPLE OF AMON at Karnak in Thebes, built during the late empire, is the culmination of the Egyptians' passion for overpowering size and grandeur. The largest columns are 69 feet high and 33 feet in circumference.

ALTHOUGH the empire was rebuilt after Akh-en-Aton's death and lasted another 150 years, it never regained its prestige. But it attained a final burst of sunset glory during the reign of the spectacular Ramses II. He ruled for 67 years, 1304 to 1237 B.C., and lived past 90. He sired more than a hundred sons and daughters. He strewed the Nile Valley with obelisks and colossal statues commemorating his deeds, and completed at Thebes the biggest columned hall ever built (*left*).

Ramses II was by no means the first Egyptian ruler with an obsession for self-aggrandizement and size. A century earlier, King Amenhotep III planted two colossal statues of himself in western Thebes (*above*). But Ramses also appropriated the ancient monuments of his forebears, substituting his name for theirs. Meanwhile, enemies of Egypt were encroaching on the frontiers. The severed head of his colossal statue at Thebes remains today as a symbol of Egypt's shattered empire. Shelley's poem *Ozymandias* refers to Ramses by a Greek version of his throne name:

> . . . Two vast and trunkless legs of stone
> Stand in the desert. Near them on the sand,
> Half sunk, a shatter'd visage lies . . .
> And on the pedestal these words appear:
> "My name is Ozymandias, king of kings:
> Look on my works, ye Mighty, and despair!"
> Nothing beside remains. Round the decay
> Of that colossal wreck, boundless and bare,
> The lone and level sands stretch far away.

Later, when their imperial glory was a memory, the Egyptians found consolation in other values. One said of the ancient sages: "Books of wisdom were their pyramids, and the pen was their child."

THE "DIVINE WORDS"
OF EGYPT

RAMSES III was the last of the great pharaohs, reigning from 1198 to 1166 B.C. After him Egypt was to have another thousand years as an independent nation (though often under foreign-born rulers), but the old power was gone. The loss of confidence that began with the collapse of the Old Kingdom and the feeling of insecurity and regimentation that set in with the Hyksos invasion seem to have killed the Egyptian spirit.

Egypt was invaded many times—by Ethiopians, Babylonians, Assyrians, Persians, and finally, in 332 B.C., by Alexander the Great, whose satrap, Ptolemy, founded ancient Egypt's last dynasty. The Ptolemaic period kindled a final flare of cultural greatness, during which the great library at Alexandria became a world center of learning. The period ended in 30 B.C., with Cleopatra's death.

The Egyptians gave the world its oldest surviving mathematical treatises, its first medical books, its first anatomical and medical vocabulary, its first pharmacopoeia (which included castor oil), its first instructions in surgery, in the diagnosis and treatment of disease, and in the use of bandages, compresses, sutures and splints.

The Egyptians had deep faith in the magic of the written word and believed that by the very act of writing they could insure the realization of the thoughts and hopes inscribed. From the Fourth Dynasty on, the tombs of noblemen were decorated with hieroglyphic texts affirming the merits of their life in this world and their hope of its continuation in the next. From the Fifth Dynasty on, tombs were painted with even more elaborate inscriptions. Although in theory a king was a god who returned to the company of his fellow deities, the Egyptians left nothing to chance. They set down prayers, pleas, ancient rituals and mystic spells designed to influence the gods and project their monarch's sovereignty into the hereafter.

The hieroglyphs that embellished royal tombs were wrought with exquisite care. Yet even in the ordinary usages of daily life, the written language entailed high artistic skill. The earliest examples of Egyptian writing—memorial inscriptions from the First Dynasty—date from 3100 B.C. The last, so far as is known, were set down in 394 A.D. At the very beginning of this enormous span, the hieroglyphic language (from the Greek *hieros,* meaning "sacred," plus *glyphein,* meaning "to carve") evolved swiftly into a rich and versatile system that could encompass any subject, from poetry and legend to business, medicine and law. Although it underwent subsequent changes, the remarkable fact is that it changed so little. By contrast, for example, with the huge mutations that have occurred in English in the 600 years between Chaucer and the present day, modifications of hieroglyphic writing were so slight that, having assumed its classic form in the Old Kingdom, it was still successfully employed for religious and official purposes 2,500 years later.

From the Old Kingdom on, anyone desirous of a government career had to read and write, and anyone who mastered these arts was assured of a comfortable livelihood. It was education that created the ruling class. To equip sons for careers in government, the priest-

REMOVING CONSECRATION BALM that had hardened into a pitchlike material, Egyptologist Howard Carter prepares to open the coffin of Tut-ankh-Amon. Many coffins contained curses on looters, inscribed in hieroglyphs.

hood or the arts, parents entered them in scribal schools at the age of five. There they memorized classic texts and took endless dictation from their teachers. The curriculum was rigid and the discipline severe, as revealed by student copybooks in which schoolboys had to write and rewrite, in order to perfect their calligraphy, such maxims as: "The ear of the boy is on his back and he harkeneth when he is beaten." To become a scribe, the Egyptian schoolboy was faced with the difficult task of learning at least 700 different characters. He also had to be able to draw them with felicity. Among the characters were intricate pictographs of people, anatomical parts, animals, birds, amphibians, ships, fish, tools and trees.

The complexity of the scribes' work and of the language was increased by the fact that the individual hieroglyphs were used in different contexts in two fundamentally different ways: (1) as ideographs, or sense signs, conveying the literal idea of the object shown, e.g., the sign for the sun ⊙ which might denote "sun," "light" or "day"; and (2) as phonograms, or sound signs, used to spell out sounds as in charades, e.g., the owl 𓅓 and the hand ⸺ which denote respectively the sounds *m* and *d,* because the Egyptian words for "owl" and "hand" were dominated by the consonant in question. Hieroglyphs

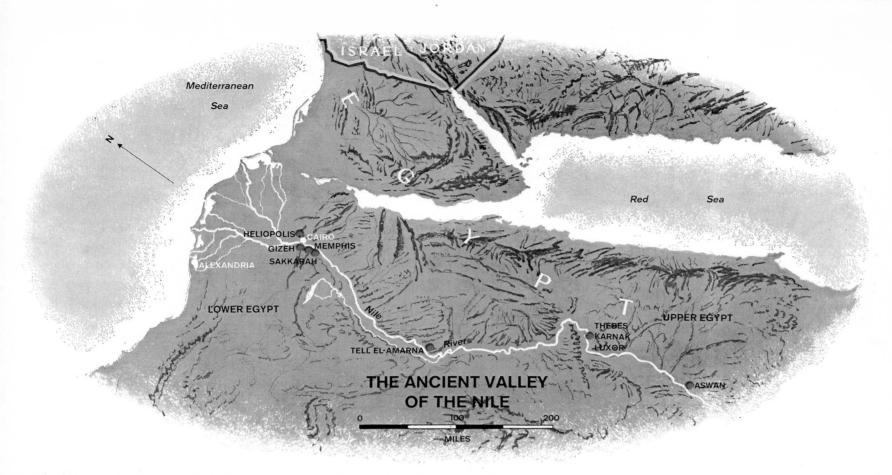

THE ANCIENT VALLEY OF THE NILE

Mediterranean Sea

ISRAEL · JORDAN

Red Sea

HELIOPOLIS · CAIRO
GIZEH · MEMPHIS
ALEXANDRIA SAKKARAH

LOWER EGYPT

Nile

TELL EL-AMARNA River

THEBES
KARNAK
LUXOR

UPPER EGYPT

ASWAN

0   100   200
MILES

doubtless evolved in prehistoric times directly out of pictorial art. But they became a system of writing only after the addition of the charade, or rebus, principle, which may have been borrowed from the Sumerians. The great Egyptologist, Sir Alan Gardiner, has suggested that the desire to convey proper names stimulated the development of the rebus principle—as in English one might represent the name Churchill by pictures of a church and a hill.

In the course of applying the rebus principle, the Egyptians evolved, by Old Kingdom times, a phonetic alphabet, consisting of 24 consonants and semiconsonants, including several glottal and gutteral sounds which do not occur in English. Although the idea of an alphabet was a unique inspiration, the Egyptians never realized its advantages and never developed it further. Nor did they ever bother to develop symbols for vowels. Their word stems consisted entirely of consonants. Vowel sounds mainly conveyed changes of tense or mood and were therefore of only secondary importance.

Far from contenting themselves with the sound signs represented by the 24 consonants of their alphabet, the Egyptians also employed signs denoting two, three or four consonants in combination—the choice depending on convention and the amount of time and space available to the scribe. Moreover, they often combined ideographs with phonograms—the former suggesting the general idea, the latter the pronunciation. Together they transmitted the precise word.

EGYPTIAN hieroglyphs could be written from left to right, from right to left, or vertically, depending on the space to be filled and the scribe's artistic fancy. Furthermore, words were run together without spacing in order to produce a handsome, continuous sequence. The clue to the direction was indicated by the signs depicting birds, snakes and other creatures; if they faced to the right, for example, one was expected to start reading from the right.

The two hieroglyphic sentences shown below—here spaced for clarity—reveal most of the considerations cited in the preceding text. They are taken from a self-laudatory inscription in the tomb of a prime minister who wanted the gods as well as posterity to know how hard he had worked for his king. Beneath each hieroglyphic word is its phonetic transliteration (the signs resembling quotation marks indicate gutteral sounds). Beneath the transliteration is the English translation.

mk	*wi*	*m*	*nfw*	*n·f-imy*
Behold,	I	(am as)	a skipper	belonging to him.

ḥm·n·(i)	*ʿwy*	*grḥ*	*mi*	*hrw*
I am ignorant of	sleep	night	as well as	day.

Hieroglyphs required such painstaking calligraphy that in time the scribes evolved a cursive, everyday handwriting called hieratic in which the elaborate hieroglyphs were reduced to simpler lines representing only the barest suggestion of the originals. As the centuries passed, hieroglyphic writing was relegated entirely to sacred and official inscriptions on temples and funerary monuments, and hieratic became the dominant form. It was in hieratic that all correspondence, legal documents and business transactions were set down. And it was in hieratic that the Egyptians left their legacy of medical science to the western world. Here is an example from an Old Kingdom medical papyrus: "If thou examinest a man having a wound in the top of his eyebrow, penetrating to the bone, thou shouldst palpate the wound, and draw together for him his gash with stitching. . . . If thou findest that the stitching is loose, thou shouldst draw it together for him with two strips of plaster, and thou shouldst treat it with grease and honey every day until he recovers."

Hieratic gave way to a still more abbreviated script called demotic. And in the Second or Third Century A.D., demotic was swallowed up in turn by Coptic. The language of the Copts, early Egyptian converts to Christianity, Coptic was written largely in Greek letters.

SURVEYING A TEMPLE AREA, French architect Jean Pierre Minost and an Arab assistant prepare for the removal of the building to save it from the waters of the Aswan High Dam. The temple, Es Sebua, was built by Ramses II.

A PHOENICIAN WAREHOUSE on the waterfront at Tyre is packed with finely crafted goods for export. The Phoenicians lived on the eastern coast of the Mediterranean and absorbed the cultures of the invaders, immigrants and travelers who passed through the area at a critical period of civilization's development. Both as traders and as colonists, the Phoenicians carried new technologies and ideas—including the new idea of the alphabet—on to Europe.

OLD STATES, NEW EMPIRES

After 2000 B.C., civilization was enriched by the clash and intermixing of peoples in the eastern Mediterranean

AT the beginning of the second millennium B.C., the principal civilized societies, located along the Tigris and Euphrates Rivers in Asia and the Nile in Africa, had lived for more than a thousand years in nearly total isolation from each other. This isolation was about to be shattered. New powers, such as the Hittites in the Anatolian mountains of what is now central Turkey, were beginning to rise around the old societies. The big powers of Egypt and Babylonia, having achieved the difficult transition to nationhood, began increasingly to move out of their own borders to meet and trade. The ideas and techniques of civilization began to reach less developed peoples, causing them to grow in strength and confidence. This was the age in which civilization first became truly international and the area of the civilized world was greatly expanded.

As historian Gordon Childe has said, by the time this era came to an end, around 500 B.C., "The several portions of this zone [from the Atlantic coast of Spain to the Ganges in India, and from southern Arabia to the northern coasts of the Mediterranean, approximately] were integrated and interconnected to a degree never before attained. An educated Persian or Greek, however vague and inaccurate his knowledge of its extremities, could feel himself an inhabitant of a humanly populated world—an *oikoumene,* as the Greeks called it— four times as large as an Egyptian or Babylonian could have dreamed of a thousand years earlier."

The great meeting place of peoples lay between Egypt and the Mesopotamian region around the Tigris and Euphrates Rivers. It was the narrow Syro-Palestinian strip along the Mediterranean's eastern shore that now includes parts of Syria, Lebanon, Israel and western Jordan. This coastal strip was the land route between Asia and Africa, and its shore was one terminus of the sea lanes that connected Europe with Asia and Africa. Here came most of the celebrated peoples of the era—Egyptians, Hittites, Babylonians, Assyrians, Hebrews, Phoenicians, Philistines and many others who make up a stirring roll call of the names of antiquity. A lively intermingling of cultures took place over a period lasting a millennium and a half. Many people helped spread the ideas of civilization. Among the most influential were descendants of the region's earliest settlers, who came to be called Canaanites and, later, Phoenicians.

The late Neolithic villages of the pioneers of the eastern Mediterranean arose about the same time as similar settlements along the Tigris-Euphrates and the Nile. But the people of the eastern Mediterranean had no lack of raw materials such as drove the river-valley peoples out to raid and trade, and they had no need to cooperate in major irrigation projects. Their first settlements grew up around small rivers and springs. In addition, they had regular rainfall, abundant forests and metallic ores.

Contentedly, they established small city-states, each with its own king. They probably had no collective name for themselves. As they absorbed successive waves of migrants from both north and west, their stock became mixed. By the time the Old Testament Hebrews came on the scene, they were being called Canaanites and their land Canaan, probably from the word of a neighboring people for "purple dye." For they had acquired fame as dyemakers, especially of "royal," or "Tyrian," purple (from their city of Tyre), which they obtained from murex shellfish. Later the Greeks began calling them Phoenicians, from the Greek *phoinix,* which means "purple red." Historians now use the Greek name to identify the people concentrated in the coastal port cities after invaders occupied most of Canaan.

As political and military powers, the people of the land of Canaan were always to be overshadowed by others. But their cultural influence was extensive. After losing most of their land, the Phoenicians devoted themselves in earnest to the foreign trade and colonization that made them one of the most important carriers of eastern ideas and technology to barbarous Europe. Among the civilizing tools they carried abroad was an invention of their own: the first true alphabet.

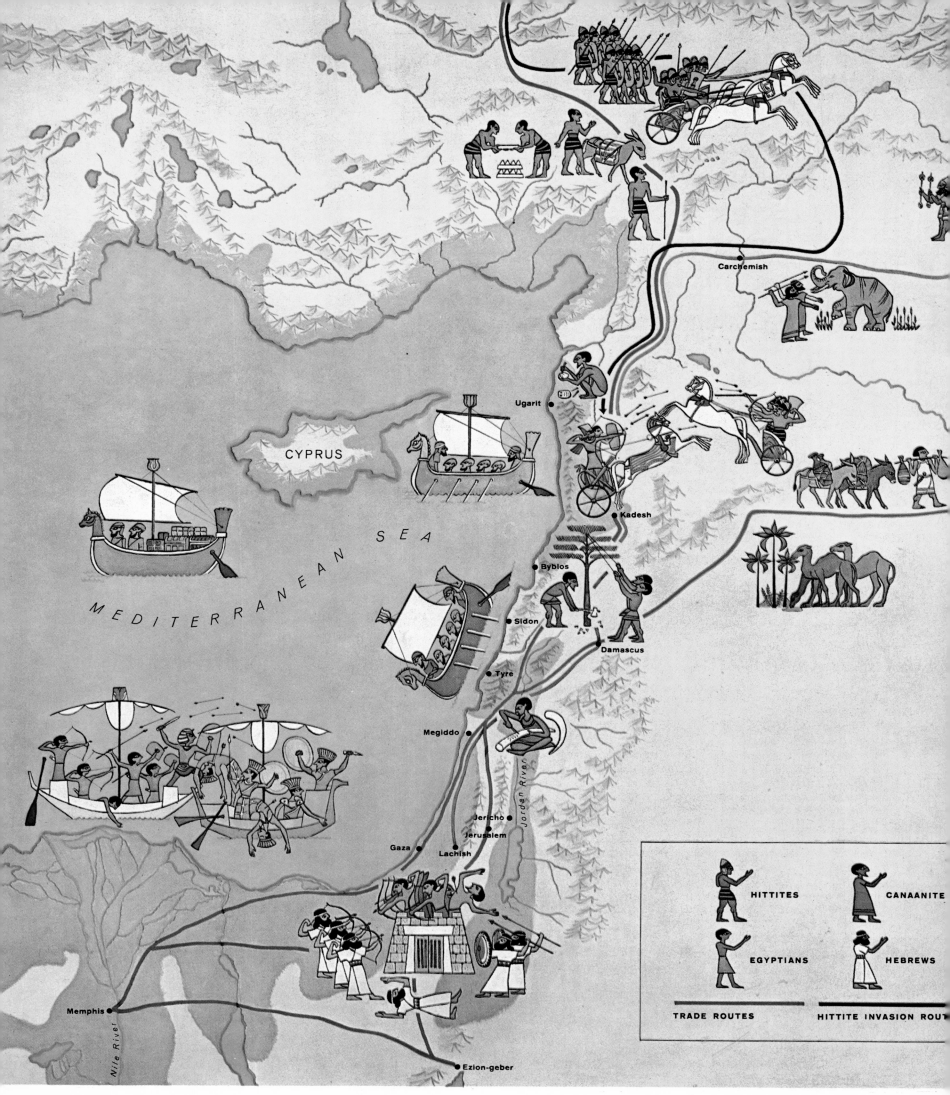

Map labels: Carchemish, Ugarit, CYPRUS, Kadesh, Byblos, Sidon, Damascus, Tyre, MEDITERRANEAN SEA, Megiddo, Jordan River, Jericho, Jerusalem, Gaza, Lachish, Memphis, Nile River, Ezion-geber

Legend:
HITTITES — CANAANITE
EGYPTIANS — HEBREWS
TRADE ROUTES — HITTITE INVASION ROUT[E]

THE MAIN INTERNATIONAL ROUTES of war and trade and the chief peoples who used them from about the 16th to the Sixth Century B.C. are shown on this map, which presents the important events of a millennium. At the top, Hittite warriors begin a sweep of conquest that will take them into northern Syro-Palestine, and Hittite miners stack ingots of silver and gold they have brought out of the Taurus Mountains. Assyrian warriors are shown at the right, and at Nineveh an Assyrian king receives tribute from subject peoples. Near him, Canaanite ivory hunters attack one of the elephants that were once plentiful in the Euphrates marshes. At Ugarit, a scribe uses an early version of that invaluable Canaanite invention, the alphabet. At sea, two Canaanite merchantmen rowed by slaves are heading west to Cyprus and beyond, and a third sails south to Egypt. At Kadesh, the Egyptians meet the Hittites in a

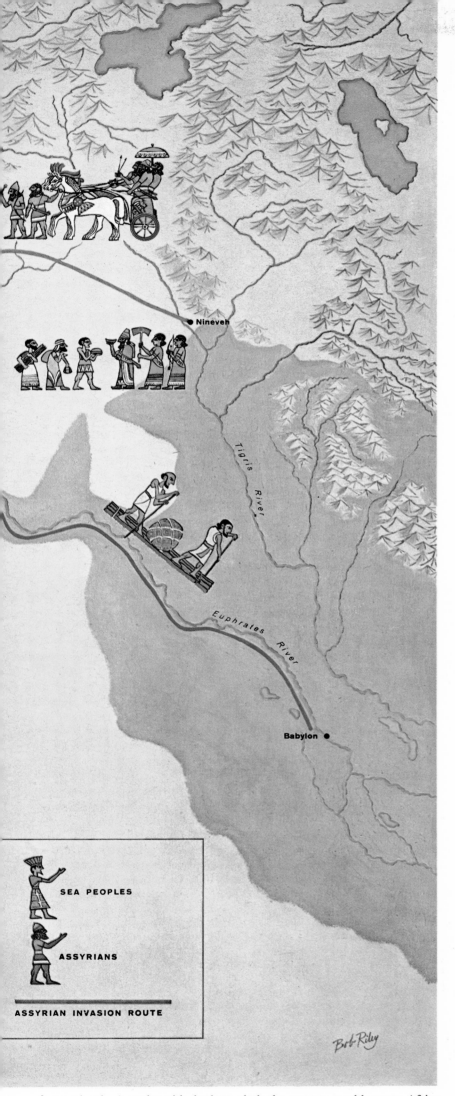

AT THE CROSSROADS OF CIVILIZATION

E GYPT'S influence in the crossroads area of Syro-Palestine was dominant from about 2600 to 1200 B.C. But to the north a new power was rising: a squat, militant mountain people called Hittites, who had invaded and conquered north-central Asia Minor sometime before 1900 B.C. They began to threaten Egyptian dominance in Syro-Palestine toward the middle of the 16th Century. About 1370, while Egypt was preoccupied with Pharaoh Akh-en-Aton's religious revolution, the Hittites made good their conquest of the northern area of Syro-Palestine. The black line at the top of the map shows their invasion route and roughly bounds the southern part of their empire. At Kadesh in 1286, Ramses II of Egypt fought a major battle against the Hittites and lost, as related on the next page.

Except for the Hittites and Egyptians, most of the famous peoples of this time and place—Canaanites, Hebrews, Babylonians and Assyrians—were Semitic. They were related to each other in language and are thought to have been racially related, too. They all came out of the Arabian Desert, drawn by the fertile lands of Mesopotamia and Syro-Palestine. Their common name derives from the Biblical account of the Flood and the supposed descent of the Hebrews from Noah's son Sem, or Shem.

The relationship of all these peoples inspired no outward sense of brotherhood. The Old Testament relates that the first Hebrew patriarch, Abraham, was a native of Haran, in northern Mesopotamia, which scholars think he must have left about 2000 B.C. After a sojourn in Egypt, the Biblical account continues, his descendants were led by Moses to the "promised land" of Canaan. As rough and hardy nomads, the Hebrews succeeded in taking the mountainous southern lands of the Canaanites with comparative ease. They encountered a more formidable enemy in one group of the raiding Sea Peoples, called Philistines, who had settled near them in the Gaza area. Aramaean nomads took a hand in the conquest of Canaanite land. After about nine tenths of their land was lost, the Canaanites turned more and more to foreign commerce. Known as Phoenicians, they became the greatest merchant mariners of their time.

The Assyrians, inhabitants of the upper Tigris region who had long been content to act as traders between the Hittites and the Mesopotamians, had built up a powerful state by 1100 B.C. After mastering Babylonia, they began to make a bid for empire early in the Ninth Century. Jerusalem was among the cities that escaped slaughter and sacking by paying heavy tribute to the conquering Assyrians. The map on these pages shows their invasion route, ending at Lachish, which Sennacherib captured in 701. Within less than half a century, the Assyrians had also conquered Egypt, uniting the entire region from the Persian Gulf to the Nile in the world's first great empire.

IRON AGE ARTIFACTS found at the sites of Philistine and Hebrew cities (*below*) show that the era began toward the end of the second millennium B.C. From top to bottom are a dagger, a plowshare, arrowheads and a sickle.

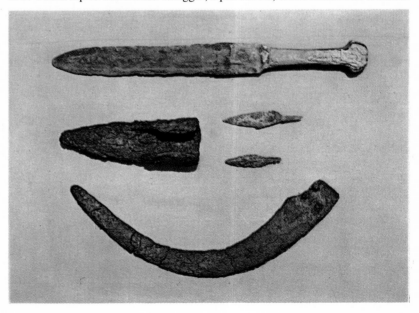

famous battle. A trader with donkeys plods the caravan road between Africa and Mesopotamia. East of Sidon, Canaanite woodsmen fell a cedar of Lebanon. Off the Nile delta, Egyptians are attacked by raiding tribes called Sea Peoples. On land, the Hebrews, having made their Exodus out of Egypt, besiege a Canaanite stronghold. The trade route at bottom connects the Nile kingdom with copper mines, later exploited by King Solomon, around Ezion-geber.

THE BATTLE OF KADESH

THE Hittites, mighty conquerors in their time, bequeathed little to posterity except relics of their fighting prowess and of their fleeting empire. Their most memorable military encounter occurred in 1286 B.C., when Pharaoh Ramses II of Egypt, whom the Greeks called Ozymandias, undertook to regain the north Syro-Palestine area where the Hittites had established control nearly a century before. Masters of ambush, the Hittites under King Muwatallis concealed their troops on the east side of the Orontes River. Ramses marched up the west side to Kadesh at the head of one of his divisions, leaving the other three straggling far behind. While Ramses camped northwest of the city, the Hittites sent the nearest of the straggling Egyptian divisions into a panicky flight that swept most of Ramses' own division along with it.

Left with little but his household guard and a few officers, the young pharaoh suddenly found himself confronted by the entire Hittite force. Mounting his chariot, he bravely led charge after charge into the massed troops of the enemy, tumbling many of them back into the river. A Hittite division that could have easily overwhelmed Ramses from the rear stopped instead to loot his camp. Finally reinforcements for the Egyptians arrived and the Hittites withdrew into the walled city for the night.

The Pharaoh Ramses promptly went back home to claim and advertise a great "victory," but he left the Hittites in control of the northern territory. He eventually acknowledged their right to it by signing with them what may have been the world's first mutual-defense and nonaggression pact. He later took a Hittite wife to cement the treaty. The Hittites held on for less than a century more. Then they in their turn fell before invaders and began to fade out of history.

THE "KING'S GATE," one of nine in the wall that surrounded Hattusas, the Hittite capital, still stands in the Taurus foothills 50 miles east of Ankara, modern Turkey's capital. The wall was probably built about 1800 B.C.

HITTITES IN PANIC (*left*) flee across the Orontes River to the walled city of Kadesh, at upper right, before the charge of a gigantic, godlike Ramses II. This relief, in the "Ramesseum" at Luxor, is one of 10 with which Ramses advertised his "victory." But the Hittites kept the territory.

HITTITE WARRIORS are carved in line (*below*) on the rock walls of the outdoor sanctuary at their chief religious shrine, two miles east of Hattusas. They wear the peaked headdresses with which the Hittites adorned their gods, suggesting that these warriors had a religious function.

CANAANITE OPULENCE

THE opulent worldliness of the Canaanites shocked the Hebrew prophets of the Old Testament, dedicated as they were to the simple ways and austerity of their nomadic ancestors. Most of the Canaanite culture was borrowed—from Egypt, Mesopotamia and the Aegean—but what the Canaanites lacked in originality they made up for in sheer lavishness. They delighted in vivid colors, and their dress was rich and elaborate; the Canaanite gentleman in the Egyptian portrait at the left is clearly a dandy. Their luxury products were in demand throughout the Mediterranean world. The ivory pieces discovered at Megiddo, including those shown on these pages, record the industry of Canaanite artists no less than their skill. Canaanite cities—Jericho, Hazor, Jerusalem, Ascalon, Gaza, Ugarit, Megiddo—were populous and well-to-do. Hazor in its prime boasted between 30,000 and 40,000 inhabitants. But even for the time, the Canaanite religion was primitive. The prophets of the Hebrews particularly inveighed against the god Baal, most popular in the pantheon of the Canaanites. The Canaanites practiced ritual prostitution and sacrificed human beings as well as animals to their gods. And their fertility goddesses supposedly took great pleasure in sex, war and bloodshed.

A CANAANITE ARISTOCRAT, one captured by Egyptians, is pictured at left with rich dress, well-kept hair and pointed beard. This portrait is on a glazed faïence tile used as a doorjamb inset in the palace of Ramses III.

A CANAANITE GOD, probably Baal, is represented in a gold-leaf statuette. The favorite of
Canaan, Baal was scorned by Hebrew prophets.

A HIGHBORN WOMAN, carved in ivory, wears
a fringed robe and has carefully plaited hair. The
carving was probably made for a furniture inlay.

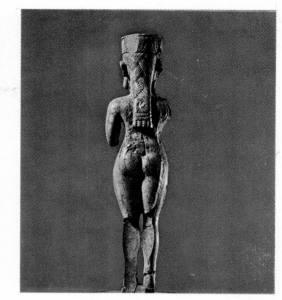

A NUDE WOMAN is carved in ivory, probably
for use as a dish handle. Hebrew prophets stormed
against Canaanites for their worldly frivolities.

THE KING OF MEGIDDO, a Canaanite potentate, receives food and drink
from his queen. This carving was executed on an ivory panel. The king's
throne is shown flanked by the Canaanite symbols of majesty. These are
winged figures derived from Egyptian sphinxes, which the Hebrews called
cherubim. At the right a soldier stands guard, while a singer accompanies
herself on the lyre. In the New Testament, Megiddo is called Armageddon.

CONSTRUCTION OF THE TEMPLE in Jerusalem is watched by King Solomon and his courtiers from the porch (*right center*). In the center foreground rises an outdoor altar for "burnt offerings." Slaves are busily moving two "cherubim," their wings detached, to flank the Ark of the Covenant in the temple. Wall panels of cedar decorated with cherubim, based on the idea of Egyptian sphinxes, lie at left. Behind them stands the huge bronze "sea" for

holy water, and beyond it, the south gate of the temple enclosure. With walls 10 feet thick, the temple could double as a fortress for a last stand against attackers of the city. The building was completed after seven years of work.

SEMITES IN EGYPT are shown in a section of a 19th Century B.C. Egyptian painting. The bellows suggests that these seminomads, possibly similar in appearance to the Hebrew patriarchs, may have been traveling metalworkers.

KINGDOM OF ISRAEL

CONTRARY to Biblical tradition, the Hebrews led from Egypt by Moses were probably only a segment of the people who began to conquer a portion of the land of Canaan sometime after 1400 B.C. Scholars now think that the Hebrews of the Exodus probably linked forces with other Semitic tribesmen already in Syro-Palestine. They were distinguished only by their faith in one god, Yahweh or Jehovah, and in the Commandments that he had given them through their prophet Moses. The new homeland was divided among the twelve tribes of Israel. For about two centuries they were loosely united by a central sanctuary at Shiloh, in the southern hills of Palestine, where the Ark of the Covenant was kept and an administration by a high priest with extensive but non-political authority was established. In times of crisis, such as arose in encounters with the Philistines, local chieftains temporarily acquired greater power. But under the Philistine menace, the simple tribal organization proved inadequate.

A demand for national unity arose after the Philistines destroyed Shiloh and carried off the Ark. A local chieftain named Saul rallied the tribes to his banner, defeated the Philistines and was made king. With the establishment of the Kingdom of Israel, in about 1020 B.C., there began a brief period of Hebrew political unity not to be repeated until modern Israel was founded in A.D. 1948. Saul was an able soldier but not a politician. He could not cement the dispersed and often feuding tribes. He quarreled with his influential son-in-law David and he alienated the powerful priesthood. He died by falling on his sword in a losing battle with the Philistines. He was succeeded by David, who was both a soldier and a statesman. David finished the war with the Philistines and carried out further conquests of Canaanite territory. Capturing the Canaanite citadel of Jerusalem, he made it the political and religious capital of the kingdom. His reign (1000-961 B.C.) was a period of growing commercial prosperity, political unity and renewed religious devotion. Israel remained a rather primitive pastoral country, however, compared to the wealthy, sophisticated coastal cities—held by the people now called Phoenicians. David's son and successor, King Solomon (961-922 B.C.) succumbed to the lure of Phoenician urbanity, and his reign took on the look of oriental grandeur, if only in a minor way.

Because the Second Commandment forbade the Hebrews to make "any graven image," the Israelites developed few skills as artists and craftsmen. Phoenician architects and artisans designed and directed the building of Solomon's palace and of his temple, supplying its carved "cherubim" and elaborate bronze containers for holy water, and decorating the interior with paneling made from cedar of Lebanon. Phoenician metallurgists operated Solomon's copper mines and refinery at Ezion-geber, and Phoenician sailors carried his produce to trade in foreign markets. For Solomon's many projects, the Israelites paid heavily in taxes and labor. The Israelites were further dismayed by their king's household. He took, according to the Bible, 700 wives, among them an Egyptian pharaoh's daughter, Sidonian princesses and Hittite women, and built temples in which these foreign women could worship their own gods. Then Solomon himself fell away from the Hebrew faith: he "went after Ashtoreth the goddess of the Zidonians and after Milcom the abomination of the Ammonites. . . ."

After Solomon's death, the kingdom split in two. The rival kingdoms of Israel and Judah quarreled, and the power of the Hebrews declined. Their end began with the all-conquering Assyrians about 800 B.C. But the magnificent faith and ethic of the Hebrews survived as an enduring current in the stream of world civilization.

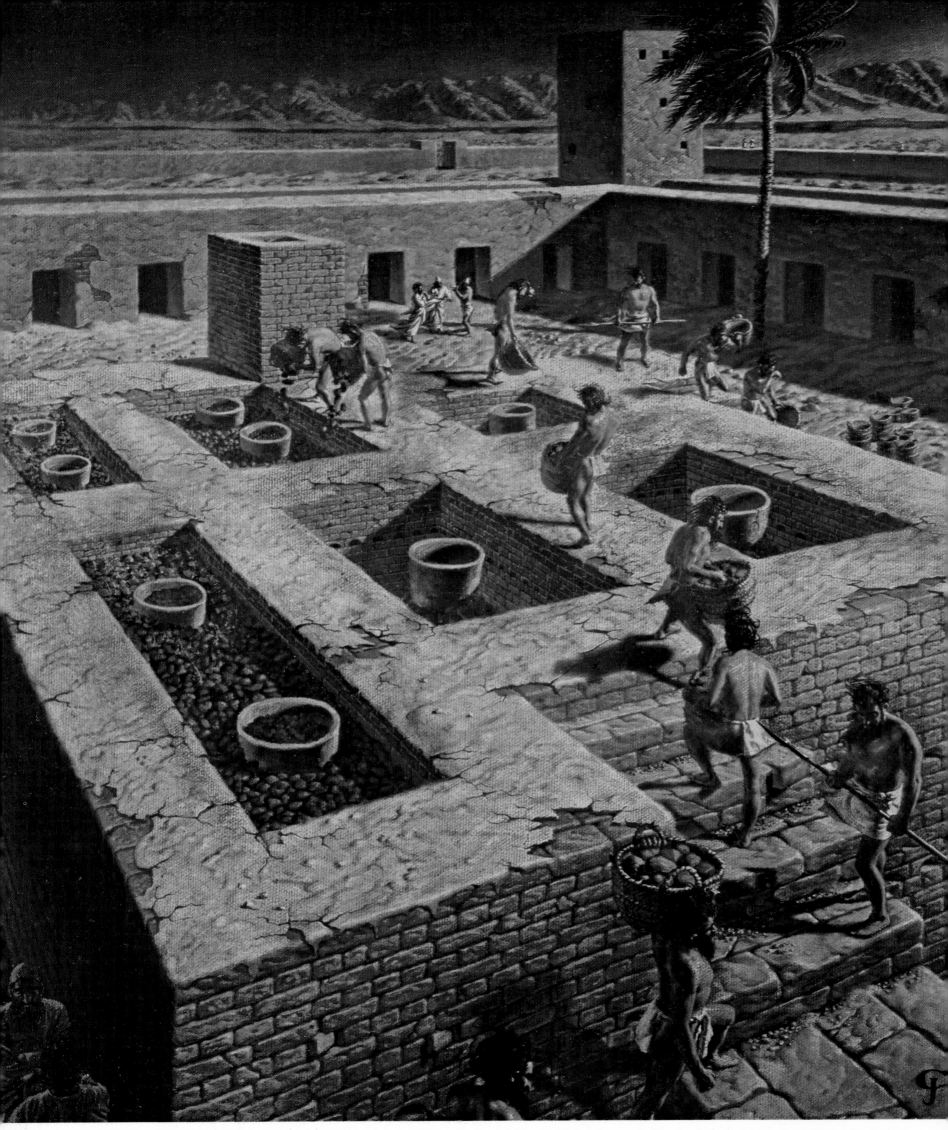

A COPPER REFINERY at Ezion-geber by the Red Sea is operated by Phoenician metallurgists for King Solomon of Israel. Copper ore has been placed in the clay crucibles, which are set in charcoal pits, and the strong winds blowing from the north fan the fires to intense heat. The refined copper was carried, in ingots, by Phoenician ships that Solomon chartered, and traded in foreign markets for such exotic goods as gold, perfume and spices.

IN AN EGYPTIAN HARBOR, seven Phoenician merchant ships lie with their gangplanks down while the mariners carry their wares ashore. At bottom center a Phoenician offers a large jar, probably containing oil. This painting, from a tomb wall in Thebes, apparently dates from about 1400 B.C. It may have been on such trading visits as this that Phoenicians acquired the idea of an alphabet from the rudimentary approach to it made by the Egyptians.

TRADE AND ALPHABET

AS the leading metallurgists (*opposite*), sailors, artisans, explorers and merchants of their time, the Phoenicians were the middlemen of civilization. Though sometimes disliked, they were valued for their usefulness as traders and craftsmen. Homer, in his *Odyssey,* described their appearance in Greece: "Thither came Phoenicians, men famed for their ships, greedy knaves, bringing countless trinkets in their black ship." They were, as a rule, adapters rather than creators, absorbing elements of civilization from their neighbors and spreading around the Mediterranean world the ideas they accumulated and the merchandise they manufactured.

Like all great inventions, the Phoenician invention of the alphabet evolved from a synthesis of ideas. The Phoenicians acquired a knowledge of hieroglyphic writing from the Egyptians. But as precision-minded businessmen they wanted to keep detailed, accurate records. A thousand years before the Phoenicians, the Egyptians had developed a rudimentary alphabet consisting of 24 signs for 24 consonants and semiconsonant sounds of their language. But the idea of a full phonetic alphabet apparently never occurred to them; they continued to use these sound symbols in conjunction with the hundreds of pictographs and ideographs that comprised their elaborate lexicon. The Phoenicians needed something more manageable than a written language devoted largely to proclaiming the glories of gods and god-kings. The first alphabet probably arose out of their mercantile necessity. "Now the Phoenicians who came with Cadmus," wrote the Greek historian Herodotus, "introduced into Greece upon their arrival a great variety of arts, among the rest that of writing." The Roman alphabet today derives from the Greeks' adaptation of the Phoenician alphabet.

It is significant that the earliest known examples of Phoenician alphabetic writing were found in the Sinai peninsula, which was under Egyptian domination at the time. The Phoenicians also used several other systems of writing, and they invented at least one other type of alphabet. The first examples of inscriptions in the fully developed Phoenician alphabet were found at the Mediterranean port of Byblos, and have been dated at about the 10th Century. (The word "Bible" comes from the name of the Phoenician port of Byblos, which was famed as an exporter of papyrus, used for writing paper.)

HIEROGLYPHS AND LETTERS are both shown on this 900 B.C. Egyptian bust of Pharaoh Osorkon I, sent to the King of Byblos. The pharaoh's name in hieroglyphs (*center*) is surrounded by a Phoenician alphabetic inscription.

131

IN THE HARBOR AT TYRE a group of shipwrights, wearing the conical caps favored by Phoenician men, work with their slave assistants to shape the ribs of a merchant vessel out of beams hewn from cedar. In the background at far left, a ship back from a long voyage unloads its cargo. At right, a soldier is directing slaves bringing timber into the shipyard. In the distance beyond them, longshoremen are loading bales and boxes of manufactured

THE PHOENICIANS' CITIES OF THE SEA

THE cities of Tyre, Sidon and Byblos, and others around which the Phoenicians concentrated after losing most of their land to invading nomads, were erected for the most part on offshore islands or promontories jutting into the Mediterranean. Here, with the tall cedars of Lebanon that grew thick on the mountains still left to them, Phoenician shipwrights built merchantmen bigger and sturdier than any before. Manned by mettlesome crews and rowed by slaves,

goods onto ships, which will carry them to ports of the Mediterranean and perhaps even into the Atlantic. Beyond the ships and the long quay lies a sea wall built by the Phoenicians to protect their busy anchorage. Situated on an offshore island and defended by strong walls and warships, Tyre was for centuries invulnerable. Though recurrently assailed by enemy armies, Tyre, like all heavily fortified Phoenician cities, carried on business as usual.

the Phoenician ships ventured ever farther from home, through waters made perilous by storms and pirates. They voyaged beyond the Aegean to Malta, Sicily, Sardinia and through the Pillars of Hercules, or Straits of Gibraltar, to the Atlantic coast of Spain. There is some slight evidence that when the tin deposits of the area began to run out, the Phoenicians may have sailed all the way to Britain for fresh supplies. According to Herodotus, their crowning achievement was the circumnavigation of Africa about 600 B.C., when they sailed in the service of Pharaoh Necho. As Phoenician commerce flourished, Tyre, Sidon and Byblos grew into cities that were known throughout the ancient world. They were crowded with warehouses and workshops where raw materials brought by their ships from abroad were manufactured into fine goods for export. And their harbors and sea routes were guarded by the most powerful navies of the ancient world.

PHOENICIAN LEGACY

IN some of the lands with which the Phoenicians traded, they set up nothing more permanent than a tent, then sailed on after a few days. Their wares included plates and bowls of gold, silver and bronze; shields of bronze; spear points and daggers of gray iron; bottles of ivory and smooth pottery filled with perfumes and unguents; fine-textured wools and linens dyed purple and red. Purple may well have become the color of royalty in ancient times simply because the Phoenician dye was so expensive to produce that few people other than kings could afford it.

At the end of their longer trade routes, the Phoenicians set up permanent colonies. These began as small fortified villages and gradually they grew into great trading cities rivaling Sidon and Tyre. One of these, founded on the Atlantic coast of southern Spain about 1100 B.C., was Gadir, which became the modern city of Cadiz. An even greater ancient city, destined not to survive, was established about 950 B.C. on a North African peninsula near the modern city of Tunis. This was Carthage, founded according to Roman legend by a princess of Tyre named Dido who had fled her native city after the murder of her husband by her brother. Carthage, which became a great maritime power and colonizer in its own right, challenged the Etruscans, the colonizing Greeks and finally the Romans. The Punic Wars, which brought about the city's destruction in 146 B.C., were so named from the Roman *poeni*, meaning "Phoenicians."

The Romans underestimated the debt they owed, if only indirectly, to their archenemies. For the culture which the Phoenicians had acquired from many sources inevitably accompanied their trade. That trade was at its height during the so-called Dark Age of Greece, when artistry and craftsmanship declined and the art of writing was apparently lost. Fine Phoenician goods like those shown in the painting at right helped to inspire the revival of Greek craftsmanship, and the Greek alphabet may have been created after its inventors had watched Phoenician scribes writing their records of goods bought and sold. In turn, the Romans acquired much of their culture from the Greeks.

Although the Phoenicians apparently used their alphabet primarily for business, tablets found at ancient sites and translated have revealed that the trade-minded Phoenicians had a well-developed literature, much of it religious. And this literature, through the Hebrews, exerted a profound influence on the Old Testament. As Dr. W. F. Albright, the American archaeologist, has observed, "Through the Bible, the entire civilized world has fallen heir to Phoenician literary art."

A PHOENICIAN PLATE of silver is decorated with scrollwork and figures showing scenes of hunting and battle. This was the kind of craftsmanship which the wandering traders took to the semi-barbarous people of Europe.

ON A BEACH IN GREECE Phoenician merchants in their conical caps display their wares. In the left foreground a Greek woman clad in homespun feels the texture of fine Tyrian wool. At the tent pole (*center*) a man who has

tried on a purple robe admires himself in a mirror. At the right a Greek husband agrees to buy his wife a pair of gold earrings from the white-bearded trader presiding over a table laden with jewelry. Outside the tent some Phoenician seamen are being offered their choice of female slaves, captured by the Greeks in battle, in trade for their goods. In addition to slaves, the Greeks often offered olive oil, grain and metals in exchange for Phoenician wares.

THE ASSYRIANS AND SEMITIC CULTURE

THE mingling of peoples and cultures in Syro-Palestine and surrounding areas reached a climax from the early Ninth to the late Seventh Centuries B.C. when, like a gigantic flail, the conquering armies of Assyria swept from the Tigris-Euphrates to the Nile, burning, pillaging, extorting, slaughtering and dispersing survivors.

The Assyrians, a Semitic people who took their name from their chief god and first chief city, Ashur, were the greatest military people of the pre-Roman world. In the 12th Century B.C., from their homeland in the upper Tigris region, they first struck west to the Mediterranean and northward to Lake Van. But this conquest was ephemeral. Not until the reign of King Ashurnasirpal II (883-859 B.C.) did Assyria become a ruthless fighting machine that struck terror through the civilized world. Ashurnasirpal boasted of his policy of frightfulness: "I stormed the mountain peaks and took them. In the midst of the mighty mountain I slaughtered them, with their blood I dyed the mountain red like wool. . . . The heads of . . . warriors I cut off, and I formed them into a pillar over against their city, their young men and their maidens I burned in the fire."

Some cities the Assyrians pillaged and destroyed, others they would spare in return for tribute. When one city rebelled, Ashurnasirpal taught all of them a lesson: "I built a pillar over against his city gate, and I flayed all the chief men who had revolted, and I covered the pillar with their skins; some I walled up within the pillar, some I impaled upon the pillar on stakes. . . ."

To forestall rebellions, the Assyrians used a system of mass deportations. Leading citizens and others from a captured city were driven to some distant land and replaced by people from other conquered territories. A fragmentary text by King Sargon II describing the capture in 722 B.C. of Samaria, capital of the northern kingdom of Israel, has been reconstructed thus: "I led away as prisoners 27,290 inhabitants of it. . . . The town I rebuilt better than it was before and settled therein people from countries which I myself had conquered." The hostility between Samaritans and Jews recorded in the New Testament is partly traceable to this resettlement.

After a century of simple pillage and extortion, the Assyrians under King Tiglathpileser III (745-729) moved on toward genuine empire, settling Assyrian governors and troops in conquered provinces, which included Megiddo and most of the northern kingdom of Israel. Tyre, Sidon and other major Phoenician cities had submitted to the Assyrians in 842 B.C. and paid tribute to avoid Assyrian interference in their extensive commerce. Now they were attacked again, and their demise began at the hand of the famous King Sennacherib (704-681). Sennacherib crushed a revolt by King Hezekiah of Judah and conquered the southern Hebrew kingdom. But he failed to take Judah's capital city, Jerusalem.

Sennacherib's son Esarhaddon (681-669) carried Assyrian rule into Egypt, boasting that he had conquered Memphis "in a half a day by means of mines, breaches and assault ladders; I destroyed it . . . and burnt it down." Assuming the title "King of the kings of Egypt," the victor boasted overweeningly: "I am powerful, I am all powerful, I am a hero, I am gigantic, I am colossal."

Esarhaddon's son Ashurbanipal (668-633) pushed on into southern Egypt, capturing Thebes. Last of the Assyrian kings, he was followed by a series of weak rulers. In 626 B.C., a Chaldean named Nabopolassar seized the throne of Babylonia. Fourteen years later he joined Medes and Persians in overthrowing great Nineveh, and the mighty Assyrian empire was no more.

Its place was briefly taken by the Chaldeans of Babylon under Nabopolassar's son Nebuchadnezzar II. In 586 B.C. he razed Jerusalem and the Temple of Solomon, and sent the Jews into Babylonian captivity. In 572 B.C., after a siege of 13 years, he occupied the mainland area of Tyre and took most of the commercial aristocracy of the port city hostage. In 538 B.C. Babylon fell to the Persians, whose King Cyrus let the Hebrew exiles go home.

FOR nearly 2,000 years the vanished empires of Assyria and Babylonia were remembered chiefly by Biblical accounts in which their kings were denounced as bloody tyrants and their cities as abominations. In the mid-19th Century archaeologists began digging at the sites of vanished Mesopotamian cities. One of the earliest and most valuable discoveries, at Nineveh in the 1840s, involved the

SOLDIER-ARCHAEOLOGIST Yigael Yadin examines pottery at Megiddo, the Biblical Armageddon. Overlooking the Plain of Esdraelon, the fortress of Megiddo dominated a key Palestinian route from Egypt to Mesopotamia.

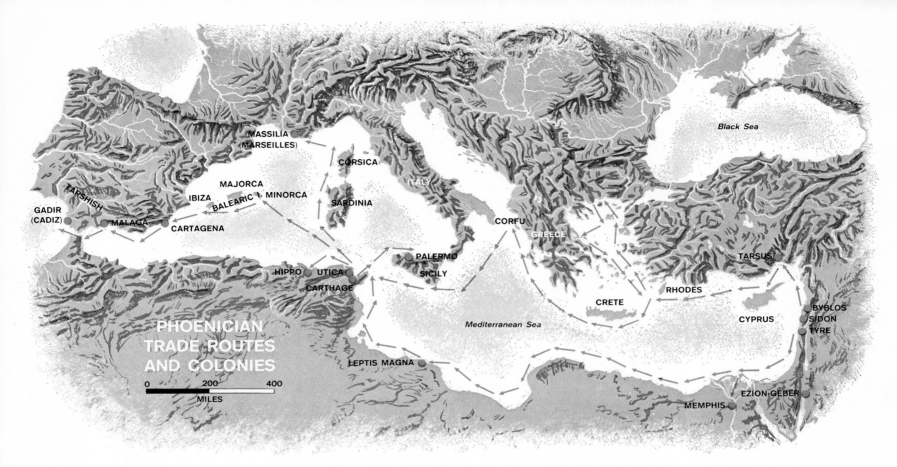

PHOENICIAN
TRADE ROUTES
AND COLONIES

0   200   400
MILES

cruel King Ashurbanipal. He had written of his youth, "I received
. . . the hidden treasure of the art of writing. . . . I considered the
heavens with the learned masters. . . . I read the beautiful clay tablets from Sumer and the obscure Akkadian writing, which is hard to
master. I had my joy in the reading of inscriptions in stone from the
time before the flood." Ashurbanipal had sent scribes throughout
Assyria and Babylonia to copy and translate any writings they found.
In his library were tens of thousands of clay tablets. Here are some
of the surprising discoveries made from this and other sources during the past century of digging and deciphering:

King Nebuchadnezzar, destroyer of Jerusalem, in addition to his
annals about military conquests, recorded his work of peace: the
restoration of Babylon, its streets, canals, palaces and temples.

The inscription of the great legal code of Babylonia's King Hammurabi (c. 1728-1686 B.C.) begins with a prologue setting forth the
king's duties: ". . . to promote the welfare of the people . . . to
cause justice to prevail in the land, to destroy the wicked and the
evil, that the strong might not oppress the weak. . . ."

A piece of Babylonian wisdom literature, written some time before
700 B.C., counsels:

> Unto your opponent do no evil
> Your evildoer recompense with good.

THE modern world's debt to the early Semitic peoples is great.
They were assimilators and transmitters of culture. The Akkadians and their Semitic successors in Babylonia and Assyria handed
on much of the civilization of the non-Semitic Sumerians—as did
the Phoenicians and the Hebrews. The later Aramaean Semites of
northern Syria might be forgotten if they had not devised a writing
so simple that their Semitic language—which Christ spoke—became
nearly universal in the ancient world and a major channel for the
communication of eastern culture to the West. The early Semitic
peoples also enriched what they absorbed—just as the Semitic Arabs
did in later centuries when they became chief preservers of the Greek
legacy during Europe's Dark Ages.

Professor Sabatino Moscati of the University of Rome says in
his *Ancient Semitic Civilizations:* "Semitic contributions to human
culture have been many and positive. In the first place, the very
means whereby we express our thought in writing, the alphabet,
came into being in a Semitic land. . . . The Akkadians have furnished literary themes, legal conceptions, astronomical data, and
mathematical lore. . . .

"The greatest Semitic contribution to human culture is . . . that
of one member of the group: the Hebrews. The conception, so revolutionary for the rich polytheism of antiquity, of the oneness of God,
of a single moral power . . . formed the essential kernel of Hebrew
religion, as it was transmitted to the European world by Christianity, and to Asia and Africa by Islam. These three great religions
. . . all came into being in a small area of the Semitic region. . . ."

EXCAVATION AT MEGIDDO reveals part of the ancient city's water system.
At the bottom of stairs descending the shaft (*foreground*) a tunnel led to
an enclosed spring. This water system was built in the 12th Century B.C.

A FAVORITE SPORT of the artistic, pleasure-loving Minoan people, who flourished on the island of Crete from about 2000 to 1400 B.C., is illustrated in this painting of "bull leaping" performed by a girl. After pulling herself up by the horns of a charging bull, the girl turns a handspring over its back while her male companion waits to steady her when she lands on the ground. Both male and female athletes wore only a loincloth when in the arena.

THE SHAPING OF THE WEST

The Minoans and the Homeric Mycenaeans of the Aegean laid the foundation for the first great western civilization

THE Greeks of the Golden Age (roughly 600-300 B.C.) had a genius in philosophy, art, politics, poetry, drama, science and the enjoyment of life that is still in many respects unmatched. Their history supposedly began in 776 B.C., the year of the first Olympic games. They themselves believed that the tales of heroes and gods recounted by Homer in the *Iliad* and *Odyssey* were authentic history, but later scholars dismissed these epics as fiction. Now it is known that the glory that was Greece did evolve from two earlier civilizations, the Minoan and Mycenaean, whose histories bear a striking resemblance to the accounts given by Homer.

The earliest roots of Greek culture appear to have grown on the narrow, mountainous island of Crete, which sprawls 160 miles across the mouth of the Aegean. Its north coast, deeply indented with large bays, furnished good harbors for the shallow ships of the ancients. But the southern coast was forbidding. As Homer described it, "there is a smooth cliff, sheer towards the sea . . . where the Southwest Wind drives the great wave against the headland on the left towards Phaestos, and a little rock holds back a great wave." The culture that evolved on this island is called Minoan, after its legendary king, Minos. Here, between 2000 and 1400 B.C., a creative maritime people, who appear from their relics to have been sensitive, versatile and peace-loving, founded a culture based on the great technological advances made earlier in the east. The Minoans built great palaces, produced exquisite works of art and manned a fleet that ranged the Mediterranean from Asia Minor and Africa to Sicily. Thus began the first major civilization of Europe.

The best known Minoan bequest to posterity is the myth of Theseus and the monster—half man, half bull—that was called the Minotaur. Excavations in Crete have shown that the bull was indeed a central symbol of Minoan life. Ancient wall paintings (such as the one on page 147) indicate that the national sport with both young men and girls was the "bull leaping" shown in the painting opposite.

Sometime after 1900 B.C., the first Greek-speaking people entered mainland Greece, perhaps from the Balkans, perhaps from farther east. Spreading from Macedonia to the Peloponnesus, they established towns that Homer and Greek myth and drama later made famous: Pylos, home of Homer's long-winded King Nestor; Orchomenus in northern Boeotia; the Argive city of Tiryns, associated with Hercules; Thebes, the capital of Oedipus; Iolcus, the port from which Jason and his Argonauts set sail in quest of the Golden Fleece. The dominant city, which gave the age its name, was Mycenae, which Homer described as "rich in gold."

As Homer related, the Mycenaean Greeks, whom he called Achaeans, were virile, hot-tempered and warlike. Unlike the Minoan kings, who had rambling, unfortified palaces brightly colored and open to the sky, the Mycenaean chieftains lived in somber, heavily fortified citadels. Their first artifacts were crude. But beginning about 1600 B.C., Mycenaean art was gradually transformed through contact with the more civilized Minoans and Egyptians. Professor Spyridon Marinatos offers an ingenious theory to explain how this came about. The Egyptians, he believed, hired Mycenaean mercenaries to help them drive out the invading Hyksos, and the fighters were ferried to Egypt, the dominant big power of the day, by the peaceful but sea-skilled Minoans. In any event, a close cultural relationship between Mycenaeans and Minoans developed, and Mycenaeans may even have ruled at Knossos in the last years of the Minoan era. For a while they dominated the sea lanes of the Mediterranean, though in time the Phoenicians replaced them.

Minoan civilization survived for only a century or so after most of its buldings were demolished about 1500 B.C., possibly by earthquake and inundation by the sea after a colossal volcanic explosion took place on a nearby island. But already, in a fruitful merging of cultures, the gently creative Minoans had joined the martial, aggressive Mycenaeans in laying the early foundations of Greek culture.

THE PALACE at Knossos, seat of power during Crete's golden age, overlooks the Great South Road, main artery of the Minoan civilization. The road swung toward the palace across the Vlychia Stream by a massive stone viaduct on nine lofty corbeled arches. Along this highway moved all of the busy cross-island traffic, traveling between the northern ports that traded with the Aegean world and those in the south that traded with Africa.

CRETE'S GOLDEN AGE

AMID the rocky and then thickly forested heights of Crete, three royal palaces arose in the first glow of Minoan civilization 4,000 years ago. One was built in the south at Phaestos, a second on the northern coast at Mallia. But the greatest crowned Knossos in north-central Crete, three miles from the sea. Its ruins survive today as the supreme monument to Crete's golden age.

The palaces sprang from no single outburst of creative genius. For centuries Neolithic men had lived on Crete in caves and huts.

Sometime before 2500 B.C., a wave of sea-borne wanderers arrived from unknown shores, bringing new blood and skills. They found no great river valley like those of the Tigris and Euphrates, the Indus and the Nile. But Crete had some compensations. A land of valleys, small plains and terraces cut by three great and many smaller mountain ranges, it offered climates ranging from north temperate to subtropical. Thus it permitted the growth of a variety of plants that made it potentially self-sustaining. It also offered opportunities for trade in every direction, plus insular security. The palaces and cities that the newcomers built were confidently unfortified. Under the impetus of immigration, Crete emerged from Stone Age stagnation

are led by a noble landowner, a gray-haired man wearing a fringed leather mantle decorated with a pattern of inverted scales. From the balconies and porticoes of the western façade of the court, the palace personnel watch the revelry. In the middle of the façade, directly behind the fallen harvester, stands a small columnar shrine with stylized white horns of consecration, dedicated to a patron goddess. To the right, a staircase and

On the palace side of the ravine, the road split into three forks. The path at the traveler's right as he approached entered the stepped portico of the palace—brightly adorned and supported on downward-tapering pillars in the Minoan style—and thence gave access to the state entrance used by palace residents, government officials and foreign envoys. The middle lane, which two men are shown descending, led to the west court, where freight and

into the changing era of metals. Beginning about 2000 B.C., wheeled vehicles were introduced, potters turned out polychrome vases of delicate texture and brilliant design, the idea of writing was adapted to Cretan use and applied to business purposes, and the three great palaces were built. This first phase of Minoan culture, known as the age of the Old Palaces, ended about 1700 B.C. with a catastrophe, probably an earthquake, that destroyed all three palaces as well as most of the outlying towns.

The Minoans rebuilt vigorously, beginning the brilliant age known as that of the New Palaces. The Minoan navy ruled the seas, and merchantmen plied them with rich cargoes of pottery, metalwork,

wine and olive oil to exchange for tin, ivory and other foreign produce. Minoan artists and craftsmen set the esthetic standards for the whole Aegean world. And though all three palaces were rebuilt on a larger scale, political power now clearly centered in the Palace of Minos at Knossos.

It may be that one or more Cretan kings used the name of Minos, or perhaps Minos was a royal title—like "pharaoh" or "Caesar." But the great palace at Knossos, one of the most elaborate structures built by man in ancient history, was unquestionably remodeled, expanded and embellished by a succession of rulers. Devoid of the symmetry and order dear to the later Greeks, it was a

ordinary citizens were received. The left-hand roadway ran northward to the harbor town on the Aegean three miles away. In the middle ground, beyond the cypress trees and olive groves, stand the houses of the city of Knossos.

maze of apartments, corridors, colonnades, light wells and staircases, rambling over more than six acres and rising at least three stories high, put together from a combination of masonry, rubble and wood. Its labyrinthine complexity may have suggested the scene of Crete's most famous myth, that of Theseus and the Minotaur. But it was airy, comfortable and adorned throughout with brightly painted pillars, frescoes and decorative façades. Around the royal residence lay the community of Knossos, a thriving city that was the greatest European city of its day. Homer sang its praises: "One of the ninety towns of Crete is a great city called Knossos, and there, for nine years, King Minos ruled and enjoyed the friendship of almighty Zeus."

TOWN HOUSES at Knossos, as painted on Minoan plaques (*below*), show flat roofs, paired windows and curious raised "attics." Some had horizontal beams (*left*), some used masonry (*right*) or showed beam ends as decoration.

A HARVESTERS' PROCESSION, making its way through the great central courtyard of the Palace of Minos, is a high point in a ceremony of thanksgiving to the deities of nature at the end of a bountiful season. In the van are four singers and a capering musician jingling a sistrum, an Egyptian noisemaking instrument. Behind them, waving sheaves of grain, come the laughing harvesters. (One of the celebrators has stumbled and fallen.) They

FOLD OUT: DO NOT TEAR

entrance hall lead to the official and administrative sections of the palace. The re-creation of the scene in this painting is based in part on the decorations on the Harvester Vase shown in the photograph at upper right.

THE HARVESTER VASE, carved from black steatite, shows home-going harvesters trailing along behind a leader wearing a fringed mantle. The lower part of the vase is restored.

A JOYOUS PEOPLE

BECAUSE the Minoans' written language has not been deciphered, their history has been called "a picture book without text." But their surviving art makes the picture book a vivid one, and reveals a gay and joyous people. Physically they were of the familiar Mediterranean type, with dark, curly hair and slender bodies. Unlike the bearded Mycenaeans, the men were usually clean-shaven, and they wore their hair long. The women used heavy lip rouge and eye shadow, and their coiffures were elaborate. The pictures of them that survive indicate that they customarily went bare-breasted. Self-assured, handsome and wasp-waisted, they carried themselves with pride.

The Minoans enjoyed a variety of sports, including boxing and wrestling, as well as their hazardous specialty in the bull ring. A gregarious people, they liked to band together on occasion to celebrate good fortune. From paintings and other works of art come glimpses of antique pageantry. Inside the palace at Knossos a long passageway called the Corridor of the Procession is decorated throughout its length with one of the most ambitious of Minoan frescoes, depicting a colorful parade of many human figures. Though time has obliterated most of the features of the fresco, some of the remaining sections portray striking individuals of various estates—stalwart and noble youths bearing votive offerings and garbed in intricately patterned kilts with gold and silver girdles, musicians in ankle-length robes, maidens, priests and priestesses.

The Minoans had much to be thankful for. Both their works of art and their abundant natural products—especially their olive oil, honey, fish, figs, other fruits and many aromatic and medicinal herbs—were renowned throughout the ancient world. Best of all, they enjoyed and mirrored in their art a freedom from war—the *pax minoica*—that the later Greeks never had. Homer describes Crete as "a rich and lovely land . . . densely peopled and boasting ninety cities." Other ancient writers called it "great, fat and well-fed," the Isle of the Blessed. Some have identified it with Plato's Atlantis. It is small wonder that the Minoans developed and passed on that zestful love of life and beauty that was to distinguish the classical Greeks who followed them as inhabitants of the Aegean mainland and islands.

IN THE QUEEN'S APARTMENT, her ladies in waiting divert themselves by spinning wool and playing games while her majesty, seated at left, gets a hairdo and manicure. Minoan women had their long hair elaborately curled and adorned with jewels, and their artists showed them with saucy and flirtatious faces. The queen's chamber is illuminated and ventilated through air shafts, a feature of Minoan architecture. A marine fresco adorns the far wall.

ROYAL CHAMBERS OF THE PALACE

THE Palace of Minos was cleanly bisected by the great central court shown on the preceding pages. The west wing housed the administrative section, throne room, shrine, business offices, halls of state, reception chambers and the royal magazines. The magazines consisted of a series of narrow storerooms, ranged along a corridor 130 feet long and 10 feet wide, stocked with jars and goatskins of olive oil, wine and grain. The east wing contained living quarters. Here, in addition to the royal suites, were many luxurious apartments and private chambers. An elaborate sanitation system was a notable feature of Cretan buildings. Until modern times, no plumbing system in western civilization was as efficient as the one devised by

the Minoans. Not even the Roman Empire surpassed it, and after Rome's fall, soap disappeared from Europe for more than 400 years.

The focus of activity in the east wing was the commodious chamber of the queen (*above*). Here, surrounded by her ladies in waiting, she held court, entertained friends and attended to the cosmetic and costuming chores imposed by Minoan custom on ladies of high rank. All evidence indicates that, by contrast with the feminine homebodies of classical Greece, Minoan women enjoyed a freedom and social status equivalent to that of men. In Minoan art, women are shown at public festivals, mingling in crowds and appearing with men at sports events not only as spectators but also as performers.

THRONE ROOM in the Palace of Minos (*above*) still has its alabaster throne. The frescoes depict mythical griffins. The broken religious objects found on the floor suggest prayer offerings in the 1500 B.C. disaster.

A DRINKING CUP found at Knossos (*left*) echoes the chief Minoan symbol. Legend has it that Zeus took the form of a white bull, kidnaped the princess Europa and swam with her over to Crete. Minos was their son.

BULL LEAPING is shown below in a fresco of about 1500 B.C. Apparently no weapons were used in this sport, and no portrayals of a bull's death have been found. The girls who took part may have been princesses.

A MINOAN TREE-CULT CEREMONY is pictured on this gold ring. The priestess at left grasps a tree while another votary raises her hands in adoration of the central figure, who is probably a goddess.

THE SACRED CAVES

UNLIKE most peoples, ancient or modern, the Minoans built no great temples or monuments to their gods. In fact, they appear to have had no gods, but only a series of goddesses—or perhaps a single goddess, the great Earth Mother, who was thought to have been the original deity of European religion and was shown in various guises. The Minoans equipped their homes with tiny sanctuaries, seldom more than a few feet square. But their principal places of worship were not man-made: a mountain peak, a forest grove or—apparently most popular—the depths of a limestone cavern such as the sacred Cave of Psychro (*right*) high in the mountains of eastern Crete. To this cave and many others the Minoans brought frequent offerings.

The labyrinth in which Theseus slew the Minotaur may have been suggested by some such cave, or by the intricate structure of the Palace of Minos. According to the myth, the sea god Poseidon punished King Minos for a broken vow by inspiring his wife Pasiphaë with an unnatural passion for a sacred bull. Their offspring was the Minotaur, a monster with a bull's head and a man's body, which Minos confined in a labyrinth. Athens was required periodically to send a living tribute of seven youths and seven maidens as fodder for the Minotaur. The Athenian hero Theseus volunteered to join the third such sacrificial party—and killed the monster with his bare hands.

Greek myth normally symbolized an attempt to explain some natural phenomenon, or a memory of actual history. The Athenian tribute may have represented a period of Cretan dominance, and Theseus' victory the turning of the tables that apparently occurred toward the end of the Minoan era. In any event, traces of the Cretan cult seem to have been absorbed into Greek religion, and Zeus himself was supposed by the Greeks to have been born in a Cretan cave.

THE SNAKE GODDESS grasps two serpents. She was one of the principal deities of ancient Crete. This statuette is carved from ivory and is embellished with gold.

THE INFLUENCE OF EGYPT appears in this panel of a Minoan sarcophagus. To the dead man (*at right, above*), three priests are offering calves and a boat. At left a priestess pours a libation.

IN THE HOLY CAVE OF PSYCHRO a worshiper (*right*) places a statuette on a rock ledge while his companions stand in silent awe. Other images are shown in this painting of a shrine for pilgrims.

IN THE GREAT HALL of a Mycenaean palace, members of a royal household gather around the hearth to listen as a minstrel strums his lyre and sings epic lays about great heroes and their deeds. Tales of Mycenaean heroes, as told by Homer, inspired the classical Greeks, who came after the Mycenaeans. The room shown here is based on the great hall of the palace at Pylos, home of King Nestor, sage counselor of the Greek armies in the Trojan War.

THE HEROES OF HOMER AND GREEK HISTORY

THOUGH the Minoans contributed notably to Greek culture, they were not Greeks. The Mycenaeans, who were the first Greek-speaking people to arrive on the mainland of Greece, reached there sometime after 1900 B.C. Their settlements grew slowly but continuously through the centuries and became flourishing communities. The pace of Greek development was speeded by contact with Crete and Egypt, beginning about 1600 B.C. Then, in the following century, the balance of power shifted from Crete to the mainland, and the Mycenaeans became undisputed masters of the Aegean world. In the next three centuries their commerce and cultural influence expanded throughout the eastern Mediterranean area. Mycenaean colonies sprang up on the islands of Rhodes and Cyprus, and the fortified strongholds of Mycenaean kings studded the mainland from the Peloponnesus to Thessaly and many of the isles of the Aegean Sea.

These were the men and times immortalized by Homer in the *Iliad* and *Odyssey*. And it was from these tales of their Mycenaean ancestors that the Greeks acquired their heroic code and outlook. The epics were staples of Greek education. They were told and retold in the old way (*opposite page*) as an oral tradition long before being written down. Seekers of glory and renown, the Homeric heroes valued personal honor above all, and their descendants also set great store by feats of war and athletic prowess. The later Greeks gradually broadened their concept of honor to include the heroic fulfillment of any other admirable capacities a man might possess. The purpose of life, they believed, was the pursuit above all of personal excellence, which they called *arete*.

Evidence that the real-life counterparts of Homer's heroes were not illiterate barbarians has accumulated since World War II. Their so-called "Linear B" writings, deciphered in 1952, point to a fairly advanced stage of social organization. Homer's "resourceful Odysseus" is merely one example indicating that these legendary heroes valued intelligence as well as physical strength and courage. Such tomb findings as the golden cup at right above testify that, after stimulation from Crete and Egypt, the Mycenaeans achieved not only a high level of artistry and craftsmanship but also impressive wealth from a flourishing maritime trade. Their palaces, with simple, functional ground plans that made them vastly different from the labyrinthine Minoan style, were clearly forerunners of the classical Greek temple. And all this was a thousand years or more before the golden age of Greece—the great age of Aeschylus, Sophocles and Euripides, of Hesiod and Pindar, of Phidias and Praxiteles, of Pericles, Alcibiades, Socrates, Plato and Aristotle.

Archaeological evidence indicates that the *Iliad* and the *Odyssey*, though probably first composed some 400 years after the event and perhaps set down in writing even later, convey a reasonably accurate picture—mingled with elements from a later time—of civilization during the Bronze Age of Greece; these are the people and the ways of life of late Mycenaean times.

The recorded narrative of European history begins, in the world's oldest literary masterpieces, with the Trojan War in the 12th Century B.C. According to Homer, the cause of the war—aside from various machinations of the gods—was the abduction of Helen, wife of King Menelaus of Sparta, by Paris, son of King Priam of Troy. In retaliation, the lords and chieftains of Greece mobilized their troops under the leadership of Menelaus' elder brother, King Agamemnon of Mycenae. Among the commanders was Idomeneus, "lord of the Cretans," now conjectured to have been a member of the Mycenaean dynasty that ruled the peaceful Minoans after about 1450 B.C. Embarking in a fleet of more than 1,000 ships, the avenging armies sailed across the Aegean and laid siege to Troy. The struggle, according to the story, lasted 10 years, traditionally from 1194 to 1184 B.C. Toward the end, the two greatest warriors of the opposing forces, the Greek Achilles and Trojan Hector, met in a personal combat which Achilles won. The Greeks eventually captured Troy and obliterated it as a power of the Aegean world.

Modern historians suspect that the Greeks besieged Troy not over Helen but to free their trade routes to the Black Sea from the control the Trojans must have exercised over traffic passing their citadel above the Hellespont. Whatever the cause, it is clear that some great conflict must have taken place. Excavations at Troy have shown that the city was destroyed by fire about the date set by Greek tradition.

NESTOR'S CUP is so called because it resembles one described in the *Iliad* that belonged to King Nestor. Found in the excavated Grave Circle at Mycenae, the cup is less than six inches high. Its handles are topped by doves.

A GOLDEN CUP found in a tomb at Vaphio displays the artistry of Aegean metalworkers. The three-inch-high cup is made of two sheets of gold, the inner left smooth, the outer decorated in relief with a bull in full gallop.

THE LION GATE, built after 1350 B.C., still guards the entrance to the citadel of Mycenae. Now headless, the lions are the oldest example of monumental sculpture in Greece. In ancient times the gate was closed with wooden doors.

CITADEL OF MYCENAE

ACCORDING to Greek legend, Mycenae, Homer's "strong-founded citadel . . . rich in gold," was built by Perseus, slayer of the Gorgon Medusa. In one version, the hero was wandering across the Argive plain when the point of his scabbard fell off. He took this as an omen that he should build a city on the spot. Another account held that he plucked a fungus from the ground and when water flowed from it he named the place Mycenae—a Greek word that can mean both "fungus" and "point of a scabbard."

Modern archaeologists prosaically say that the city was founded by pre-Greek peoples about 3000 B.C. After the arrival of the first Greeks more than a thousand years later, Mycenae prospered. In time it became the capital of a mainland and Aegean empire. Overlooking the fertile plain of "horse-rearing Argos . . . home of lovely women," the city enjoyed an abundance of figs, olives, grapes, barley and other crops. It may also have grown rich from copper mines in the nearby hills. Probably the chief reason for its dominance was its strategic location at the mouth of several mountain passes.

Then, as in later times, Greece was split by its many natural barriers into a patchwork of city-states. Homer confirms archaeological indications that these cities were bound in a loose confederation under the King of Mycenae. Real unity came to Greece only after its conquest by the Romans.

By the end of the 13th Century B.C., Mycenae had attained the full grandeur depicted in the painting at right. Later Greeks believed that its massive walls must have been built by the Cyclopes, one-eyed giants descended from the gods of earth and sky, who bore huge stones from the mountains and fitted them together with smaller stones to fill the crannies. Access to the citadel was by way of a road ascending from the Argive plain to the Lion Gate shown above. Towering over all was the king's palace, equipped with gracious apartments, a splendid throne room and a great hall, or *megaron,* decorated with frescoes of military scenes.

No Grecian city is more legend-haunted than Mycenae. After Perseus came King Eurystheus, for whom the hero Hercules performed his 12 mighty labors. Other famous names of Mycenae's mystohistory were immortalized by Aeschylus in *The Oresteia,* which tells the story of Agamemnon's return from Troy, his murder by his wife Clytemnestra and her lover Aegisthus, and their murder by Orestes.

AGAMEMNON'S CAPITAL, the Acropolis of Mycenae, crowns a craggy hilltop high above the rich Argive plain. Surrounding the entire citadel are massive walls, 20 to 25 feet thick and perhaps 60 feet high. The walls are made of

huge, irregular limestone blocks. The towering royal palace was built in the 14th Century B.C. and remodeled in the 13th. This painting shows only its state portion, containing the great hall, grand staircase and throne room.

The residential section is beyond. Houses for court officials and retainers —flat-roofed, two-storied, and built of stone, brick and timber—stand before the palace, and three private homes appear at left outside the walls.

ALL CARRIED WEAPONS

FOR ancient Greeks, early and late, warfare was an integral part of human existence. Homer's Odysseus observed: "Zeus has appointed the accomplishing of wars, from our youth even into our old age until we are dead, each of us." By classical times, fighting was confined to battlefield and arena, but the historian Thucydides wrote that "in ancient times all Hellenes carried weapons."

With natural barriers of mountain and sea fragmenting their land into small autonomous domains, the Greek cities fought one another to defend their limited and often poor soil. But individuals also fought for glory and renown, seeking out danger to test and prove the heroic stuff of which they were made. And in the Greek martial character there was a unique esthetic element which distinguished the Homeric warrior from belligerents of other ages: a pride in the grace and agility of the human body, a love of beauty in weapons and a glorying in the human spirit that showed itself in veneration of the individual hero. Both Greek and Trojan soldiers delighted in their glistening armaments: "First he [Paris] placed along his legs the fair greaves linked with silver fastenings . . . . Afterwards he girt on about his chest the corselet . . . . Across his shoulders he slung the sword with the nails of silver, a bronze sword, and above it the great shield,

huge and heavy. Over his powerful head he set the well-fashioned helmet with the horsehair crest, and the plumes nodded terribly above it. He took up a strong-shafted spear that fitted his hand's grip."

There was no uniformity of equipment in either the Greek or the Trojan army. Corselets might be of leather or bronze; helmets were variously made with cheek plates, horsehair crests, horns or boar's teeth (*far right*). Each warrior equipped himself as his station in life permitted. In battle there appeared to be little organized maneuvering of troops, and no indication of over-all military direction or planned strategy. Agamemnon was not a general in the modern sense. His army made no attempt to blockade Troy, or even cut off its food and water supply. Fighting usually ended each evening as darkness fell.

It was presumably for reasons of this kind that the Trojan War lasted 10 years—a drawn-out succession of disorderly melees, punctuated by chance encounters between individual antagonists and occasional formal duels between famed heroes. The emphasis was all on the individual champion and his honor. Achilles was admired rather than condemned when he sulked in his tent and refused to join his comrades against the foe, because his honor was slighted. And so decisive was the role of the hero that at one point Achilles turned the tide of battle by simply appearing, unarmed, while: "Three times across the ditch, brilliant Achilles gave his great cry, and three times the Trojans and their renowned companions were routed."

FIGHTING AS INDIVIDUALS, not as an army, warriors battle outside a Mycenaean city. In the foreground, soldiers fight over the body of a fallen attacker; his foes seek to divest him of weapons and armor while his friends (*right*) strive to preserve his honor and their own by dragging him off for burial. Although the weapons described by Homer differ in some respects from those the Mycenaeans are known to have used, the Homeric poems

A WARRIOR VASE, found at Mycenae (*left*), shows six long-nosed soldiers who wear corselets, greaves and horned helmets, and carry spears and shields. Barely visible at left is a figure waving the age-old farewell of women to men going off to war.

A WARRIOR'S HEAD, carved in ivory, is protected by a helmet with boar's teeth (*right*). It was found at Mycenae. This type of headgear is described in Homer's *Iliad:* ". . . on the outer side the white teeth of a . . . boar were close sewn . . . with skill."

do provide a fairly accurate picture of Greek warfare in the Bronze Age. The chief defense of the warrior was his great shield, often shaped like an 8, which protected his body from neck to below the knee but was so cumbersome that a fallen fighter might be pinned beneath it. The principal offensive weapon was the spear, supplemented by the sword and the bow and arrow. The horse-drawn chariot was used for transport rather than as a tactical weapon.

THREE LIONS are shown in a hunt scene on a bronze dagger blade with an inlay of gold, silver and black niello. Two lions flee. The third, turning to attack, has struck down one huntsman. Three spearmen and an archer are still facing the charging beast. The blade was found in a tomb.

A LION HUNT in the highlands turns to tragedy. In this painting a fallen huntsman, encumbered by his heavy shield, is mauled by the quarry while his comrades seek to save him. Homer explained that it was vital to hunt lions in order to safeguard livestock: ". . . lions which as they prey upon the cattle and the fat sheep lay waste the steadings where there are men, until they also fall and are killed under the cutting bronze in the men's hands."

"THE BALEFUL BEAST"

THE Mycenaean Greeks found danger, and opportunity for displays of courage and prowess, in hunting as well as in war. Necessity was added to sport when, from the mountain fastnesses of ancient Greece, bears, wolves and lions descended to harry the domestic flocks. A lion hunt is vividly described in Homer's account of the fight between Achilles and Aeneas: "From the other side the son of Peleus [Achilles] rose like a lion against him, the baleful beast, when men have been straining to kill him . . . and he at first pays them no attention but goes his way, only when some one of the impetuous young men has hit him with the spear he whirls, jaws open, over his teeth foam breaks out, and in the depth of his chest the powerful heart groans; he lashes his own ribs with his tail and the flanks on both sides as he rouses himself to fury for the fight, eyes glaring, and hurls himself straight onward to the chance of killing some one of the men, or else being killed himself in the first onrush." If the lion won, there was probably no great mourning, for the Greeks regarded a courageous death as the proper fulfillment of a hero's life. Even the classical Greeks had a hazy notion of immortality, sometimes regarding the hereafter as reserved for heroes only, sometimes conceiving it as a world of wraiths. But about 1600 B.C., apparently as a result of Egyptian influence, the Mycenaeans began to build elaborate royal tombs (*below*), richly furnished and decorated.

A ROYAL FUNERAL takes place in a Mycenaean tomb in the side of a hill. The bodies of the king and queen lie on the floor of the chamber, surrounded by mortuary gifts. Behind them stands a group of mourners, including a servant (*second in line at left*) and a dog, who will be killed to accompany their rulers in death. In the background at left, workers prepare the place of interment. Just inside the doorway a flaming pyre consumes perishable offerings.

FORERUNNERS
OF THE CLASSIC GREEKS

THE power of the Mycenaeans began to wane in the late 13th and early 12th Centuries B.C. Their decline was long attributed to invasion by the Dorians, a backward and illiterate people who moved down through central Greece and the islands from the northwest mountains, perhaps themselves being pushed by upheavals in the vast barbarian hinterland. However, historians now regard the Dorian migration as only one phase of the downfall of the Mycenaeans. The fall of Mycenae itself they count as merely one result of a far larger disturbance extending over several hundred years.

Spearheaded by that conglomeration of tribes known collectively as the Sea Peoples, this great movement of various peoples by land and sea brought about a period of tremendous upheaval in the eastern Mediterranean. During this period the civilized world witnessed the end of the Hittite Empire, the collapse of Egyptian power in the Near East, the sack of Troy, and the destruction and looting of cities throughout Greece, Anatolia and the Levant. The long-nurtured commercial and political organization of the Bronze Age peoples was disrupted in this time of troubles, which marked the beginning of the Iron Age. Iron, abundant and easily worked, was soon to become the "poor man's metal." Bronze swords and spears could not prevail against the slash of iron blades.

It may have been their very success that made the undoing of the Mycenaeans inevitable. Their city states depended for their livelihood on an extraordinarily active and widespread foreign trade. The trade conducted by the Mycenaeans was far-ranging: timber and metal from the eastern Mediterranean, grain from Egyptian and Black Sea ports, and amber from the Baltic were exchanged for pottery and other manufactured goods. The increasing prosperity that resulted nurtured a Mycenaean population of considerable density. When the trade routes were gradually severed by the raids of the Sea Peoples, disaster became inevitable. Economically isolated, city turned upon city, and many Mycenaeans emigrated to Asia Minor and its offshore islands or joined the marauding Sea Peoples in raids on cities in the area from Greece to Palestine. There is evidence at Athens, Tiryns, Pylos and Mycenae itself of hastily erected fortifications—and often of their violent destruction.

It was at about this stage that the Mycenaeans moved against Troy. Some authorities say that it was a last major effort to free the grain route to the Black Sea. But the effort was made too late. Those cities which, like Athens, were not wiped out, gradually withered. Then the Dorians infiltrated the stricken land, introducing additional chaos to an already prostrate civilization.

The Mycenaean world crumbled. Art and craftsmanship declined, and no scrap of writing dating from this period has been found. The so-called dark age of Greece ensued, during which tales of Mycenaean heroes lived on in oral tradition, eventually to be immortalized by

AMATEUR Heinrich Schliemann is credited with the discovery of the Homeric world.

Homer and passed on to later ages as a glorification of the mythical ancestors of the Greeks.

Homer's tales were believed to have no factual basis whatever until the second half of the 19th Century A.D. Two men were responsible for the change in attitude that occurred then. One was a rich and romantic-minded German merchant named Heinrich Schliemann, who began to excavate the site of Troy in 1871. The other was Sir Arthur Evans, an Englishman who in 1899 uncovered the ruins of the palace of Minos at Knossos in Crete. Together Schliemann and Evans opened a new chapter in history, a chapter which is still being written.

SCHLIEMANN had been fascinated by the stories of Homer since his childhood. Later he wrote, "I talked of nothing else to my playfellows but of Troy. . . . I was continually laughed at . . . ." After acquiring a fortune in business, Schliemann retired in 1863 when he was 41, divorced his wife and married a 16-year-old Greek girl. Together at Hissarlik they began to excavate what they thought was Troy. Here Schliemann found several superimposed towns, none of which was the Homeric city. Abandoning Hissarlik, he was digging at Mycenae five years later when he found mummified bodies—three with golden face masks—in the ruins of a Mycenaean cemetery. Believing he had discovered the remains of Homer's heroes, he triumphantly telegraphed to the King of Greece: "I have gazed upon the face of Agamemnon." Years of controversy about both of these discoveries followed, but scholars now agree that Schliemann did find the site of Troy, if not the proper layer, and that his finds at Mycenae belonged to a period several centuries earlier than the Trojan War.

Schliemann had supposed that Homer was a contemporary of his heroes. But as more Mycenaean relics were unearthed, discrepancies appeared. The Trojan War had been fought in the late Bronze Age, but Homer knew about iron. As Leonard Cottrell pointed out in *The Bull of Minos*, the Mycenaeans buried their dead, but the Homeric heroes burned theirs. Mycenaean swords were designed for thrusting, Homer's for slashing. Though memorized folk tales had preserved many details of Mycenaean life with astonishing fidelity, Schliemann finally conceded that Homer must have lived several hundred years after the Trojan War. The important fact, confirmed by continuing discoveries at Mycenae and elsewhere, was that there had been a high civilization in Greece a thousand years before the golden age. Finds in the shaft graves and in the tholoi, or hillside tombs, indicate that Mycenaean culture and prosperity lasted for some 500 years.

The mystery of the origin of the classical Greeks was still not solved. Were the Mycenaeans really Greeks? Or were they simply good fighters and traders of some other stock who had flourished in Greece for a while? Here Sir Arthur Evans made his contribution. Like Schliemann, Evans was a rich man. As a boy he spent summers with

THE
AEGEAN
CIVILIZATION

0   50   100
MILES

his father collecting flints in Britain and France. When he was 33, he took his wife to Greece where they called upon the Schliemanns, then engaged in excavations at Tiryns. In 1894 he went to Crete for the first time. There he traveled to the legendary site of Knossos where he found that a Greek—appropriately named Minos—had already dug trenches uncovering massive walls. Evans returned to Crete five years later, and acquired the lease for the remainder of the site. By the spring of 1899, his digging had revealed a great labyrinth of buildings, which Evans described in his diary as an "extraordinary phenomenon—nothing Greek—nothing Roman—perhaps one single fragment of late black varnished ware among tens of thousands . . . its great period goes at least well back to the pre-Mycenaean period."

In 1900 at Knossos Sir Arthur found some clay tablets. The Minoans, it appeared, had started out as the Egyptians had begun—with picture writing—and then developed two linear scripts that seemed to be closely similar though not identical. Evans tagged them Linear A and Linear B.

For 40 years Sir Arthur tried in vain to decipher these scripts. The task was then taken up by a young English architect and amateur cryptographer named Michael Ventris who employed a variety of laborious code-breaking techniques. In 1952, he scored a success. The language of Linear B turned out to be an extremely archaic form of Greek. The oldest European language ever found, it was the ancestor of classical Greek. Linear A, presumably the Minoans' own language, remains undeciphered.

S INCE Evans' find at Knossos, numbers of similar tablets have been discovered in the ruins of Mycenae and other mainland cities, though no others have turned up on Crete. Unhappily, the tablets contain no history, no philosophy, no poetry. They are devoted to inventories and lists of animals, farm products, people and military equipment. They do, however, tend to confirm the evidence, already established in painting and pottery, that the Minoan-Mycenaean link was a close one, and to strengthen the belief that Mycenaeans may have ruled in Knossos after 1450 B.C. They leave little doubt that after the decline of Minoan civilization, Crete was absorbed into the mainstream of Hellenic life.

Accumulating discoveries about Europe's Dark Ages have suggested that the darkness was mainly in the minds of the historians. Will the same prove true of the Greek dark age? The classical Greeks borrowed their alphabet from the Phoenicians, and the earliest known example of their adaptation of it belongs to the Eighth Century B.C. Some of the Linear B tablets may be almost as late. Did the two overlap? Or, as the late Professor Wace of Princeton asked: "Is it likely that such an inventive, intelligent and wideawake people as the Greeks would ever have stopped reading and writing once they learned to do so?" Wace thought not. Schliemann and Evans, he wrote, "revealed a new world for archaeology and for classical studies, but if much has been learned, much still remains to be learned."

DISCOVERER OF KNOSSOS, Sir Arthur Evans stands near a wall of the famous Cretan palace. Keeper of the Ashmolean Museum at Oxford, Sir Arthur spent five years on his archaeological investigations in the Aegean.

159

THE HEAD OF A WARRIOR bespeaks many of the qualities of the Etruscans: strength, intelligence and martial prowess. At their height, Etruscan cities controlled most of Italy, even Rome itself, which later acknowledged its indebtedness to the Etruscan genius. This fine terra-cotta head, nine inches high, was made in the Fifth Century B.C., when the Etruscan power was beginning to decline. It probably formed part of the decoration of a temple.

THE GAY, GIFTED ETRUSCANS

Great fighters on land and sea, the early masters of Italy were also magnificent craftsmen and industrious traders

AT the turn of the first millennium B.C., a prolonged period of restless movement began among the civilized peoples of the eastern Mediterranean. Some turned west to new frontiers, looking for land, trade or raw materials. They carried with them the patterns and techniques of civilizations already about 2,000 years old. It was this urge to move westward that brought civilized men and their societies to new lands in the Mediterranean, to the European shores of the Atlantic and eventually across the ocean to the New World.

Among those who moved out of the eastern world—a world already too old and too confining for the more vigorous of the peoples it had produced—were Phoenicians from the Levant, Greeks from the Aegean isles and mainland, and a mixed lot of seafarers from various areas. The Phoenicians, hardy seamen and canny traders, founded Carthage in northwestern Africa, near the site of modern Tunis. In time, their colony became the capital of an empire so rich and powerful that Rome itself felt insecure, and a Roman senator proclaimed: *Delenda est Carthago* (Carthage must be destroyed). The far-roving Greeks colonized a stretch of coastal Europe from Sicily to Spain. But the Greek cities, like those of the Phoenicians, remained fundamentally cultural outposts of the older civilizations from which they had sprung. Only one truly new civilization emerged from the great Mediterranean migration. This was the civilization of the Etruscans, a talented people who live on in the frescoes, sculpture and craftwork shown on these pages. The Etruscans founded their urban society around 800 B.C. in Etruria, which roughly corresponds to modern Tuscany on the western coast of Italy.

Did the Etruscans migrate in a body from some coastal region of Asia Minor, or did an early people native to the Italian peninsula somehow draw upon the vigor and genius of one or more eastern races? The question is still being disputed by scholars. Certainly the language, religion, habits and attitudes of the Etruscans represented a fusion of Italic and some eastern elements into a unique cultural pattern. The Etruscans not only brought civilization to Italy, but through trade and cultural interchange across the Italian Alps greatly accelerated the movement of the peoples of central Europe from barbarism to civilization.

The Etruscans at their height dominated the Italian peninsula from the Po valley in the north to Salerno in the south, and surged to riches and power when Rome was still a hamlet amid rural hills. Indeed, Etruscan kings—the famous Tarquins—ruled Rome from about 616 to 510 B.C. Much later, when Rome was in its prime, long after the Etruscans had lost their identity as a distinct people, the Romans proudly traced much of their own strength and glory to their Etruscan heritage. Through Rome, every western society that followed owes something to the gay Etruscans.

Few people in history have displayed a more varied genius. The Etruscans were skilled mariners and naval fighters, as well as formidable horsemen and warriors on land. They were creators and conquerors of cities, adventurous and successful traders, industrious miners and fashioners of metals, enthusiastic sportsmen, gamblers and musicians, and magnificent painters and sculptors. They loved life and lived it joyously.

The Etruscans never brought their autonomous city-states together in an effective union. A succession of enemies—colonial Greeks, native tribesmen, Celtic and other invaders from central Europe—gradually chipped away at Etruscan power. In the end it was Rome, with its political cohesion and superior system of organization, that overwhelmed the separate Etruscan cities and absorbed Etruria. The civilization of the Etruscans disappeared in the last century of the pre-Christian era. It left behind only a sparse written record, in a language that scholars are still trying to master. But another kind of record happily survived. It is the record in gold, bronze, terra cotta, silver, clay, stucco carvings and vivid painted frescoes of their daily life that the creative Etruscans left in their subterranean tombs.

A FUNERAL BANQUET is depicted in this famous fresco in the Tomb of the Leopards at Tarquinia, a chief Etruscan city. The figures eating, drinking and reclining on couches at the rear represent the tomb's departed owners, enjoying themselves in the afterworld with friends and relatives. Musicians play for the gathering, and a servant at right center carries a wine jar. Funeral artists traditionally painted women with light skins, men in a darker red.

162

A BURIAL URN of the Seventh Century B.C. resembles the huts of the early Etruscans. In or beside vessels of this type, survivors placed objects such as men's weapons and women's jewelry that might be used in the afterlife.

HOUSES OF THE DEAD

IN life, the Etruscans were constantly preoccupied with death. The idea of death, says French scholar Raymond Bloch, "weighed on them perpetually and terribly." But a natural gaiety tempered their fears and they prepared for the afterworld as if it were a place where earthly joys would be renewed. It is this attitude that inspired the Etruscan "houses of the dead," where most of the treasures pictured on these pages were found.

The tombs are either carved in the volcanic *tufa* that underlies much of the Italian peninsula or constructed from blocks of it. On the outskirts of their cities, wealthy Etruscans arranged to rest forever in replicas of the rooms where they had slept, dined and entertained in life. In some tombs, bodies of the dead were placed; in others, cremated ashes were preserved in finely wrought urns of bronze, terra cotta and alabaster. The costly trappings of an extremely wealthy society were enshrined with the dead: richly engraved armor of bronze and iron, splendid pottery, incised mirrors and gold ornaments. On the walls of the tomb, painters sometimes depicted their employer and his family, with friends and servants, at war, in sport, at the banquet table.

A STONE CHAIR stands in the vestibule of a huge tomb at Cerveteri (*right*), with many rooms carved from rock. The shield above the chair was also carved from the rock. Entrances to wealthy homes probably looked like this.

AN ETRUSCAN FARMER with his yoked oxen is immortalized in bronze. This statuette, dating from about the Fourth Century B.C., is one of the few Etruscan works found that show any interest in life outside the cities.

SOCIETY AND MUSIC

ETRUSCAN society was extremely rigid. From beginning to end, the aristocracy that dominated Etruscan life never permitted the lower orders—merchants, hired artisans, slaves—to rise to places of privilege and power as their equivalents in Greek and Roman societies sometimes did. Partly because of this fact, the Etruscans who are seen in frescoes, in statuary and in the accounts of Greek and Roman chroniclers were mostly members of the wealthy upper classes. Thus Etruscan life now appears to have a sheen and a brilliance that probably would have seemed unreal to many of the people who actually experienced it. In any case, the daily life of Etruscan aristocrats must have been a lush round of wining, dining and pleasure. "Twice a day," the Roman writer Diodorus Siculus said, "sumptuous tables are laid and everything brought that goes with exaggerated luxury—flowers, robes, and numerous silver goblets of various shapes; nor is the number of slaves who are in attendance small." The servants, musicians and other attendants portrayed in the tomb frescoes seem to be as happy as their masters, but there is no record to indicate whether they really were or not. A disapproving Greek historian of the Fourth Century reports that Etruscans were served by naked slaves. Diodorus, blaming the eventual decline of the Etruscans on their excessive love of luxury, complains on the other hand that they clothed their servitors in garments "more costly than befits the station of a slave."

Etruscan men usually wore short jackets. Later they adapted the Greek *khiton,* a short tunic, and in cold weather wore over it a more ample *tebennos,* or cloak, forerunner of the Roman toga. Etruscan women wore a light, pleated tunic and a thick outer cloak, often dyed in brilliant colors. Both men and women took pride in their shoes, which were made of leather or embroidered cloth and were long, pointed and curled at the toes—a style borrowed from Asia Minor. They also wore ankle boots and sandals. In early times, both men and women affected long hair, and the men were bearded. Around 500 B.C., the men began to cut their hair short and to go clean-shaven. The women also shortened their hair, and wore it in tight curls that framed the face, or tucked it behind their necks in the Greek fashion.

The Etruscans ate, danced, made love, hunted, raced and died to the sound of music. Their favorite instruments were the stringed lyre, the curved trumpet with a piercing note and, above all, the double flute, which appears in many of their frescoes. In paintings and statuary, Etruscan husbands and wives are shown in loving companionship—a reflection of the rare equality that upper-class Etruscan women enjoyed at a time when men generally regarded women as inferior creatures to be kept in subjection and seclusion.

A FOND COUPLE is depicted on the lid of a funeral urn (*above*). The Greeks sometimes misinterpreted scenes such as this one as evidence that the Etruscans were addicted to shameless displays of public lechery.

GAIETY marks this scene from a rich man's tomb fresco (*left*). The winebearer leads two musicians, one playing a lyre, the other a double flute. This fresco shows how high living was enjoyed by well-to-do Etruscans.

165

ETRUSCAN SPORTS

THE Etruscans were avid hunters and sportsmen. They tracked deer and wild boar with dogs. A Greek account says that they also used flutes in the hunt, luring animals into nets and traps with "the purest and most harmonious melody." Horses were bred both for war and for racing and were harnessed to chariots or carried riders. Mounted horsemen competed in conventional flat races and also in an Etruscan game (later adopted by the Romans) called the *truia*, in which the horses had to be maneuvered over a course shaped like a maze. Naked riders on barebacked horses vied at shifting from one mount to another at full gallop. The Etruscans had sports arenas, which were predecessors of the Roman circus, but seats (on wooden stands) were available only for important personages. Both men and women were enthusiastic spectators at the sports events.

On a single day in an Etruscan arena, the spectators might see chariot and horse races, foot races, pole vaulting, wrestling and boxing, and perhaps acrobats, trick riders and clowns. These spectacles may have originally had a religious and ceremonial aspect. Actors and ritualistic dancers performed along with the athletes, usually to the sound of flutes or other musical instruments. Elaborate games were staged as the climax of the funerals of wealthy people. The funeral games sometimes involved duels to the death between combatants, probably slaves, who were in effect offered up as human sacrifices in honor of the deceased. In one fresco depicting such a duel, a masked man sets a ferocious dog upon his opponent, who is

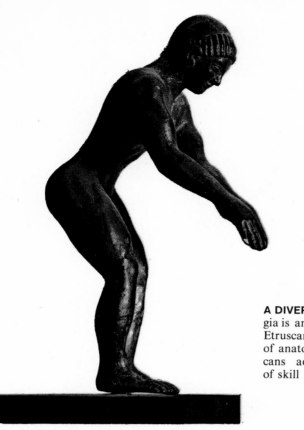

A DIVER found at Perugia is an example of the Etruscan artists' mastery of anatomy. The Etruscans admired displays of skill in sports events.

armed with a cudgel but has his head covered by a sack. Later, the Romans adopted human combat from the Etruscans as a funeral rite. Out of it, according to Roman historians, grew the mortal contests between troupes of professional gladiators which, in arenas all over the Empire, entertained the populace.

From an early date Etruscan warriors were accustomed to carry out a war dance which was by no means part of their military training but seems to have had a religious and magical value. This rhythmic dance, accompanied by the sound of lances beaten on shields in a regular cadence, was intended to draw the attention—and the favor —of the gods of war to soldiers who were about to go into combat. Music and the dance were omnipresent in Etruscan life. The dancing generally seems to have been performed by professional entertainers: single dancing girls accompanied by a pipe player, and chorus groups of dancing men and women. The jerky leg movements and the rapid arm gestures suggest that the dancing was usually highly animated and possibly orgiastic. Aristotle, one of many Greeks who wrote of the Etruscans with a curious mixture of distaste and fascination, complained that the Etruscans "fight, knead dough and beat their slaves to the sound of the flute."

The Etruscans (or their ancestors) were supposed to have invented dice. According to legend, the Etruscans originated in an ancient country of Asia Minor called Lydia. When a famine afflicted them there, they devised dice as a means of keeping their minds off their hunger. But dice games and similar diversions proved to be poor substitutes for food, and as the famine persisted, half the people of Lydia set off on the ocean trek that finally brought them to Etruria.

A DISCUS THROWER is depicted on a fresco adorning a tomb found in 1958 at Tarquinia. Believed to have been painted in the Sixth Century, the Tarquinia tomb was the most important Etruscan tomb discovered since 1892.

WRESTLERS have locked their hands over a stack of three bronze basins that will be awarded to the winner. At the left, with a curved staff, stands the referee. The figure at the right is engaged in a gladiatorial contest.

A FOOT RACE resembles the Olympic games, but whether the Etruscans staged intercity contests on the Greek model is unknown. This and other Etruscan sports show traces of Greek and earlier Mesopotamian customs.

CHARIOT RACING, a popular Etruscan spectacle (*left*), is pictured here with a three-horse team. Etruscans raced more often with two horses harnessed to light chariots, magnificently embossed with bronze and gold figures.

167

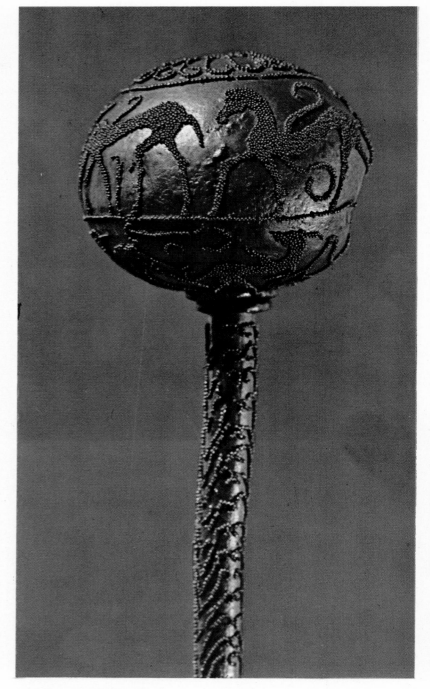

A GOLDEN BROOCH with an Oriental air has interlaced palm leaves framing five lions on the top disk; below two mesh links, griffins and lions adorn a smaller disk. It was buried with the wealthy woman who owned it.

GOLDEN GRIFFINS and other mythical animals decorate the head of this fine *spilla,* or pin, much enlarged in the photograph. The golden pin is eight inches long. It was found at Vetulonia, one of the richest of Etruscan cities.

WEALTH FROM METALS

APART from the vigor and intelligence of the people, the chief source of Etruscan wealth and power was metal. The western coast of the Italian peninsula and the off-lying islands, particularly Elba and Sardinia, were among the areas of the ancient world where iron, copper, tin and other metals were found in useful quantities. It was partly this profusion of metal resources that drew the Greeks, the Phoenicians and the migrants of Asia Minor to the west and embroiled them in ceaseless conflicts over possession of the mineral riches. Their knowledge of how to extract and work the metals was an inheritance from the more civilized east.

The export of extracted metals and finished metal products, including art of the kind shown here, earned the riches with which the Etruscans imported a great variety of goods from as far away as Egypt. They were masters in working all of the metals known to them. Trade in metals and the things it bought sent them coursing through the seas both as merchant sailors and as naval warriors defending their routes and ports. In the sense that iron as well as copper and bronze were already in use, the Iron Age preceded the Etruscans to the Etrurian area. But the Etruscans brought iron into abundant use, along with other metals, and so they may be given credit for having first made the use of iron a decisive factor in western societies.

A TWO-HEADED BIRD with four legs (*left*) is mounted on wheels to imitate a chariot. Fashioned of bronze in the so-called Villanovan period (Eighth to 10th Centuries), it was probably a cult object, used for perfume or incense.

ETRUSCAN FIGURINES are fashioned in bronze (*above*). The second and third figures from the left wear the peaked hats of *haruspices*, or soothsayers. To the right of the elaborate, curvaceous oil lamp, a goddess raises her skirt.

AN ETRUSCAN TEMPLE is shown here in a plaster model. The temples faced the south, which was believed to be the dwelling place of the more favorable gods. Inside the temples in three rooms stood images of deities. The statues of the gods and the temple walls were often gaily painted.

HOUSES OF THE GODS

LIKE everything else that the Etruscans built above ground, their temples or "houses of the gods" have vanished except for a few fragmentary remains. From those remnants and later descriptions, scholars have reconstructed models of the kind shown above.

The Etruscan houses of the gods represented a transfer to earth of the conception of holy areas in the sky: the Latin *templum* originally connoted a space reserved to the gods. Fear of the gods and an obsessive need to discern the will of the gods dominated the lives of the Etruscans. Their religion was laden with a sense of mystical gloom and foreboding. A powerful caste of priests incessantly sought to determine the will of the gods from three principal indicators—lightning, thunder and the entrails of sacrificed animals. The priests themselves were called *haruspices.* They looked to the sky as the seat of divine power and to the liver as a readable replica of the sky. The intensity of thunder and the direction of lightning flashes indicated the will of the gods and, through it, the prospects of men and nations. Many of the names of Etruscan gods were closely related to those of the Greeks: Aplu to Apollo, Artums to Artemis, Hercle to Herakles, Turms to Hermes. The chief Etruscan god, Tinia, came to resemble the Greek Zeus and the Roman Jupiter. His wife, Uni, became the equivalent of the Greeks' Hera and the Romans' Juno. The Roman augurs, or readers of omens, were patterned after the *haruspices.* There came a time, in fact, when the Romans hired Etruscan *haruspices* and placed much faith in them.

The Etruscans considered that the precepts of their religion had been specifically revealed to them by Tages, a spirit who had sprung from the earth with the face of a child and the wisdom of an old man. The Greeks and Romans simply derived their religions, and their gods, from the universe around them, without specific revelation. In time the Greeks and Romans came to regard their gods rather lightly and to ascribe many natural events to natural causes. To the very last, the Etruscans viewed theirs with an awe amounting to dread and believed that every single occurrence on earth was of divine origin.

ABDUCTION SCENE from a temple frieze shows a satyr making off with a robust maiden. The frieze, found at Satricum, was made in the 5th Century B.C. Life-size terra-cotta decorations like this were lavished on temple roofs.

"APOLLO OF VEIIO" bears the name of the city where it was found. It represents the god whom the early Etruscans called Aplu, and is thought to be the work of Vulca, the only Etruscan sculptor whose name has survived.

A TRITON, or minor sea god, with a fishlike body and a human head and feet, is depicted in the bronze frieze at the left. It once embellished the side of a chariot. The figure crouching at the right represents an archer.

171

A WAR CHARIOT, reconstructed from bronze fragments (*left*), shows a woman giving armor to a warrior on the front panel. Two warriors fight on one side; a winged chariot and a centaur appear on the side not shown.

FINE ARMS AND ARMOR

THE Etruscans' mastery of metals contributed not only to their wealth but to their martial prowess. Etruscan warriors probably had the best arms and armor of their day; certainly they went into battle with a wide assortment of bronze and iron weapons. Seventh Century Etruscans fought with battle-axes, lances and daggers; for protection they had sturdy, round shields of bronze and helmets with elaborately figured bronze peaks and crests. In the next century they adopted Greek-style helmets of several kinds and also developed their own distinctive morion, a one-piece helmet without a visor. They had round and oval shields, such refinements as metal shin guards, and both curved and straight swords. They prided themselves on their splendidly armed and mounted cavalry, and they also fought from horse-drawn chariots of the kind shown above. Later accounts emphasize the power of their naval fleets, which were greatly feared by Greek and other rivals of the time. It was the Etruscans who first gave the Italic peoples the urge to conquer and dominate the sea. From ancient times, the Greeks, whose literature may not be completely objective on the subject, since they were bitter contemporary rivals, set down records of the supremacy of the Etruscans both in eastern and in western seas as deplorable and unceasing piracy. In any case, according to legend, Etruscan maritime activity spread Etruscan civilization along the shores of Italy, Sardinia, Corsica, North Africa, Greece, southern France and Spain. But it was as infantrymen, and through a still mightier people, that the Etruscans made their major contribution to the science of warfare. From the Etruscan infantry formation, the Romans derived the organization of the invincible legions that ultimately turned Rome into the master of its world.

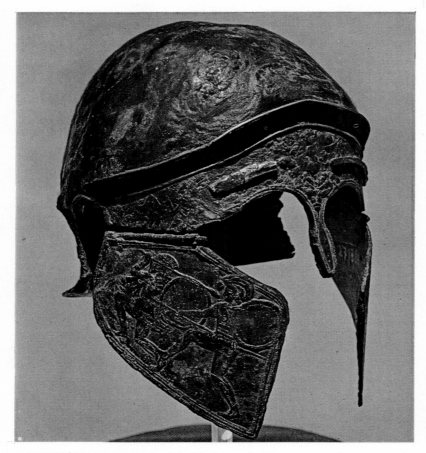

A CEREMONIAL HELMET is of the kind worn by Etruscan warriors at parades and similar occasions of display. The scene of two foot-soldiers fighting is typical of the decorations with which Etruscans liked to emboss their armor.

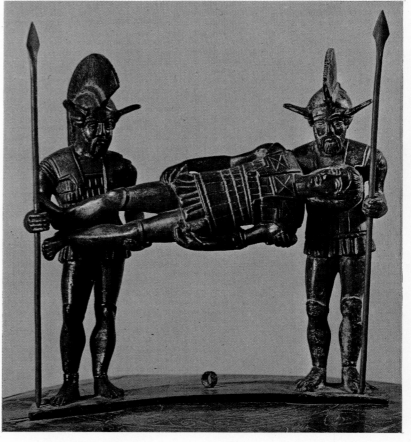

ARMORED WARRIORS with a slain companion wear helmets of Greek design. This carving on a chest shows that Etruscan armor and weapons were like those used by Greeks and Romans in the Fourth and Third Centuries B.C.

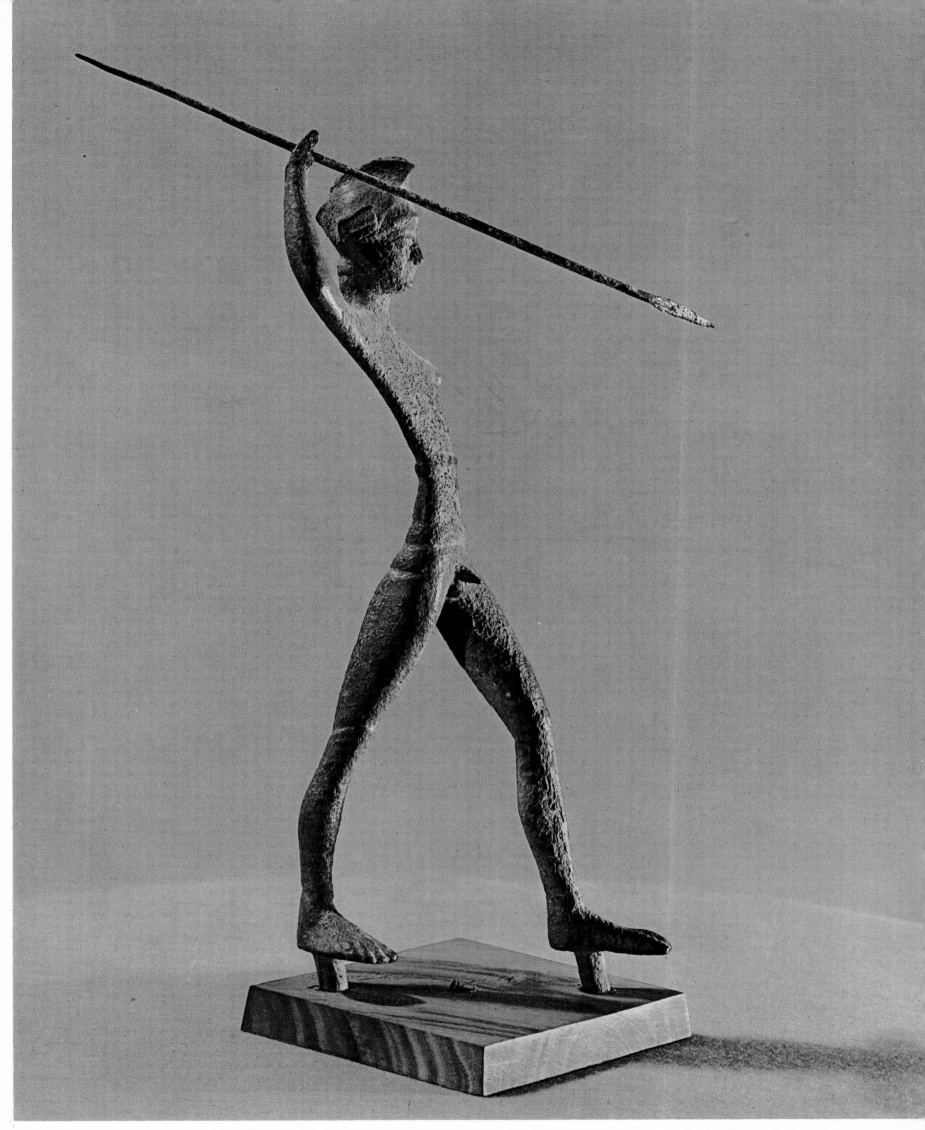

A NAKED LANCER in bronze is a Fifth Century artist's representation of an Etruscan warrior. As offensive weapons, the Etruscans used a heavy lance with a point of iron or bronze; a light lance, or javelin; a long sword (a relic of the armament used during the late Bronze Age); a short sword, or glaive; a curved saber (used between the Sixth and Fourth Centuries); a dagger; and a battle-ax, which in the oldest times had two blades.

ENIGMAS AND IRONIES
OF THE ETRUSCANS

THE Romans called the people of Etruria the Tusci or Etrusci, and they are generally termed Etruscans today. But they were widely known in their own time by the Greek name of Tyrrhenoi, or Tyrrhenians, and the waters off the coast of Etruria are still called the Tyrrhenian Sea. This is a tribute to the influence of Herodotus, the Greek historian of the Fifth Century B.C., who traced the origin of the Tyrrhenians to Lydia in Asia Minor and who named them for Tyrrhenos, the prince who supposedly led them across the seas to Etruria. Another Greek historian, Dionysius of Halicarnassus, disputed Herodotus' account some four centuries after it was written and argued that the Etruscans were natives of the Etrurian region.

A still later theory, now generally discredited, held that the first Etruscans migrated south to Etruria from northern Italy or perhaps central Europe. The many variations upon these major suppositions

about the Etruscans include a possibility that they were related to the dimly known Turshas, who were one of the Sea Peoples described in earlier chapters. And another possibility is that the Etruscans were originally migrants from Asia Minor who paused and settled for a time on the Aegean island of Lemnos and then moved on to Etruria. A growing school of scholarship is now inclined to believe that various people from Asia Minor and the eastern Mediterranean reached Etruria in small parties or even as individuals, settled there and by gradual social merger with the natives evolved an Etruscan or Tyrrhenian strain.

Wherever they may have come from originally, the Etruscans, like the Romans, were powerfully affected by the warm climate and the rugged terrain of Italy. As Alfredo Signoretti, a modern authority on the Etruscans, puts it: "Industrious, excitable, attached to life;

A NEW TOOL FOR ARCHAEOLOGISTS is a camera fitted with a periscope and a light attachment (*left*), here being used to examine an unopened Etruscan tomb near Rome. A hole was dug through the roof of the tomb and a photograph taken. The picture that resulted (*center*) revealed urns and dishware in the 2,500-year-old tomb and led to a decision to open it (*right*). The camera-periscope was invented by Carlo Lerici, whose hobby is archaeology.

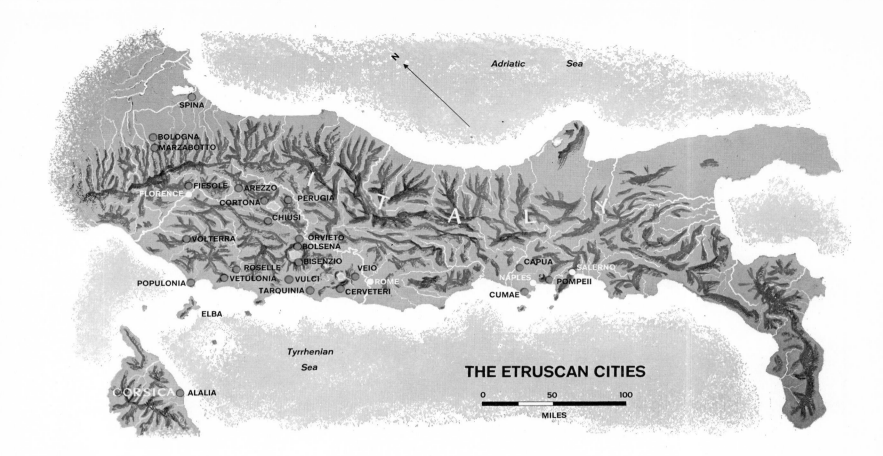

The map labels (reading from the figure):

SPINA, BOLOGNA, MARZABOTTO, FIESOLE, AREZZO, FLORENCE, CORTONA, PERUGIA, CHIUSI, VOLTERRA, ORVIETO, BOLSENA, ROSELLE, BISENZIO, VEIO, VETULONIA, VULCI, ROME, POPULONIA, TARQUINIA, CERVETERI, CAPUA, NAPLES, SALERNO, CUMAE, POMPEII, ELBA, CORSICA, ALALIA

Adriatic Sea, ITALY, Tyrrhenian Sea

THE ETRUSCAN CITIES

0   50   100

MILES

superstitious, mischievous, with a love of luxury; quick and intelligent, but with a tendency to anarchy; wanting to use every means to hand and make their prestige felt, but ready to sacrifice themselves for their own blood; loving their home town without going beyond this in the idea of the state as such. This is the Etruscan; and this is the Italian of all time."

The earliest written accounts of the Etruscans came from Greek and Roman chroniclers who made no pretense of treating their subject with detachment. Presumably because at one stage of their history the Etruscans hindered and occasionally thwarted Greek expansion in the western Mediterranean, the Greeks tended to write of them with envy and scorn alloyed with reluctant admiration. The Etruscans in these accounts often appear as thieves, pirates, rapists and lechers. The Roman attitude toward the Etruscans varied with circumstances. At first the Romans looked on them as rivals, enemies and conquerors. The attackers who were opposed by "Horatio at the bridge" were Etruscans. The Etruscan dynasty of the Tarquins governed Rome from 616 to 510 B.C., and are generally given credit for making a city out of what previously had been a collection of villages. Among other things, they gave the city an effective drainage system. But after the Etruscans had finally been conquered by Rome, the Romans swung to the opposite extreme and sometimes exaggerated their very real Etruscan heritage.

The written Etruscan record is all but useless as a guide to Etruscan life and culture. Scholars now understand the rudimentary Greek alphabet of Etruria, recognize many individual words and have wholly translated the thousands of brief tomb inscriptions to the dead and to the gods. In addition, one longer writing—a cloth manuscript found wrapped around an Egyptian mummy—has been translated. But the brief inscriptions contain little more than dates and names of places and people, and the longer text contains a compilation of ritual rules that tells relatively little.

It is, Professor Massimo Pallottino points out, as if later generations had tried "to assess the thought and literature of a modern nation from tombstones in a few cemeteries, inscriptions on a handful of buildings and some pages torn from its Book of Common Prayer. The fundamental obstacle . . . is the poverty of these primary documents." So far the Etruscan writings have revealed one fact of major importance about the Etruscan people: because the language is so different from all known languages (despite its Greek alphabet), the Etruscans who used it must have been different in vital respects from other peoples of their time and world.

Thanks to Greek and Roman accounts, the formal history of the Etruscans is fairly well known. The first cities they built were probably Vetulonia and Populonia, on the Etrurian coast near the island of Elba, and the cities of Cerveteri, Tarquinia and Vulci. Thereafter they expanded through Etruria until they were able to bring 12 cities into the confederation which modern scholars call "the Etruscan League." By the standards of the time and place, all 12 deserved the

name of cities, although the biggest of them probably never exceeded five or six thousand in resident population.

Between approximately 700 and 500 B.C., the Etruscans extended their dominion north into the Po valley, east to the upper Adriatic, and south through Roman Latium into Campania. In this period of almost continuous expansion they also occupied the island of Corsica, which was prized for its metal resources, and intermittently maintained footholds on Sardinia. At one time or another, there were some 42 Etruscan cities, including Rome itself and storied Pompeii.

Early in their expansion the Etruscans allied themselves with the Phoenicians of Carthage against the Greek colonial complex in the western Mediterranean. At Alalia in Corsica, in 540 B.C., the Greeks claimed victory over the combined Etruscan and Carthaginian fleets in a great naval battle, but it was probably either a draw or a narrow victory for the Greeks: they soon abandoned Corsica to the Etruscans, who founded a city called Victory there. Possibly inflated with their success, the Etruscans sought to expand their hold on southern Italy and thereby overreached themselves. The Greeks defeated them at the southern port of Cumae in 524 B.C. In the next century the Etruscans suffered successive defeats at the hands of the emergent Romans, the peninsular hillsmen called Samnites, the Celts from the north and the Greek colonists of Syracuse. Thereafter they declined almost steadily, and by 250 B.C. they had submitted to the Romans. During the last century before Christ, Etruria and all of its once proud cities formally became Roman territory, and Etruscan culture ceased to exist as a separate entity.

It is one of the ironies of the Etruscan story that the very symbols associated with Roman authority and power—the golden crown, the golden ring and scepter, the fasces and the *toga palmata*—had originated with the Etruscans. The French scholar Raymond Bloch of the Sorbonne has well summarized the debt that Rome and the later western world owe to the Etruscan people and civilization: "These people," Bloch has said, "were an active civilising agent in the heart of Italy, and their impetus, together with that of the Greek colonisers, released the peninsula from the obscurity of early barbarism. Their civilisation was extremely complex, eastern in its remote origins and strongly Hellenised from the archaic period onwards. They brought eastern ways of thought and expression to Italian soil, but they also transmitted the art and the religion of Hellas. Rooted in the soil of Italy, the Etruscans did not have an autonomous or isolated history, but participated in the evolution of the peoples living around them. The true beginnings of Rome are to be found in their presence on the seven hills. Rome rid herself at an early date of the Etruscan tyrants, but she preserved a great part of their heritage. And the hatred Rome bore Etruria for centuries must not lead us to underestimate the importance of the debt owed to Etruria by Rome. The Etruscan influence was to live on in Rome in her Constitution and *mores,* in her religious thought and in the arts; it was to form part of the cultural heritage which Rome, in her turn, would leave to the West."

A BAND OF MIGRATING CELTS passes through rough terrain in quest of a new home, sometime around 400 B.C. The tribesmen bring their livestock and carry their possessions, heaped in ox-drawn carts or strapped to their backs. Their chieftain, astride his small, shaggy horse, directs the march from a rocky ledge at right center. During their period of expansion, many ever-restless, ever-moving Celtic tribes spread across the face of Europe.

WANDERERS OF THE NORTH

Searching for new land, Celtic and Scythian tribesmen carried elements of civilization through Europe and Asia

WHILE early civilizations rose and fell around the Mediterranean and in the Middle East, wandering groups of people far to the north ranged the forest lands and steppes from western Europe to the borders of China. From time to time these restless tribes erupted into the civilized areas of the south, often raiding, sometimes conquering and settling in new lands. The Greeks and Romans disdainfully referred to these tribes of the northern plains and forests as "barbarians" because they lived outside the pale of civilization, and historians have perpetuated the use of the word.

There were many of these so-called barbarians. The Aryans swept down upon northern India and Iran. Other tribes penetrated to the shores of the eastern Mediterranean, founding such states and empires as those of the Mitanni and the Hittites. Still others crossed the Balkan passes to overthrow the tottering Mycenaean Empire in Greece. Many of these raiders settled down to make a contribution to the growth of civilization in the lands where it had begun.

For many centuries, the barbarians were in contact with the more advanced peoples of the south, through trade or armed forays. Although their Bronze and Iron Ages came much later than they did for the peoples in the south, some of the barbarians reached a level close to civilization in the first millennium B.C. They became transmitters of the techniques and culture of their more civilized neighbors. And in the long perspective of history, these people of the northern hinterland made rich and lasting contributions to the later growth of civilization in Europe and western Asia.

The Celts and the Scythians were the two main groups of barbarians who roamed through the forests of Europe and migrated over the plains of Asia. The two shared a common cultural tradition as nomadic tribesmen. Through trade channels, and probably later through direct contact, they exchanged ideas and inventions. The Scythians, who lived on the plains of Asia, probably acted as middlemen between the ancient civilizations of the Mediterranean and China.

The first major glimpse of Celts and Scythians is to be found in the pages of Herodotus, who wrote his history of the ancient world in the Fifth Century B.C. He has little to say about the Celts (*Keltoi*), although they were trading with the Greeks of Massilia (Marseilles) and were in contact with the Etruscans over the Alps. But he devotes a whole book of his histories to the Scythians, the mounted nomads who carved out an empire in southern Russia, along the shores of the Black Sea, about 700 B.C. In an excursion westward, the Scythians probably met the Celts in Hungary and taught their fellow barbarians the art of horseback riding, which turned out to be a more effective technique in warfare than the chariot. Much of Herodotus' historical writing is a mixture of legend and hearsay, but he paints a detailed picture of Scythian life based on firsthand information obtained on his own visit to Olbia, the Greek colony in south Russia. Olbia carried on a bustling trade in wines, pottery and art in exchange for grain from the Scythian farms of the Ukraine and probably gold from the mines and rivers of the Altai range.

Rome finally pushed its civilizing rule out into the lands of the Celtic and Scythian barbarians, thus temporarily stemming the nomadic forays into the south. Widely scattered at the peak of their historical prominence, the Celts never evolved any formal political system. Though they recognized the strength of Rome and were aware of their own disunity, they never progressed beyond the stage of tribal or clan organization. They remained a feudal society, with a warrior aristocracy bestriding a peasant population. The Scythians disappeared from history about 100 B.C. But the Celts, or at least such vigorous and imaginative descendants as the Irish and Welsh, are still active in English-speaking countries everywhere. The wandering Celts settled in many lands, from Spain to Asia Minor, where St. Paul addressed his epistle to the Galatians. (The Galatians, like the Gauls, were of Celtic stock.) To western man they transmitted the Roman heritage in law and language, and the Christian heritage in religion.

AT A CELTIC FARMSTEAD in southern Britain, a farmer raises his arm to greet a friend. According to the Celtic custom of "fosterage," the guest is delivering his son to live here as a foster child, thus forming a bond between the families. Their bright-checked woolen clothes reveal the Celtic love of color. The owner's wattle-and-mud house stands at left. A woman (*right*) ladles out coarse grain for bread from an underground storage pit. Beyond

CELTS AND THE LAND

SOME early Celts gave up the roving life to settle down. The first major signs of Celtic settlements in the early Iron Age in Central Europe appear to date from about 850 B.C. This was centuries after the Hittites had learned the use of iron. Though Europe was a primary source of iron ore, it lagged far behind the Middle East in working the ore. The La Tène Iron Age (named for a Swiss lakeside village settlement where the first archaeological remains of the period were found) began about 500 B.C. and lasted for five centuries. A combination

of iron weapons and tools gave the Celts mastery over their central European homeland. The iron ax enabled them to clear forest lands. The iron plow drawn by oxen broke virgin soil, gave them a surplus of grain and vegetables that spurred the growth of population and sent them wandering in quest of fresh fields and pastures.

But the Celts never seem to have become wholly domesticated. The agricultural and pastoral life never completely supplanted their inclination for hunting and warfare, which was the basis for a Celtic aristocracy. Their farms on the uplands of France and Germany and on the downs of southern England seldom comprised more than 20 acres in all, and their dwellings were primitive thatched houses of

the timber palisades lie new-plowed fields. An abandoned storage pit (*lower right*) is filled with assorted trash. Though untidy and littered, these farmsteads gave a stable home to many Celts at the end of their wanderings.

IRON TOOLS that enabled the Celts to become skilled carpenters (*below*) include the adz (*top*), the saw (*center*) and the chisel. These implements were found at the site of a village at Glastonbury Lake in the south of England.

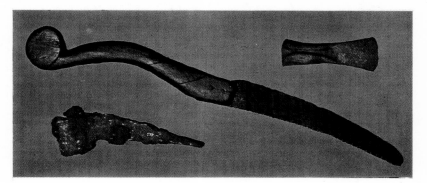

timber, twigs and clay. Later, sometime in the Second Century B.C., defensible clusters of dwellings began to be grouped together in southern France and in central Europe. These townships (*oppida*) were hardly cities or even towns, but they marked a real break from the basically scattered, rural character of archaic Celtic society. There were cities in the south of Europe and also in the cradles of civilization in the Middle East, but not in the hinterland of Europe. To the Celts, who had only small tribal strongholds, bringing together large numbers of people permanently was an innovation. The development of urban life had marked effects on tribal life, not the least of which was a lessening in importance of the old rural kingship.

179

A BRONZE MIRROR, decorated with a flowing design, filled in with a basketwork pattern (*right*), is a discovery from the English Midlands. The mirror's back is shown here; the reflecting surface is on the other side.

IN A METAL SHOP, where workers are forging iron weapons and molding bronze ornaments, a customer admires herself in a mirror while the master smith praises his product. A worker in the rear of the shop keeps the fire going.

MANNING THE RAMPARTS, the Celtic defenders of a fortress in Britain prepare to repel enemy tribesmen advancing against them raggedly on foot or in chariots. The Celts' chieftain (*left*) waves aloft the tribal emblem, while

WAR AND THE SMITH

THE smith held a high place in Celtic society. He not only produced the iron swords, plowshares and axes that were vital to war and farming, he also catered to the self-esteem of the warrior aristocracy by providing them with beautifully decorated shields, helmets and jewelry. Celtic design was almost entirely abstract, characterized by non-representational patterns of flowing scrollwork and bold, eccentric curves. Sometimes its bizarre motifs hinted at convolutions of grotesque petals or the tendrils of vines. The smith enjoyed almost supernatural status; he was regarded more as sorcerer than craftsman. His art was magic, but his most important role was as a

manufacturer of weapons of war, in which the Celts were frequently engaged. In combat, Celtic warriors impressed the cool-headed Romans as madly courageous, temporarily terrifying and strategically stupid. They dashed into battle with wild shouts and a piercing clamor of horns and trumpets, relying heavily on daring, noise and confusion.

The Celts relied for static defense on hilltop forts, the remains of which are to be found studded throughout western Europe. Some of these were improvised earthworks. Others were elaborate fortifications of stone, which provided a refuge for Celtic families and their animals. These afforded adequate protection against marauders, but could not resist Roman siege catapults. In his *Commentaries on the Gallic War*, Julius Caesar describes how easy it was to capture them.

buglers sound the alarm on their boar's-head trumpets. At left foreground, farmers of the neighborhood are pouring through the gates to find shelter. The row of stakes along the parapet of the fortress is crowned with the skulls of enemy chiefs killed in previous battles, which were prized trophies among the Celts. The kind of fortress shown here, made of stone but used only as a temporary refuge in time of battle, would have been built around 150 B.C.

WAR EMBLEMS include animal motifs as talismans to bring good luck in battle. The bronze helmet (*left*) has the horns of an ox. The trumpet (*right*) has a boar's-head shape.

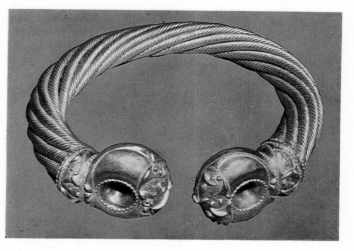

A COLLAR PIECE, worn by a chieftain in Britain, is made of strands of electrum, an alloy of gold, silver and base metals. This torque is part of a trove of Celtic remains found in Norfolk.

DRUIDS AND MAGIC

THE Celtic tribes owed allegiance to no state until their subjugation by Rome, beginning in the First Century B.C. They were loosely bound together by a religion incorporating ancient beliefs in various tribal gods who exercised magical powers over man. The inner secrets of this faith were known only to the priestly caste of Druids, who had to serve a novitiate that sometimes lasted 20 years. But the Druids were more than priests. They were also advisers to the tribal chiefs, judges, teachers and transmitters of oral tradition. The Celts worshiped their gods in sacred groves and forest glades, often where there was a spring-fed pool. In Britain and Gaul, the oak, particularly when clad in mistletoe, was considered a sacred tree. (The use of mistletoe at Christmas today is a relic of the old religion absorbed by Christian custom in northern lands.) Celtic rites were awesome. Although the Druids preached abstention from wrongdoing, they permitted human sacrifice, a practice the Romans eventually stamped out with some difficulty. The Roman poet Lucan, writing in the First Century A.D., tells of "ruthless altars" and of trees "stained with human gore" on which birds would not perch. Long before the Christian faith took root in Celtic lands, the old gods had merged with their Roman equivalents, but many superstitions surrounding the old Celtic gods were still flourishing.

A SILVER CALDRON, wrought by Celts around 100 B.C., is embellished with symbolic figures and scenes. The bearded male with upraised arms (*center*) is probably a god. This caldron was used in religious ceremonies.

IN A SACRED OAK GROVE beside a pond (*left*), Celts gather to worship one of their three-faced deities, on the pedestal at left center. The chief Druid invokes the god and other priests cast offerings into the pond.

A FUNERAL FLAGON for Celtic libations, made of bronze and richly inlaid with coral and enamel, shows Greek-Etruscan influences, but the beasts on the handle resemble Scythian work.

CELTIC DEATH RITES

THE Celtic warriors were preoccupied with death, partly because of their violent way of life, partly because of their conviction that the soul was immortal. They envisioned the hereafter as a continuation of earthly existence, involving all the same pleasures and physical needs. When a man died, his family put into his grave the things he would require in the world to come—weapons, jewelry and vessels filled with food and wine. Poor people were more casual about their dead, but nobles and important chieftains were often buried in full battle regalia. Leaders were laid to rest in their chariots. At such royal funerals, trenches were dug in the bottom of the burial pit for the wheels so that the chariot could lie level with the bottom of the grave. The deceased was stretched out on the earth with his head in the chariot. Sometimes his horse and all of its trappings were buried with him.

A CHARIOT WHEEL about three feet wide, unearthed near the River Tweed in southern Scotland, is made of wood with an iron tire. The iron rim was wrought separately in circular form, and then shrunk onto the wooden wheel.

AT A CHIEFTAIN'S FUNERAL in the Fifth Century B.C. (*right*), retainers lower his war chariot into the grave. The containers in the foreground will be filled with food. A Druid keens over the body; another pours an offering of wine.

SCYTHIAN WARRIORS on horse and foot are depicted on the crest of a gold comb. The foot soldiers' trousers were probably of leather and their belted jackets of felt. The horseman has an armored shirt with metal scales, and a helmet and greaves in Greek style. The Scythians developed small bucklers for convenient use on horseback. This elaborate piece was discovered in a royal tomb at Solokha in the Dnieper valley, together with copper vessels

NOMADS FROM ASIA

THE mounted nomads known as Scythians, a name embracing a great conglomeration of tribes, wandered for centuries from place to place in the heart of Asia in search of fresh pasture lands for their horses and cattle. On the march, they were a formidable sight. First came wave after wave of cavalry astride shaggy, fierce-looking mounts. Following them came thousands of mounted tribesmen driving huge herds of beasts dusty from the long trail. Behind rolled a huge caravan of lumbering, ox-drawn wagons carrying wives, children and chattels. Footsore slaves came limping in the rear. At nightfall the horde halted to raise its yurts, or cylindrical tents of hide, against a bleak sky often filled with snow.

Driven from their grasslands by other nomads, the Scythian hordes moved southwest between 800 and 700 B.C. In Asia the early Huns were repulsed at the borders of China, and as they retreated, other tribes were set in motion throughout much of Asia until the shock wave eventually reached the Scythians. Pushed from one desirable pasture land to another, the Scythians eventually reached the suburbs of civilization along the shores of the Black Sea. They came to rest in the country of the Cimmerians (another nomad people) and drove them across the Caucasus into Asia Minor to add to the turbulence that may have caused the Etruscans to migrate to Italy. Some of the Scythians settled down and began to cultivate the rich Ukrainian soil. Later, groups of Scythians penetrated as far west as Hungary, Romania, Bulgaria and Prussia.

In their heyday (about 600-100 B.C.), the Scythians were a prosperous people who obtained much of their wealth from trade, especially with Greece. Scythian settlers in southern Russia supplied Greece with valuable consignments of grain, salt, sturgeon, tuna, honey, meat, milk, hides and furs—and, most important, slaves. In return, the Greeks furnished the Scythians with jewelry, metalwork and pottery of the finest quality.

The mounds and barrows of Siberia and the Ukraine, where the Scythians buried kings and their consorts, tell modern scholars most of what they know about Scythian life. The Pazirik tombs of the Altai Mountains, dating back to the Fifth Century B.C., began to be excavated in 1947. The timber roofing had been removed by looters centuries ago and rain water had seeped in on the corpses and objects buried with them. The water froze; the bodies and fragile items of clothing, wood, leather and felt were preserved. Russian archaeologists are still searching into their nation's past, and it is possible that there are other finds to come as spectacular as those from Pazirik.

filled with meat, and clay jars full of wine and oil to refresh a king on his long journey to the world beyond. It was fashioned for a Scythian, probably on special commission, by a Greek craftsman in the Fifth Century B.C.

BINDING A WOUND on a comrade's leg, a Scythian warrior is portrayed on a vase found at Kul Oba (Hill of Ashes) near the Caucasian city of Kerch. As part of their riding garb, Scythians wore peaked hats tied under their chins.

EQUESTRIAN NECKPIECE comes from the tomb of a man found at Kul Oba in the Kuban region on the Black Sea. Fashioned of gold, it has a blue enamel inlay and is probably of Greek design. The horsemen confronting each other at each end of the ornament are riding stubby-maned Mongolian horses. Most Scythian warriors owned a fair number of fine horses, and the important tribal chiefs generally possessed large herds of stallions and brood mares.

A REIGN OF HORSEMEN

MASTERY of the horse, which men had learned to control in central Asia about 2500 B.C., was the most significant factor in the life of the Scythian nomads. Their cavalry and light, horse-drawn chariots gave extreme mobility to their warfare and made them the terror of enemies on foot. Historians say little about the Scythians except when they became involved with the big world empires. Darius, the great Persian, had an indecisive war with them before his ill-fated attempt to conquer Greece. More than a century later, Philip of Macedon, father of Alexander the Great, fought another indecisive war with the Scythians.

Scythian battle steeds wore elaborate ornaments of bronze, silver and gold. For protection against enemy weapons, they wore handsomely worked eyepieces and nose shields, richly decorated with the likenesses of animals. Some carried metal breastplates and were almost as heavily caparisoned as the war horses of the Middle Ages.

Pet stallions were cosseted and pampered. Great magnates measured their wealth by the size of their studs, and at their death some of their horses were slaughtered and entombed with or near their masters in the manner of Celtic burials. One of the Pazirik tombs discovered in the Altai Mountains contained the remains of five saddle and four chariot horses, a wagon of Chinese design and a saddle cloth with decoration of Persian workmanship. The taming of horses for riding also produced revolutionary changes in clothing fashions. Trousers seem to have appeared first in the steppe area, and the first Europeans to wear trousers were the Celts. Before them, men wore skirts or wrapped themselves in skin robes.

Some of the equine art of the Asiatic Scythians, who were a connecting link between China and western Asia, is strong evidence of an interchange of goods and artistic techniques among early cultures. Their mineral wealth made it possible for the Scythians to buy ornaments and textiles from various civilized nations. But over the centuries they also evolved a true artistic style of their own, which penetrated as far north as Scandinavia and as far west as the British Isles.

A RIDER AT REST sleeps in the shade of a tree on which he has hung his quiver, while his wakeful companion holds the reins and his wife looks on. This scene was executed on a gold-plated plaque used as a belt decoration. Part of a collection started by Peter the Great and now in the Hermitage Museum, it may have come from the Pazirik tombs, probably one of many objects that were stolen years ago by looters but retrieved by Peter in the 18th Century.

A MOUNTED CHIEFTAIN is shown approaching the throne of the Great Goddess, most revered of Scythian deities. This is a detail from a felt-decorated cloth measuring 14 by 21 feet, found at Pazirik. The design consists of felt cutouts stitched onto an off-white background. It was probably used by a nomad ruler as a decorative tent hanging. Representation of the human figure rarely appears in Scythian art, but here it is of religious significance.

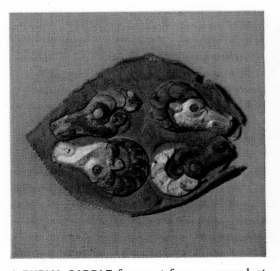

A BURIAL SADDLE fragment from a mound at Bashadar, in southern Prussia, is decorated with four gilded rams' heads attached to the leather.

A WOMAN'S BOOT, fur-trimmed, is an unusual relic of Scythian clothing. Thieves amputated the owner's foot, probably to take her ankle jewelry.

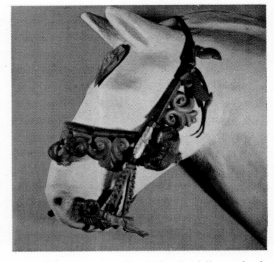

A WOODEN BRIDLE from the Pazirik tombs is part of a horse's harness decorated with flowers, a ram's head and the figure of a charging ram.

A WORLD OF ANIMALS

IN the Altai or Golden Mountains, the ancestors of the Asiatic Scythians lived the life of hunters, pursuing or being pursued by wild beasts and birds of prey. It was a land of lions and leopards, elk and buffaloes, wolves and bears, eagles and vultures. On the steppes below the mountain massif that lies athwart Siberia, Mongolia and Turkestan, before the sands of the Gobi desert encroached on the wasted grasslands, there were wild horses ready for audacious men to bridle and tame. Further to the west in European Russia, where the Scythians finally made their home, wild boar wallowed in the swamps of the Kuban River, along with many lesser and milder creatures such as mink, beaver and otter.

For the early Scythians, these beasts and birds were the source of life or the cause of death. Prehistoric rock paintings by their predecessors, which closely resemble those that have been discovered in the Dordogne in France, were full of animals, and the Scythians' later artifacts carried on the theme. Because the lives of the Scythian nomads were so closely bound up with animals, they developed a sharp awareness of the animal world and a deep understanding of it. Except for huge felt hangings, the Scythians' art was decorative and small, and for a good reason. The Scythians were always on the move, and they had to carry their possessions with them. Their craftsmen showed great respect for, and great skill in, the wide variety of materials they used. They worked not only in bronze and gold but also in wood, leather and felt.

The Scythians' interest in animals molded their artistic outlook and resulted in an art that is mainly concerned with animal shapes. Their sword hilts were topped with animal heads. Caldrons, vases and pitchers often had handles shaped like animal bodies. Trousers, boots and rugs were embroidered with animal figures. Most of these decorations were realistic, but sometimes the Scythians depicted dragons, griffins and other fantastic animals borrowed from China and Persia. Often the extremities of one animal were shaped into an attribute of another. The single most characteristic motif found in Scythian art is the use of antlers. Originally an object of religious significance among early Eurasian nomad tribesmen, stags were apparently believed to transport the souls of the dead to the world beyond, and this idea may have been held down through Scythian times. Stags often appear on funerary objects. Antlered masks were made for horses interred with their masters. These masks suggest that the mourners hoped to speed the journey of the dead by endowing the horses, through their headdresses, with the swiftness of a stag.

A BELLIGERENT DRAGON devours the head of an elk, antlers and all, in a wood carving that has antlers covered in leather to accentuate their religious significance. Much Scythian art depicts animals in almost frenzied motion.

A BOAR AND A TIGER tangle in combat in a gold sculpture four inches wide, which was used as a belt ornament. The Hermitage Museum in Leningrad has 10,000 plaques of this sort, many of them probably mass-produced.

A CROUCHING LEOPARD, plated with gold in angular planes, comes from the Black Sea region. The figure is exceedingly elaborate—the leopard's eyes are inlaid with amber and the paws are fashioned in the shape of kittens.

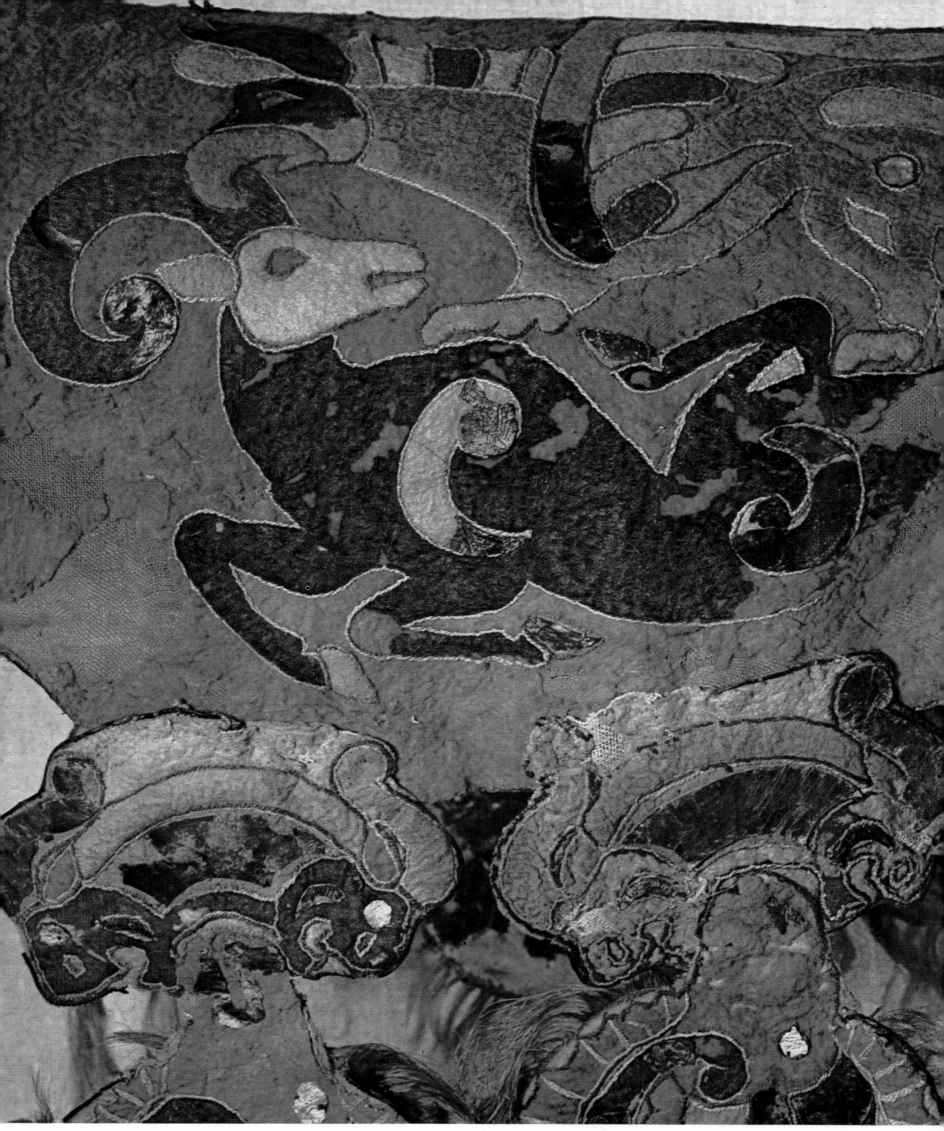

AN EAGLE-HEADED GRIFFIN and a ram are depicted in a felt saddle cloth found at Pazirik. The theme of birds of prey attacking beasts of the field is recurrent in Scythian art from the Caucasus to Siberia. The idea of fantastic animals may have come to the Scythians from the Middle East, where fabulous creatures were common in Babylonian and Assyrian art. The Persians may have been the intermediaries in passing the fashion on to the Scythians.

THE ENDURING CELTIC TRADITION

AT STONEHENGE in England, British prehistorians Stuart Piggott (*rear*) and Richard J. C. Atkinson make measurements for the restoration of the prehistoric religious center. Stonehenge was also used in the later Celtic period.

WITH a dogged capacity to endure and to outlast a succession of alien overlords, the Celts managed to survive and emerge into modern times with vitality. On the other hand, the Scythians, similar in many ways to the Celts, disappeared as a people before the birth of Christ. The reasons for the disparate fates of the two are geographical, political and cultural.

The Scythian domain had no natural barriers against invasion by hostile hordes from east or west. It occupied a central position in the steppeland, and its frontier rivers, the Volga and the Danube, could be easily bridged. The rich grassland of the Scythian steppes was a magnet for the dispossessed peoples of Central Asia, who were driven westward by the growing aridity of climate and the expansion of the Chinese empires that barred the road to the east. The Scythians collapsed before a chain of tribal movements comparable to that which had earlier brought their ancestors to the Black Sea region. Their immediate conquerors were the Sarmatians, a kindred people. Like the Scythians, the Sarmatians were superb horsemen and had developed technical improvements for battle, especially the use of metal stirrups. Among their ranks were women warriors, the source of the later legends of the Amazons.

The flourishing Scythian townships and grazing grounds between the Volga and the Don fell quickly to the Sarmatians. At the same time, balked on the west by barbarian Germanic tribes and the Macedonians, the Scythians were driven back from the Danube and the Dnieper. Pushed from both sides, the Scythians were swallowed up. The flourishing Greek colonial cities of the Black Sea littoral—Olbia, Panticapaeum and Chersonesus—which had catered to the Scythian taste for luxury, were deprived of the hinterland on which they depended for both food and trade, and so they withered away and died.

Yet the Scythian tradition was not entirely lost. The Sarmatians handed it down to the Alans, another tribe of Iranian stock. They in turn passed the heritage on to the Khazar empire, the first on Russian soil. The Khazar empire flourished from A.D. 750 to A.D. 1000, and its ruling class became converts to Judaism. The Khazar monopoly of the great trade route from Sweden to Byzantium (Istanbul) and Baghdad was bitterly resented by the Slavs, who summoned Rurik the Norseman to help them break the Khazar stranglehold over the trade routes. In A.D. 878, Rurik's successor, Oleg, captured Kiev and laid the foundations of the Russian state. The road was soon reopened between north and south to traders and missionaries from Byzantium. A later Greek tradition, the Orthodox Church, brought Christianity to the Slavs, the last of the European peoples to emerge from barbarism into civilization. Thus the traffic in ideas begun by the Greeks and Scythians 14 centuries earlier was restored.

While their strategic vulnerability denied survival to the Scythians, the more resilient Celts were partly protected by their geographical situation. Despite the fact that even the island of Britain was penetrated by invaders, the wilderness of Scotland and Wales and all of Ireland offered sanctuary to many groups of Celts and allowed many

Throughout the map the following labels appear: NEWSTEAD, GLASTONBURY, LONDON, North Sea, MOSCOW, Irtysh River, Ob River, Pazirik Tombs, EUROPE, Celts, LA TENE, Rhine River, U.S.S.R., Scythians, MASSILIA (MARSEILLES), The Alps, KIEV, Dnieper River, Volga River, Jaxartes River, Aral Sea, ROME, Danube River, OLBIA, SOLOKHA, PANTICAPAEUM, KERCH, Oxus River, CHERSONESUS, KUL OBA, Caucasus Mountains, Caspian Sea, Black Sea, BYZANTIUM (ISTANBUL), ATHENS, Mediterranean Sea, AFRICA, Tigris River, Euphrates River, SCYTHIAN AND CELTIC REGIONS, 0 500 1000 MILES

of their traditions to be kept relatively intact down to modern times.

After about three centuries of Celtic dominance, the powerful Roman legions overran Italy and Spain, subjugated all of Gaul, invaded the British Isles and reduced the far-flung Celtic dominion to a mere hinterland of Rome.

UNLIKE the Scythians, who found themselves overwhelmed by a people of similar culture, the Celts, particularly in Gaul, responded eagerly to a superior civilization and became in turn its active transmitters to their neighbors. Four hundred years of Roman occupation and civilization left so deep an impression on most of the Celtic lands that it could not be erased by the destructive invasions of such later barbarians as the Teutons, Goths and Vandals. There were many islands of Roman order and culture that survived barbarian depredations. The Dark Ages were never completely dark. Feudalism eventually bound the restless Celts to the soil, and even when they were under the domination of masterful peoples who crossed the Rhine and the North Sea to become their rulers, they still retained their culture and customs, and imposed many of them on their conquerors.

Britain was dominated in part by the Romans. But after a bloody conquest, the rule was lenient because Rome looked on its conquests as sources for taxes and tribute and not for colonial settlement. Despite the Roman occupation, which lasted for four centuries, from A.D. 43 to about A.D. 400, the Celts preserved their identity as a people. The Romans failed to implant their culture in the British Isles as permanently as they had succeeded in doing in Gaul. They built roads and towns, maintained commerce, recorded the history of their time and enforced a period of law and prosperity. Their skills and learning pervaded much of England. Latin was the official language, but Celtic remained the language of the peasantry, and Celtic folkways were not erased. The pressure from barbarian invasions in Gaul forced the Romans to draw back, first from Britain and eventually from all the Celtic lands. With their departure, the invaders poured into the most desirable, settled areas, pushing the Celts to isolated strongholds. In Britain, the Saxons drove many of the Celts into the mountainous northern and western extremities of the island —Scotland, Wales and Cornwall. There followed 200 years of barbarism, lighted briefly by the ideals and exploits of the legendary King Arthur. The many versions of the Arthurian legend handed down by the Celts in Britain have long contributed to the scholarly complexities of establishing his identity. This period also saw the beginning of the influence of the Church of Rome, which was to govern the surviving Celts' religion as well as much of their secular life. Through the agency of St. Patrick, beginning about 432, a monastically based system of Celtic Christianity was founded in Ireland, the outermost Celtic land that was never subdued by Roman arms. Eventually allied closely with the Church of Rome, Celtic Ireland formed the base for one of its most secure and loyal strongholds.

Throughout the Saxon and the subsequent Danish and Norse invasions during the 500 years after the Roman exodus, a substantial proportion of the Celts stayed on their lands to mingle their blood and folkways with those of their new masters. When the last invaders of England, the Normans, crossed the channel from France in 1066, they found a native people who were strongly tinged with Celtic stock and tradition.

In Gaul, where Celtic settlements had come into existence long before they took root on British or Irish soil, the Roman conquest consolidated and gave permanence to tribal centers, which had already reached the size of towns and were well on their way to becoming cities. Many of them that retain names of Celtic origin still flourish today. Paris was the capital of the tribe of the Parisi, Rheims of the Remi, Chartres of the Carnutes. The Sequani gave their name to the River Seine. The French language, although its origin is basically Latin, is Latin as it was spoken by the Celts and as it was adapted to their needs and style.

APART from a few sprinklings of Scythian words in Herodotus, no other trace of the language remains, for it was never written. The Celts still handed down their law and lore by word of mouth long after the Druids had disappeared. Their first alphabet, the Ogham script, probably devised by Irish monks, did not appear until about A.D. 600. Although the Celtic language does not now exist anywhere as the main language of a whole society, the uses of it that remain are due to its preservation in the islands beyond the boundaries of the Roman world. But today a revived Celtic speech is very much alive in Ireland, where it is an official government language, and in Wales, where it is used in religious services, on radio and television, and in the manifestoes of the Welsh Nationalist Party as a language of spiritual, cultural and political assertion. Manx is still spoken in the tiny Isle of Man in the Irish Sea. Gaelic lingers on in the western Highlands and the islands of Scotland; the clan system in Scotland is directly descended from the tribal organization of the ancient Celts. And in Brittany, the Breton tongue, a mixture of Old Welsh and Old Cornish, brought to France from the southwest of England in the Fifth Century A.D., is still widely spoken.

Adventurous, independent-minded, often rebellious, the latter-day descendants of the Celts—the Irish, Scots and Welsh—have carried the spirit of their remote ancestors to countries all around the world. They have distinguished themselves in many fields—as explorers, scientists, engineers, doctors, captains of industry and organizers of labor. But perhaps the finest continuing legacy of the Celts to civilization lies in their literature, which is richly endowed with poetry, fantasy and humor.

Celtic culture made a long journey from the days of the late Iron Age; but the seeds sown a long time ago among the barbarian forerunners of western man, so faithfully nurtured by them and transplanted with such care, have everlastingly enriched the western world.

A MEMORIAL MASK shows the marked resemblance of the Shang people to the present-day inhabitants of North China. Designed to hang on a wall, this mask was found in a tomb at Anyang. The civilization created by the Shang Dynasty strongly influenced all of the subsequent history of China and the art, language and customs of much of the Far East. The Shang developed a distinctly Chinese script and some of the finest bronzework ever known.

THE SHANG, MOLDERS OF CHINA

The zestful people who established the first civilization in the Far East left a lasting mark on the entire region

NOT until about 1,500 years after civilization first flowered in the Middle East did it come to eastern Asia with the Shang Dynasty, which created a rich Bronze Age culture on the flat, fertile Yellow River plain of North China. For about six centuries—roughly from 1700 to 1100 B.C.—the Shang dominated the vast North China plain as far south as the Huai River valley and eastward into the hilly Shantung peninsula. They were a robust people, delighting in the turmoil of war and the hubbub of the chase, fond of lavish banquets and fine silks and furs. Their exuberant spirit was expressed in bold and fanciful carvings in marble, jade, ivory and bone. Their craftsmanship in bronze has hardly been excelled in all the thousands of years since their dynasty was overthrown. The Shang left behind them few impressive architectural remains except their colossal tombs, carved deep into the yellow earth to shelter the bodies of their kings and the chariots, weapons, jades, bronze vessels and retinues they valued so highly in life.

The Shang people created a way of life fully comparable to the great early civilizations of Egypt and Mesopotamia. But to a greater extent than some of the better known early civilizations, the Shang left an enduring mark on all the generations that followed them, down to the present day. Many elements of the Shang culture that have survived form the basis for the civilization of China and Japan as well as other parts of the Far East.

The Shang were unmistakably Chinese. They looked much like the North Chinese of today. They raised silkworms and wove the fibers into delicate fabrics. In their religion they developed a tradition of ancestor worship that has persisted throughout Chinese history. Their complex ideographic script is the direct ancestor of modern Chinese writing. Most of the Shang writing that survives today is found inscribed on tortoise shells and ox bones that were used for divination, and takes the form of oracle questions addressed to the powerful spirits of departed ancestors. The most important ancestors worshiped

by the Shang were those of deceased kings, for each of the hereditary kings, or *wang*, was deified after his death. According to an ancient Chinese classic, the *Shu Ching*, or *Book of History*, the Shang kings ruled at various times from five different capitals, only one of which, the ancient city of Yin (last of the five), has been definitely located. Near the modern city of Anyang in northern Honan Province, at a place called Hsiao-t'un, are widespread foundations of royal residences and ancestral temples. A hundred miles south, at modern Chengchou near the Yellow River, extensive ruins may represent the remains of another, earlier capital, the city of Ao. These wealthy cities and the dozens of other Shang towns and villages formed an island of civilization surrounded by primitive villages whose peasantry still lived in the Stone Age. The Shang cities were inhabited by a warrior nobility, served by a professional class of scribes and diviners and by skilled artisans and metalworkers. The Shang kings spent much of their time waging war against "the people in the four directions all around"—the more barbaric peoples who fought periodically with this isolated civilization. The Shang war equipment included handsome horse-drawn chariots and fine weapons of bronze, and they are known to have used elephants in battle on at least one occasion.

The rise of the vigorous Shang civilization in a China otherwise completely barbarous raises intriguing questions about its origins. Certain elements of the civilization—its basic agricultural economy, its building methods, its production of silk, its use of "oracle bones" in divination—had their roots in the local Neolithic culture. But other aspects appeared suddenly with the Shang: the use of horse-drawn chariots, the elaborate burials and above all a highly developed bronze-working technique and a complex system of writing. There is little undisputed evidence for the transmission of culture to China from the far more ancient civilizations of the Middle East. Nevertheless it is widely assumed that some kind of impetus must have traveled the vast distance across Asia from the civilized West.

SHANG INVADERS in red fight green-clad Tung-I, or Eastern Barbarians, on the plains of western Shantung Province. This painting depicts an imaginary incident in a three-year war waged by Chou Hsin, the last king of the Shang. The well-disciplined Shang used chariots and fought with bows and arrows, bronze spears and dagger-axes. The barbarians were skillful warriors, but were finally overcome by the superior military organization of the Shang.

HELMET OF BRONZE is fitted with a socket for an ornamental plume and probably once had a liner. On the front appears a mythical beast with bulging eyes and stylized brows.

"THE GREAT TERROR"

KNOWN to their weaker neighbors as "the great terror of the east," the Shang enjoyed warfare both for sport and for the spoils of victory. The king probably kept only a small standing army, but he could raise at short notice bodies of troops ranging from raiding parties of 1,000 to expeditionary forces of 30,000 men. Shang inscriptions disclose the existence of specialized military officials in charge of horses, dogs and archery, but the most important Shang weapon was a reflex bow equipped with arrows of bronze, stone or bone. In close combat, the Shang employed a unique but not very effective weapon called a *ko*, or dagger-ax, a pointed double-edged blade hafted at right angles to a wooden shaft. The Shang chariots had two huge wheels nearly five feet in diameter, were pulled either by two horses or by four, and were handsomely embellished with bronze and turquoise ornaments. They were probably used to protect the commanding officer in the field. There is one record showing that the Shang used elephants in battle in a war against the Eastern Barbarians, natives of the Shantung peninsula. The campaign was carried out during the reign of the last ruler of the dynasty.

SHANG WEAPONS, made of bronze (*right*), include a curved *tao* knife at left, a *mao* spearhead at center and a *ko* dagger-ax with a six-inch, double-edged blade. The principal weapon of the Shang was the bow and arrow.

A SACRIFICIAL CALDRON, called a *chi,* is embellished with water buffalo flanked by a pair of phoenixes with a row of dragons above. Nearly three feet high, the huge vessel was used to make offerings of meat to royal ancestors.

WINE CONTAINER, or *fang-i,* is 10 inches tall. Holding 2.2 quarts, it was found in the same tomb as the tripod cup at upper right on the opposite page. The decoration of square vessels probably evolved from wood carvings.

A TRIPOD CUP, or *chüeh*, displays a stylized *t'ao-t'ieh* on its bowl. Just under 11 inches high, it was used for libations of millet wine. The cup's handle is ornamented with a naturalistic water buffalo.

ARTISTRY IN BRONZE

THE Shang ritual bronze vessels are considered among the finest objects of metal ever created by the mind and hand of man. Boldly conceived and vigorously executed, they were cast in a rich variety of shapes and sizes. No two vessels have ever been found that are exactly alike. All of them were used for ceremonial purposes. They were employed in the preparation and offering of sacrificial meats, grain and wine during the solemn rites of ancestor worship. The vessels range from massive four-legged caldrons to graceful goblets and exotic sauceboats in the forms of various birds and beasts. There are three-legged kettles and two-piece steamers for cooking, low bowls for serving solid food, shallow basins for water and covered jars for storing millet wine.

The surfaces of these bronzes are richly ornamented with geometric designs and an imaginative proliferation of animals—wild and domestic, indigenous and imported, real and imaginary. The Shang craftsmen sometimes rendered animals naturalistically in a style that made them readily recognizable. However, the Shang preferred a form of stylization achieved by manipulating the component parts of the animals into fantastic creatures that defy taxonomic classification. Their best-known motif is the so-called *t'ao-t'ieh,* a symmetrical mask composed of right and left profiles facing each other and joined together to form a grotesque face. Scholars hold strongly to the belief that this sort of ornamentation must have had some special religious or magical significance, but the Shang writings offer no explanation of the complex beliefs that may have inspired the Shang obsession with animals.

Ruins of bronze foundries have been found both at Anyang and at Chengchou, still littered with the equipment and materials employed by the Shang workmen: copper ore, pottery crucibles for melting the metals and complex earthenware piece molds for the casting. The craftsmanship of the Shang bronzes is technically superb.

BIZARRE BIRD, called *k'uei-feng,* and perhaps related to an owl, measures 4.75 inches from claw to crest. It decorates a *chi* similar to the one shown at upper left. The two caldrons were found together in a royal tomb at Anyang.

199

A BONE OCARINA with *t'ao-tieh* carving is a simple wind instrument used by the Shang in their social festivities and religious rites. Only 2.2 inches long, it has five finger holes; three are visible here and two more are on the far side.

THE JOY OF LIFE

SHANG society was divided into at least two classes—a warrior nobility and a peasantry still following a primitive way of life. Within their capitals the ruling classes led lives of considerable sophistication. Both men and women dressed in furs and fine silk fabrics. They wore trinkets and baubles made of bone, shell and jade. The women had elaborate hairdos kept in place by long ivory and bone hairpins. One skeleton found in a tomb was surrounded by dozens of hairpins. The nobility were devoted to the hunt and organized large expeditions to distant hunting grounds, returning with enormous bags of game and occasionally even live animals for the royal zoo. One Shang oracle inscription from the reign of King Wu-ting asks the question, "We are going to hunt at Ch'iu: will there be any capture?" Later it was recorded: "Hunting on this day, we actually captured one tiger, 40 deer, 164 foxes, 159 hornless deer. . . ." Such a hunt might have been celebrated by a banquet like the one shown in the painting at right.

Other diversions favored by the Shang were music and probably dancing. Four different Shang musical instruments have been found: ocarinas, bells, drums and the kind of large hanging soundstone shown at left in the painting on these pages. Ssu-ma Ch'ien, the Chinese Herodotus, gives a vivid description of the Shang enjoyment of life. Although the historian probably exaggerates the degeneracy of the last Shang monarch, he scathingly describes King Chou Hsin in these words: "He loved the pleasures of the cup and debauchery, and was infatuated with his consort, the beloved T'a-chi, whose words he obeyed."

TONGUELESS BELLS (*left*) give out varying sounds when struck with a stick. They were made of bronze, like those shown, or of pottery, and were used not for pleasure but only for ceremonial or military purposes.

AT A BANQUET, perhaps celebrating a successful hunt, Shang lords and ladies dine on assorted meats and heady millet wine, and laugh heartily at a joke that their host (*center rear*) has just told. The diners kneel on rush matting and eat with chopsticks, as the Chinese still do, from elaborate dishes of pottery, ivory and bronze. A small orchestra provides music. The murals on the walls were suggested by wall paintings found in Shang royal tombs.

AN OUTLANDISH OWL, carved in white marble and only seven inches high, has ponderous feet and spreading ears, while its body is marked with stylized designs. All of the sculpture shown on these pages, except the jade elephant at lower right, came from a single royal tomb at Anyang.

BULGING-EYED BIRD, an eagle or perhaps an owl, has human ears and eyebrows, unaccountable horns and patterned feathers rendered in low

A FROG AND A TURTLE, carved from limestone, are simple and realistic sculptures and thus differ from the general trend of Shang art. The turtle was especially esteemed by the Shang because its shell was used in divination.

A BESTIARY IN STONE

IN addition to their mastery of bronze, Shang artists were also superb craftsmen in stone, a medium that virtually disappeared from Chinese sculpture after the eclipse of the dynasty and was not revived until the Han era eight centuries later. Most of the statues discovered are small, like the objects illustrated here, but there is evidence that Shang sculptors sometimes liked large-scale work. An oxhead, larger than life, has been discovered fitted with a pin that may have joined it to a missing body. The three monsters above were carved from a soft, white marble called *ta li shih,* quarried within 20 miles of Yin. The elephant (*right*) is of jade, that rare material in which the craftsmen of China have excelled since they first began to work it in Neolithic times. The stone was both expensive and tediously difficult to work, and it had to be imported over great distances from Chinese Turkestan, some 2,000 miles away, or from Lake Baikal, Siberia, more than 1,000 miles distant. Scholars are still debating what motivation lay behind the Shang passion to combine different parts of birds and beasts into monsters. Some experts believe that they may have been totems with a religious meaning.

relief. About 13.5 inches high, it has a vertical groove in its back, apparently used to attach the sculpture to some other object as an ornament.

A MENACING MONSTER with sharp fangs and jagged teeth has the head of a tiger and the body of a simian or semihuman creature. Fifteen inches in height and made of white marble, it has a body incised with characteristic Shang motifs similar to those of the owl on the opposite page.

A JADE ELEPHANT is about 11 inches long, the largest example of Shang jade sculpture found so far. Its chunky contours reflect the shape of the stone. Stylized lines are used for eyes, ears and other anatomical parts.

203

PRISONER-OF-WAR FIGURES represent victims for Shang ceremonies of human sacrifice. The man at left has his hands tied behind his back; the woman has hers tied in front. These figures were found in a storage pit at Hsiao-t'un.

EQUINE ORNAMENTS, designed for chariots as well as horses, are of bronze and turquoise. It was the Shang custom to slay the steeds of a dead ruler and entomb them, together with their rich gear, alongside the owner's chariot.

EXECUTIONER'S AXHEAD is decorated with an open-mouthed animal's face. Once used to decapitate human beings, it has a blade six inches broad and was hafted to a wooden shaft by means of the projecting tang shown at left.

ROYAL RITES

THE Shang built lasting structures for their dead if not for their living. All eleven of the royal tombs unearthed lie in one cemetery at Hsi-pei-kang, or Northwestern Mound, near the hamlet of Hou-chia-chuang, a few miles across the Huan River from Yin. The largest of them was 60 feet square, laboriously dug by hand in the shape of an inverted pyramid 43 feet into the yellow earth. The main entrance was always a sloping ramp facing south, sometimes as long as 150 feet. Entrances in the other three directions—west, north and east—were steeper and consisted of stepped passageways. After the main pit was dug and the bottom carefully leveled, a *yao-k'eng,* or small "waist pit," was opened directly in the center of the tomb floor to house the remains of a dog and sometimes a watchman to guard the dead ruler. One royal tomb had nine such small pits, one in the middle and the others around the edge of the square tomb floor, each with a dog and a kneeling human guard holding either a jade or a bronze *ko* dagger-ax. Above them a coffin chamber was constructed out of thick cypress planks to contain the royal remains. On the inside, the walls were smoothed with a fine white lime and then decorated with traditional Shang motifs rendered in red paint and white boar's-tusk inlay. Only the barest fragments of these murals have survived. The empty spaces between the chamber and the pit walls were refilled with soil, closely packed and stamped down tightly, layer by layer, to provide a flat shelf. Then costly offerings—the biggest bronze ritual vessels, the best jades and marbles, the finest silks and pottery, entire armories of elaborate weapons, enough musical instruments for an entire orchestra—were laid on this shelf, within the wooden coffin chamber and in the four entrance passageways. Then the whole pit was filled up again with hard stamped yellow earth. The zoo of one ruler—monkeys, birds and an elephant—was put in burial chambers near the main pit. Human sacrifice, sometimes on an awesome scale, invariably accompanied these royal burials—and sometimes accompanied ritual consecrations of royal buildings as well. The Shang, like the Sumerians, indulged on occasion in mass human slaughter to provide a suitable retinue after death for a powerful monarch. The victims, probably slaves or prisoners of war, were decapitated in groups. Frequently their heads and bodies were buried separately, sometimes in the great royal grave, sometimes in separate nearby tombs. The victims may have been intended to propitiate the vengeful gods or perhaps were slated to become the slaves and concubines of the dead ruler. The origin and purpose of this monstrous practice may never be known.

AT A ROYAL BURIAL, in a huge underground pit excavated from yellow earth, an executioner (*bottom left*) lifts his ax to behead a human victim. Others wait their turn in the stepped entrance passageway in the foreground.

The coffin with the royal remains stands at the bottom of the pit in a painted wooden chamber. Valuable offerings have already been placed in the grave. The main entrance to the tomb is a sloping ramp out of sight at the right.

THE SCAPULIMANCY OF THE SHANG

SOMETIME in the 12th or 11th Century B.C.—scholars differ on early Chinese chronology—a people called the Chou swept out of the western highlands and ended the Shang Dynasty after it had endured for about 600 years. The Chou were led by Wu Wang, or the Martial King, son of Wen Wang, the Accomplished King, who had once been a prisoner of Chou Hsin but had been ransomed. Wen had plotted to overthrow the Shang but did not live to accomplish his revenge. Wu, carrying out his father's plans, invaded Shang territory at the head of an army of 50,000 men, and conquered. The last of the Shang monarchs fled to his palace, put on fine clothes and rich jewelry, and committed suicide by throwing himself into the flames of his burning palace. His consort strangled herself.

The Chou were at first inferior in culture to the Shang, but they soon absorbed almost all of the Shang cultural legacy. They continued and encouraged this culture and eventually enhanced it. Politically, they seem to have advanced beyond the Shang system of government. Wu Wang is believed to have set up a full-fledged feudal system, parceling out lands in his name to trusted nobles and chieftains.

STUDYING A SHANG VESSEL, Dr. Li Chi works at the Institute of History and Philology of the Academia Sinica in Taipei, Formosa. Dr. Li directed the archaeological work on the ruins at Anyang from 1929 to 1937.

The Chou carried on the intellectual pursuits of the Shang, including the art of writing. Proof of the Shang mastery of the art exists in a great collection of oracle bones and shells. Most of them came from the royal archives at Hsiao-t'un, the residential area at Anyang, but a few have also been found at Chengchou. The Shang script was relatively sophisticated and obviously had undergone a long period of evolution—and yet it is the earliest Chinese writing so far known. Presumably writing in China began in much the same manner as it did in the Middle East—with simple pictographs—but in China the process of development cannot be traced. All of the important methods of character formation employed in modern Chinese writing were already in use during Shang times. A few Chinese characters are straightforward pictographs (pictures representing things); others are ideographs (symbols representing ideas). But most of the characters are compounds made up of a phonetic portion, which shows the pronunciation of the word, and another portion that indicates the meaning. All of these different categories of characters are found in the writings on the Shang oracle bones and shells.

THESE bones and shells led to the rediscovery of the Shang. Fifty years ago, scholars were inclined to dismiss as unfounded legend the traditional accounts of an ancient Shang Dynasty that was supposed to have preceded the Chou, for no Shang site had ever been excavated. From time to time, strangely inscribed bits of bone were found in fields around Anyang. These were considered to be "dragon bones"—a staple in Chinese folk medicine—and were ground up by druggists. Eventually archaeologists became interested in the number and variety of "dragon bones" that turned up. As a result, the ancient Shang site at Anyang was excavated between 1928 and 1937, largely under the direction of Dr. Li Chi. The Shang probably also used wooden tablets, bamboo slips and silk for writing purposes, but none of these has survived.

Most of the Shang writing has been found on the shells of a species of tortoise that no longer exists in North China and on the shoulder blades, or scapulae (hence the term "scapulimancy" for divination), of oxen. Over 100,000 specimens of these have been found, as well as hundreds of examples of inscriptions on bronze, a few on pottery and such oddities as writing on hairpins, on trophies of the chase and, in one grisly case, on a human skull—describing the sacrifice of the chief of the Jen-fang tribe to a Shang ancestor king. Only about a third of the 3,000 different characters used in Shang writing have so far been deciphered, and a small army of some 300 scholars is at work in this field, with an output to date of more than 1,000 books and learned papers. The study is known as chiakuology (from the Chinese *chia-ku-hsüeh,* or the study of bone and shell writings).

The bulk of Shang writing was devoted to the divination of the future by communication with the spirits of the dead. This was the function of a class of diviners who applied heat to specially prepared cavities in the bones and shells, causing them to crack. The size,

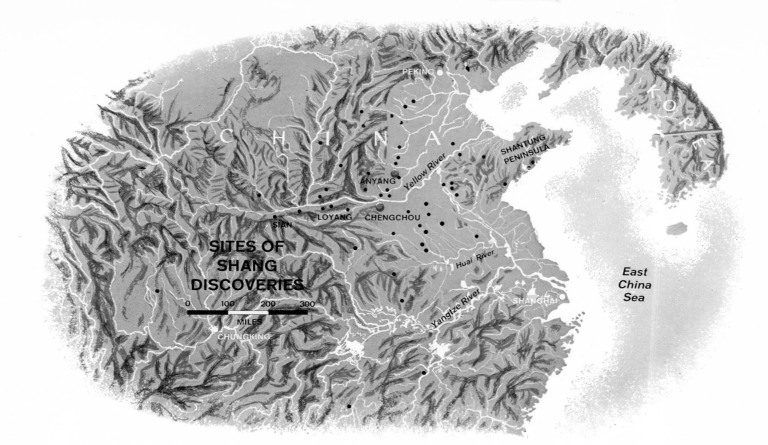

SITES OF SHANG DISCOVERIES

shape and direction of the cracks determined the oracle's answer. After this process, the questions that had been asked were sometimes written out on the surface of the bone or shell, presumably first with a brush, then incised with a jade or bronze tool.

Scapulimancy was used by the Shang kings for various purposes: to make inquiries about the weather, about the prospects for hunting or about the success of a projected military campaign. Some of the questions betray royal anxieties: "When will the crown prince recover from his illness?" "Will the queen bear me a son or a daughter?" King Wu-ting resorted to divination to find out which of his ancestral spirits was responsible for a toothache. Tortoise shells were also used to advise ancestors on the progress of the family fortunes.

These records, written by different scribes over a period of about 300 years, are the source for the chronology and names of the kings of the Shang Dynasty. They confirm the list found in Ssu-ma Ch'ien's famous *Shih Chi*, or *Historical Records*, written in the First Century B.C. They also provide information on how the Shang government operated. All government decisions are described as those of the *wang*, or king. About 20 civil, military and secretarial officials are mentioned by title. The *yin* councilors seem to have been among the most important. They were charged with such duties as the overseeing of the royal household, feasts and agriculture. The *tso-ts'e* were official archivists, the *chen-jen* diviners, the *shih* priests in charge of sacrifices, and the *kung* provided the king's music. Records on bones

also reveal that the Shang religion was not confined to ancestor worship; there were deities derived from natural phenomena as well: a god of wind, of clouds, of the sun and moon, and of the hills. The most powerful of these was Shang Ti, or the Ruler Above, who had power over the weather, agriculture and war. (Shang Ti is thus the Chinese word commonly used by Christian missionaries to translate the name of God.)

THE Chou took over from their predecessors much of the Shang law and religion. Chou officials were enjoined: "Follow the penal laws of Yin [Shang], which were right-ordered," and "Employ the ceremonies of Yin and sacrifice in the new city."

Historians divide the Chou Dynasty into two principal periods, identified with the sites of two different capitals: the Western Chou and the Eastern Chou. The earlier western capital on the Wei River near modern Sian succumbed to a barbarian attack about 770 B.C. The center of government was then moved to Loyang, some 200 miles to the east. After this, there was a decline of Chou influence until the dynasty reached the verge of foundering in the period of the Warring States, from 481 B.C. to 221 B.C. This was an epoch of continuous conflict. The Iron Age had come to China, bringing about a struggle for domination. In the struggle, a number of autonomous states eventually emerged. The state of Ch'in, which gave its name to modern China, finally swallowed up its rivals, says historian Ssu-ma Ch'ien, as "a silkworm devours a mulberry leaf."

The Shang Dynasty had been the cradle of Chinese civilization. The Chou Dynasty was its forcing house. In the tumultuous period that saw the decline of the Chou, the great Chinese philosophies of Confucius and Mencius were set forth, and the famous literary classics—including the *Shu Ching*, or *Book of History*, and the *Shih Ching*, or *Book of Poetry*—were compiled. Under the Ch'in, China was united for the first time as a great empire. It was the Ch'in who built the Great Wall of China.

China became the heartland of a great civilization that gradually penetrated a vast territory from Inner Mongolia to Vietnam, and from Tibet to Japan. Chinese farmers carried the rice economy—and the Chinese culture—with them wherever they could. The strongest Chinese influence was exerted on Korea, Japan and Vietnam. Korea was at times part of the state of China, and from Korea, Japan borrowed the major elements of Chinese civilization: writing, the national diet, clothing, art and literature. The Japanese today still kneel on the floor, a custom they inherited from ancient China, although the Chinese themselves eventually took to chairs.

For a thousand years, Japanese and Korean culture was almost wholly dominated by Chinese civilization. Then Japan and Korea began to grow into separate but related cultures. As Edwin O. Reischauer has written, "Korean culture and experience seem like variations on Chinese themes. Japanese culture and experience show what very different tunes can be played with the same set of instruments."

ORACLE BONES from the time of the 28th Shang king are inscribed with inquiries about a royal hunt (*right*) and about sacrificial offerings to ancestral spirits and a river god (*left*). Both bones are ox shoulder blades.

THE ROBING OF A HIGH PRIEST is shown in a wall painting at the Eighth Century Maya temple city of Bonampak. The Maya raised the arts of astronomy and mathematics to great heights. Their civilization, considered the most spectacular of the Middle American cultures, honored the high priest above all. The painting shows him resplendent in a jaguar skin, jade ornaments and a headdress plumed with the tail feathers of a quetzal bird.

PRIESTLY PEOPLES OF THE NEW WORLD

The ancient Maya, Aztecs and other Middle Americans were driven by faiths that demanded human sacrifice

THE New World is called "new" for no better reason than that it was new five centuries ago to its discoverers from the Old World. In fact, the Americas are just as old as the other continents and anything but new to mankind. Scientists keep tracing man further and further back in the New World. Man-made obsidian flakes have been found at the Tule Springs, Nevada, with giant bison bones dating back 24,000 years. Most scholars are now convinced that man migrated from the Old World to the New across the Bering Strait thousands of years ago, and made his hunter's way across the Americas even to the remote Strait of Magellan, where remains of campsites more than 10,000 years old have been found.

By 2000 B.C., the inhabitants of Middle and South America had made a decisive turn: from hunting to the cultivation of the native American plant called corn or maize. Founded on maize agriculture, village societies like those of the Neolithic peoples of the Old World grew up. Out of this ancient ground sprang three civilizations of splendor and power: the Aztec and Maya in Middle America and the Inca in South America. The achievements of these long-vanished American civilizations easily merit comparison with those of the Old World long ago. The Incas never learned to write but, with a genius for organization comparable to Rome's, they governed an empire. The Maya apparently never thought of the true arch but they raised stone masonry-roofed temples using the corbel or "false" arch, as nobly proportioned as the buildings of the ancient world.

To western man, scanning the night of history for light on his past, these outpost civilizations may shine so distantly and faintly that, like Neptune and Pluto, they hardly seem to belong to his system at all. Yet a dictator praising corn and a housewife cooking potatoes alike owe a debt to the inventive agriculture of ancient America.

Of the early American civilizations, among the first to flower in creative glory was that of the Maya in the tangled jungles of lowland Guatemala and the Yucatán peninsula. Around the Third Century

A.D., the Maya, already an advanced people, were building great, gleaming temples and pyramids of stone and mortar amid their corn patches in the rain-soaked Guatemalan forests. They adorned their buildings with elegant sculpture and wall paintings. They evolved a grotesque pictographic writing, preserved on stone, that has not yet been completely deciphered. They created a calendar more accurate than that of contemporary Europe. They evolved the concept of zero sometime during the Third or Fourth Century B.C. They excelled in the study of heavenly bodies.

Still producing handsome stelae, or decorated pillars, and other sculptured monuments in the style of its Classic age, the Maya civilization suddenly faltered and began fading out around 900 A.D. Eventually the beautiful ceremonial cities in the southern lowlands stood silent and deserted. Later there was a Maya renaissance in the more northern part of the Yucatán peninsula. New cities and temples rose amid old corn patches in what is designated the Post-Classic period (900-1450). New prodigies of art and architecture were executed. And at some point a fusion of the Maya took place with invading Toltecs, a barbaric but gifted people who wandered east to Guatemala and Yucatán from their homeland in central Mexico. The Mexicans were apparently the masters; they exerted a strong influence on architecture, art and religion. But eventually this northern flourish of the Maya ended and they fell into a decline as calamitous as that of the Classic era. When the Spanish conquerors arrived in 1527, the finest buildings of the renaissance were already abandoned, and the political structure consisted of small city-states continually at war with one another.

Why did the Maya civilization, for all its brilliance, thus break down? Soil exhaustion, climatic changes, disease, social revolution, foreign conquest and plain funk among the rulers have all been suggested by scholars. The fall of the Maya civilization, like its rise, remains one of the great mysteries and wonders of the old New World.

IN THE TEMPLE CITY OF TIKAL a priest on a pyramid unfolds a jaguar skin, and a red-daubed, quetzal-plumed high priest prepares to raise his scepter as the assembled worshipers reverently watch the offering of copal incense in the sanctuary. This Classic-period city had an imposing Great Plaza dominated by the huge Temple of the Giant Jaguar (*right*) and the Temple of the Masks (*extreme left*). The plaza, flanked by lesser shrines

A STAR-STRUCK CITY

THE Great Plaza of Tikal, overlooking the Guatemalan jungle, was one of the most impressive city squares ever built. Like the other big Maya Classic centers, Tikal does not seem to have been a place to live. It was a ceremonial shrine, dedicated to the religion that dominated Maya life to a degree hard to imagine. Long before the Fourth Century A.D., when Tikal became a ceremonial center, Maya religion had developed from a primitive personification of jungle animals into a philosophy that deified the stars and worshiped time. From the lowliest grower of corn to the most exalted priest, all believed that there were many gods and that they could be manipulated by anyone who understood the stars that governed them.

Ordinary Maya lived in wood and thatch houses near their cornfields outside centers like Tikal. Burning off the jungle growth, they planted enough corn in the thin forest soil to support not only themselves but their priests and rulers. The priest-astronomers spent their time studying the skies and consulting calendrical tables in their beaten-bark manuscripts—three of them, now only partially understood, survive—for clues to the best times for getting around the gods. These priests of the stars measured eternity by several interlocking time counts comparable to our days, weeks, months and years. The Maya worked out for themselves all of the mathematical basis for the applied sciences, but never went beyond that. It has been inferred that one of their time markers at Quiriguá reckons a day and month for an event 90 million years before, and that another was calculated 400 million years back, a feat about as difficult as computing the date on which Easter would have fallen 400 million years ago.

The lives of the Maya remained rigidly adjusted to the joys and sorrows of their predestined days. Certain gods would reign for a day, a month, a year or some longer period. If they were not propitious, then more favorable deities would have their turn. The priest could counsel tribe, clan or family that it would be all right to plant or sell corn or hold a wedding. Of these centuries of the Classic period, we know only that comparative peace and stability suggest a theocratic rule. There are evidences, in smashed thrones and defaced carvings, that the people may have risen against the priests at the end. The more frequent depiction of human sacrifice during the time of the Yucatán civilization suggests the presence of influences from highland Mexico. But the old gods continued to be propitiated.

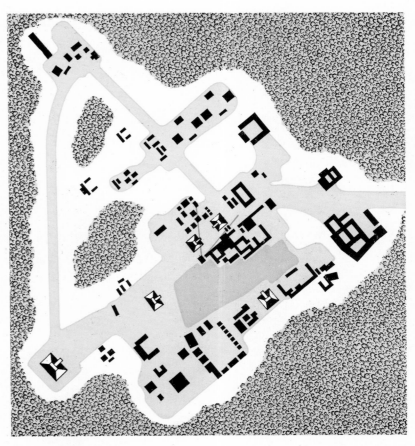

FIVE TEMPLES are shown in black and white on this map covering close to a square mile of Tikal's holy city. The Great Plaza is the tiny area at the center. The red lines mark the area shown in the painting at the left.

and carved and plain stone time markers, was paved. Its massive temple buildings were made of lime concrete faced with cut limestone blocks, quarried in the hills nearby, and covered with dazzling white coats of plaster.

THE CLASSIC AGE

AT a time when western Europe was plunging into its Dark Ages, the Maya entered into their own golden age. Cemented by the commands and consolations of a communal religion, their social order reached mature development. Their population multiplied, their priests explored new intellectual realms, their arts flourished.

The Maya talent for architectural form and embellishment reached its prime in such recently repaired structures as the Temple of the Sun at Palenque (*below*). The Maya excelled at stucco and stone friezes like those seen on the temple's roof, and also at carving scenes and hieroglyphs on the tall stelae that were reared to honor the endings of particular periods of time. The smaller sculptures in clay and jade that have survived show that they also made beautiful objects for more private occasions of worship.

In this religion-centered world, perhaps as much as a third of the people's time was taken up by public ceremonial. But on occasion even the priests went to ball games, called *pok-ta-pok* in Maya. The object was apparently to knock a solid rubber, volleyball-sized ball around an area as big as a basketball court. Players could advance the ball by bumping it—with hip, elbow, wrist or posterior—and the game must have been pretty boisterous: contemporary carvings show players padded at elbows and knees and with chests and backsides protected to soften the blow when they threw themselves forward to intercept the ball, or fell to the ground after delivering a solid bump.

THE TEMPLE OF THE GIANT JAGUAR at Tikal (*above*), also shown in the painting on the preceding page, is seen here as it looked before archaeologists of the University of Pennsylvania began digging it out of the jungle in 1959.

THE TEMPLE OF THE SUN at Palenque (*below*) sits like a jewel in the lowland rain forest. In this superbly proportioned example of classic Maya architecture, stucco friezes cover the sloping roof and centered roof comb.

AN ELABORATE HEADDRESS is shown on this molded pottery figurine. The headdress represents a bird with a rosette in its beak, and the figure has the large nose and soft facial contours the Maya apparently admired.

A MAYA MAN, as depicted in this Classic pottery figurine, sits cross-legged, robed from chest to ankles and topped with a coronet-like headdress. Elaborately jeweled, he wears enormous beads, earplugs and mosaic bracelets.

A TIME MARKER at Copán shows the elaborate hieroglyphs carved on the back of a stone monument, or stela. These pillars were set up to commemorate the passing of five-, 10- and 20-year periods in the Maya calendar.

213

THE OBSERVATORY, so called because its windows are thought to be cut in such a way as to enable officiating priests to observe both sun and moon at the vernal equinox, is an example of new building ideas introduced among the Maya after the Toltecs arrived from Mexico. A spiral staircase in the original building's inner core led to the small observation chamber at the top. The Toltec influence in Yucatán was particularly strong at Chichén Itzá.

THE MEXICAN MOTIF

AROUND the 10th Century A.D., not long after Emperor Charlemagne briefly unified western Europe, the Maya began to abandon the centers of their Classic age. The focus of Maya culture shifted northward to the Yucatán peninsula, but there it changed: at the major city of Chichén Itzá, Maya styles in architecture, sculpture and ideology mixed with influences brought by Toltec invaders from Mexico.

The Toltecs brought with them their god Quetzalcoatl, who became known as Kukulkán in Yucatán. They also brought such architectural innovations as colonnades, round temples and the ornamental use of the feathered-serpent motif. With the coming of the Toltecs, the themes of sculpture and reliefs also grew more warlike.

In the north in this period, the Maya placed increasing emphasis on human sacrifice. At times of famine or prolonged drought, they threw living victims, preferably children, into Chichén Itzá's 130-foot-deep "Well of Sacrifice" to appease the rain gods. Their new cosmology, like the old, held that the sun, the source of energy, had to be fed after its night of sleep. War was waged to obtain captives for the best solar nourishment: human blood. The captive would be spread-eagled on the high altar; four elders, or *chacs,* would pinion his arms and legs; and a priest would slash open the victim's breast, rip out the heart and wave it aloft as an offering to the rising sun.

THE TEMPLE OF THE WARRIORS at Chichén Itzá stands on the summit of a pyramid whose terraces are typically Toltec. The temple itself is ornamented with the feathered-serpent motif of the invading Mexicans. The colonnades at the foot, much like those of the Toltec city of Tula in central Mexico, suggest profane uses for the temple area. These areas, once roofed, may have served as council chambers, throne rooms and even public markets.

THE FEATHERED SERPENT, at the base of a column guarding a sacred portal at Chichén Itzá, is the emblem of Kukulkán, or Quetzalcoatl, to whom the pyramid temple of El Castillo (*center of picture*) was dedicated. Five centuries after his supposed departure for the east, his memory was so venerated that Montezuma, emperor of the Aztecs, yielded to Cortés in the belief that the Spaniard was Quetzalcoatl returning as the myth prophesied.

AN OLMEC HEAD of basalt looks out enigmatically from the swamps of La Venta, on the Mexican Gulf Coast, where American diggers found it in 1940. Eight feet high and perhaps 2,500 years old, the head was left by the ancient Olmecs, who developed a high culture before the Maya.

THE SUN GOD at far right in this carving on a stone tablet at Palenque is actually part of a hieroglyphic, and represents an attempt to put into human form the counting of time. The figure at left has just put down the god after carrying him for a Maya month—the equivalent of 20 days.

216

THE MANY CULTURES OF MIDDLE AMERICA

WHEN archaeologists began to dig the ancient cities of the low-land Maya out of the jungle more than 60 years ago, they believed that this civilization must have risen to its heights in splendid isolation. Now more is known about its origin. Diggers have pushed back the horizons of Middle American culture to 1500 B.C., and even at that misty frontier they find pottery of an excellence that implies long years of development. Some scholars are now cautiously ready to say that it was Middle Americans rather than South Americans who first cultivated corn, and all agree that in the thousand years before the Maya flowering, advanced cultures were evolving on a broad front from the villages of El Salvador in the south to the valley of central Mexico. In fact, at least three other major centers of cultural development are now known to have shared with the Maya the same general maize economy, architecture, calendar and religion, though they differed from the Maya in speech, local customs, and skill and style in art.

All three of these cultures arose in what is now Mexico. There were the cultures of Teotihuacán, the great city on the outskirts of Mexico City; of the Zapotecs and Mixtecs of Oaxaca, which was unearthed in the 2,500-year-old constructions and later tombs of Monte Albán; and of the Olmecs in the lowland regions of Veracruz and Tabasco. Of them all, the Olmecs appear to have been at least slightly in the forefront. They carved masterfully in stone, particularly in jade. They sculptured huge stone heads, some of which have been found buried in the jungle (*opposite page*). They modeled porphyry human figures with stylized jaguar faces. Some Olmec monuments bear calendar inscriptions that have been interpreted as older than those of the earliest Maya, leading Mexican scientists to claim for these gifted people the right to be called the originators of Middle American civilization.

Be that as it may, the Maya unquestionably rose side by side with other cultures which grew the same crops, built the same kind of pyramids and worshiped gods which differed from one another no more than the gods of the Greek and Roman pantheons. Two of the three Mexican cultures mentioned above—and there were others—continued to flourish throughout the centuries of Maya pre-eminence. The Zapotec builders, obsessed with the hereafter, lost themselves in funeral art. In the Valley of Mexico, the people of Teotihuacán built some of the most majestic monuments of the pre-Columbian world, the 2,000-year-old pyramids of the Sun and the Moon.

The Valley of Mexico, the broad mile-and-a-half-high mountain pocket in which the capital of modern Mexico stands, is one of the older areas of human habitation on the American continent. Bones of fossil man claimed to be 11,000 years old have been found at Tepexpan. The Teotihuacán culture grew up on the ruins of older cultures, and was in turn succeeded by the warlike Toltecs, who rose to power northwest of the Valley of Mexico. The Toltecs absorbed the monumental style in architecture, sculpture and public rites and carried it to Yucatán when they subjugated some of the later Maya in the 10th Century A.D. The Toltec warriors also spread far and wide the image of their god, Quetzalcoatl, the Plumed Serpent.

The Aztecs, the last to emerge in the Valley of Mexico, were a small, nomadic tribe who grew up on the northerly fringe of this intensely developed Middle American world. Fighting their way southward into the valley, they found lodgment on an island in Lake Texcoco at its center. The Aztecs were warriors of the god Huitzilopochtli, who, in order to live, had to be fed human blood. By the time the Spanish landed in 1519, Aztec organizing energy had subdued much of Mexico and had begun to shape its heritage, including the arts of smelting and the working of soft metals, which had finally penetrated north from South America. Cortés and his conquistadors heard only that the halls of Emperor Montezuma were filled with gold, and that is what posterity has mainly remembered.

Alfonso Caso, dean of Mexican archaeologists, has said that to speak only of the Aztecs and Maya in appraising the culture of the ancient peoples of Middle America would be practically equivalent to saying that all European art of the 18th Century is represented by that of France and of England. The Aztecs and the Maya were only the first among the many cultures of a Middle America that can be traced back to a past so remote that it has not yet been fixed in time.

MEZCALA STONE FIGURE, eight inches high, comes from the state of Guerrero in the southwestern part of Mexico. The style, which is distinctly modern in tone, differs from that of Olmec pieces found in the same region.

SACRED ARCHITECTURE

TWENTY centuries look down upon the environs of the modern capital of Mexico. Standing massively above the northern outskirts of Mexico City are the majestic monuments of Teotihuacán, notably the 208-foot-high Pyramid of the Sun. The pyramid is as old as any Maya structure and 20 times as big: it is about one half the size, in total volume, of the Great Pyramid of Egypt.

Of all the peoples who created the upland cultures of Middle America in Maya times, those of the Valley of Mexico and the Zapotecs of Oaxaca in southeastern Mexico left the most imposing ruins. The Zapotecs built many lavish burial chambers, and the people of

Teotihuacán raised pyramids. By 300 A.D., Teotihuacán must have become one of the religious and civic centers of Middle American culture. Seven square miles in area, it boasted plazas lined with palaces and avenues, paved with polished stucco and drained by an elaborate system of underground conduits. The religious sculpture was as monumental as the architecture, but the people of Teotihuacán also made small clay figurines, some so realistic and carefully molded that they appear to be individual portraits. Among the decorative symbols in the friezes and sculptures that covered Teotihuacán walls were emblems of the cult of the rain god and the Feathered Serpent. Taken over by the conquering Toltecs, the Feathered Serpent, sign of the god Quetzalcoatl, spread throughout the whole of Mexico, even to the cities of the Maya renaissance in the Yucatán peninsula.

THE EMBLEM OF QUETZALCOATL, the Plumed Serpent, is a sign and ornament that is found throughout Mexico. The hollow eyes of this one glare ferociously from the side of a Fifth Century pyramid at Teotihuacán.

THE PYRAMID OF THE SUN, just north of Mexico City (*above*), is a monument of the 2,000-year-old city of Teotihuacán. Its construction is estimated to have taken all the spare-time labor of 10,000 peasants for 20 years.

"ABODE OF THE DEAD" was the Zapotec name for this burial city at Mitla (*right*), near the modern city of Oaxaca. Their grave-centered cult led the Zapotecs to build mosaic-covered palaces that hugged the ground.

CEREMONIAL SHIELD made of tropical bird feathers and emblazoned with symbolic head is a remnant of an Aztec warrior's ritual costume.

AZTEC ASCENDANCY

THE Aztecs who were found in Mexico by the Spanish invaders were heirs to a high culture that had existed far longer than the 450-year period that has passed since western civilization was planted in America. Their heritage could be traced ultimately to the Maya and other ancient races. More immediately, it was influenced by the Toltecs, who spread their religious symbols of the eagle and the serpent throughout Mexico and left monuments in their 11th Century capital of Tula, northwest of Mexico City. The Aztecs, who built the last big civilization before the coming of the Spaniards, thought of the Toltecs as supermen of a legendary past.

Nomadic warriors from the wild northwest, the Aztecs learned to live and worship by the calendar like their ancient predecessors. They too tried to discover, for the well-being of their community, the rhythm of nature's violent power. Living under the more uncertain skies of central Mexico, however, the Aztecs probably took more care to propitiate the rain gods than the Maya ever did in their rain-drenched jungles.

Though the Aztecs had learned to work and cast in metals, little practical use was made of the art. Protected by armor of cotton and carrying stone-tipped spears, they more or less subdued the thickly settled countryside and ruled it from probably the biggest capital city known in the Americas before 1840. The Aztecs were a hard and imperious lot, and to modern eyes their art seems both brutal and grand. Their less warlike neighbors, on the other hand, were capable of producing figurines, like those shown on the opposite page, with a dirt-floor realism that compensates for their lack of sophistication.

A WARRIOR is represented in this 15-foot-high Toltec statue at Tula. This figure, along with a number of other big statues found nearby, appears to have served as a column that helped hold up the roof of a temple.

A CODEX, or graphic historical record (*below*), is unfolded to show four rain gods perhaps revered by the Mixtecs, contemporaries of the Aztecs. The hieroglyphs along the bottom of the pages mark days of the calendar.

FIGURES FROM WESTERN MEXICO depict domesticity with lively realism: one plays a drum, one holds a child, one holds a plate. They wear rings in their noses, ornaments on their ears and bangles on their biceps.

TWO-HEADED SERPENT is coated with a mosaic of turquoise, which, with jade, the Aztecs prized more highly than gold. It is fitted with fangs of shell. The two heads probably symbolized the duality and continuity of life.

A DARK PARTNERSHIP

THOUGH religion and religious sacrifice absorbed the lives of all Middle American peoples, none gave themselves over with such tremendous passion to the literal sacrifice of life as the warlike Aztecs. In the elaborate ceremonies ordained by a calendar that was deemed to be sacred, human sacrifice, usually by the removal of a still-beating heart, was the common culminating act. Long racks of victims' skulls adorned the temple squares in the principal Aztec cities and towns. It is recorded that at one festival, just before the Spaniards arrived, priests slaughtered no fewer than 20,000 captives on the high altar in the Aztec capital of Tenochtitlán.

The dark partnership of the Aztecs with death became the basis of their whole philosophy and of their best art. "The Aztec," says Alfonso Caso, "stamps the horror of death on all of his creations. Warrior of a cruel god who demanded the blood of his victims in order to live, the Aztec perceived with particular clarity the eternal tragedy of the world in which life is rooted in death."

In their sculptures of the gods, Aztec artists expressed the vision with brutality and grandeur. The massive architecture of the temples focused attention on the sacrificial drama. The Aztec calendar, though never so finely calculated as the elaborate timetables of the Maya, enforced the community's belief that all life is meted out daily by divine favor.

By the third decade of the 16th Century, Tenochtitlán, that shining lake-city of 60,000 households, the seat of warriors, artists, seers and far-trading merchants, held sway over the richest and biggest of all Middle American empires. But Aztec civilization was doomed. It took just a handful of Spaniards, forcefully marshaling their cannon, horses and western statecraft, to subdue the proud Aztecs.

SKULL MASK OF GOLD is a tiny pendant hung with dangling rattles. Almost all gold objects of the Aztec period went into Spanish melting pots. Many of those in existence, including this ornament, were unearthed in Oaxaca.

GORGET OF GOLD, which may once have hung on an Aztec warrior's chest, shows a man with a jaguar's jaws, possibly intended to represent Tepeyollotli, the jaguar god. This four-inch-high ornament was found near Veracruz.

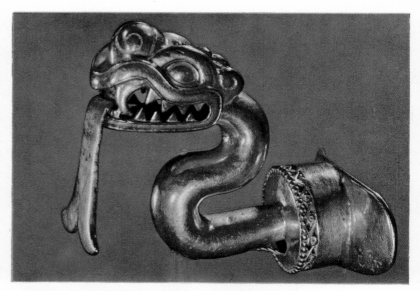

A LIP ORNAMENT once worn by an Aztec is a long-tongued serpent with golden fangs. The part at the right fitted into a slit specially cut in the wearer's lower lip. Such ornaments were worn by priests on ceremonial occasions.

A CEREMONIAL MASK in the Aztec style has eyes of white shells. At their very center are holes for the wearer to look through. The mask, which is six and a half inches high, is made of cedarwood inlaid with mosaics of variously colored and shaped turquoise. The teeth are also made of shells. This spectacular trophy was probably sent by the conquistador Cortés to Spain at the time of the conquest, but it has since found its way into the British Museum.

223

THE FIERY END
OF THE AZTEC EMPIRE

IN the years preceding 1519, omens and portents flooded in upon Montezuma the Younger, Emperor of the Aztecs. Priest as well as emperor, Montezuma brooded long over the familiar prophecy that Quetzalcoatl, the bearded, white-skinned god of all Mexicans, would return from the east "and his sons would be lords and owners of the land." His own soothsayers told the emperor that 1519 was a likely year for Quetzalcoatl's return. In stunning succession, temples had caught fire, a comet had been seen by day, a column of flame had risen to the sky on successive midnights, and Montezuma himself had looked into a mirror and seen a host of armed men. Finally a watchman came to Montezuma. "Lord and king of ours," he said, "forgive my daring. I walked to the seashore and I saw a kind of mountain or big hill moving about in the midst of the sea without touching the shore."

In such an unsettling manner and in such an unsettled mood, Montezuma learned of the arrival of Hernando Cortés, with 11 vessels, some 500 men, 16 horses and 10 cannon, to explore his realm. Cortés was a vagabond student from Medellín who had landed in the New World some years before, announcing: "I come to find gold." When he formed his fleet in Cuba, his banner bore the device: "Friends, let us follow the Cross and under this sign, if we have faith, we shall conquer." No Spaniard in 1519 saw a contradiction in his two missions.

Landing first at Tabasco, Cortés stayed for a time to gain knowledge of the natives. The shrewd cavalier quickly noticed that the Indians took his musketeers for gods carrying lightning in their hands and his horsemen for four-legged monsters with human bodies growing out of their backs. When the local chiefs visited his camp, he filled them with terror by galloping his horses past them and firing off his cannon. The chiefs gave him gold and 20 women. One was beautiful Doña Marina, as the Spaniards called her, or Malinche, as the Indians said, who became his mistress and interpreter.

Sailing on to land near what is now Veracruz, Cortés was met by ambassadors from Montezuma, who had gloomily informed himself about the white men and their leader, and their eagerness for gold. The Aztec nobles presented Cortés with a helmet filled with gold dust and other rich gifts, and asked him to go away. Meanwhile Cortés learned through Malinche that the Totonac people of the coast were spoiling to throw off the harsh Aztec tyranny, and hoped to make the invaders their spearhead for a march against Tenochtitlán, Montezuma's capital.

Thereupon the dauntless Cortés scuttled his ships and with Malinche at his side led his handful of adventurers against the unknown world that lay beyond the mountain wall of volcanoes, some of which were over 17,000 feet. Urged by Malinche, Cortés marched his men over the passes and into the land of the Tlaxcalans, who were neighbors and bitter enemies of the Aztecs. The Tlaxcalans put the power of Cortés to a practical test in open battle and, when the Spaniards won, became Cortés' allies against their hated enemies, the Aztecs. Marching on, the Spaniards sighted the smiling Valley of Mexico with its white-towered lake city of Tenochtitlán shimmering in the distance. "The promised land!" cried the cavaliers.

REJECTING all Montezuma's threats and blandishments, Cortés entered the city with his small force and only 1,000 Tlaxcalans. Bernal Díaz, soldier in Cortés' army, has told of Tenochtitlán's palaces and flower-decked avenues, of its blood-spattered temples and priests whose hair was caked with human blood, of the regal raiment of its ruler as he was borne to meet Cortés on the causeway crossing the lake. For Montezuma, believing Cortés to be the god Quetzalcoatl returning from the East, received him with honor.

Thus knowing nothing of the language or the land, without chart or compass to guide them, Spanish chivalry and Christian faith had won their way into the capital of the "kingdom of gold," and in this astonishing human adventure, armored knight met priest-warrior, each masked in the symbols of his faith.

Undeterred by a spectacle of pomp and power such as his men had never dreamed of, Cortés struck with blinding violence, treachery and

ROYAL WIDOW from an imperial Maya dynasty is the Empress Eduarda Xiu, 81, shown near ruins of the temple at Uxmal in Yucatán. The Xiu family is descended from the last rulers of the Maya cities in the Yucatán peninsula.

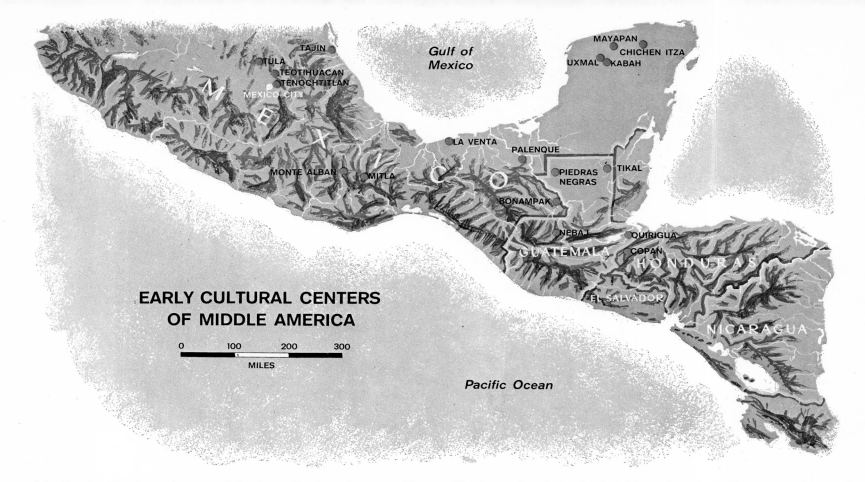

EARLY CULTURAL CENTERS OF MIDDLE AMERICA

0   100   200   300
MILES

Gulf of Mexico

MAYAPAN
CHICHEN ITZA
UXMAL KABAH

TAJIN
TULA
TEOTIHUACAN
TENOCHTITLÁN
MEXICO CITY

LA VENTA
PALENQUE
PIEDRAS NEGRAS
TIKAL
BONAMPAK

MONTE ALBAN
MITLA

NEBAJ
QUIRIGUA
COPAN

GUATEMALA
HONDURAS

EL SALVADOR

NICARAGUA

Pacific Ocean

originality, hurling Aztec throne and theology alike into the gutter. He seized Montezuma as a hostage and burned some of his ministers alive. Then he demanded that the emperor have gold tribute fetched before him, and for three whole days the Aztec goldsmiths labored to melt the beautiful ornaments into the gold bars the conquerors demanded. There was $6.3 million worth, and the foot soldiers, allotted a mere $300 share apiece, called for more. But at this point Cortés smashed the idols of Tenochtitlán in their temples.

THE Aztecs rose in revenge, and when Montezuma tried to quiet them, they stoned him to death. The Spaniards, besieged by enraged Indians, were forced to abandon Tenochtitlán: so loaded were many of them with Aztec gold that when they fell from the causeway in their retreat they were dragged under and drowned. In that one bloody passage, which they came to call *la noche triste,* or sad night, the Spaniards lost three quarters of their men. Cortés sat down under a cypress tree and wept.

As the Spaniards withdrew painfully toward their allies in Tlaxcala, an Aztec army of an estimated 200,000 fell on them at Otumba. Stones and arrows rattled against their armor, but the weary conquistadors held their discipline. Late in the day, writes historian William Prescott in a classic passage, Cortés, "rising in his stirrups descried at a distance in the midst of a throng the chief who from his dress and military cortege he knew must be the commander of the barbarian forces. To the cavaliers at his side he cried: 'There is our mark. Follow and support me.' On they swept with the fury of a thunderbolt and Cortés, overturning [the Indian commander's] supporters, sprung forward with the speed of a lion and striking him through with his lance, hurled him to the ground." The Indians fled in defeat, and Cortés led his survivors into Tlaxcala.

Gathering their scattered forces together, the Spaniards marched a second time on Tenochtitlán. This time, under a resourceful new emperor, Cuauhtémoc, Montezuma's nephew and son-in-law, the Aztecs fought back with desperate fury. Deserted by their tributary tribes, they resisted with a unity never before seen. The fighting spread from the causeways to boats in the lakes. Cortés was narrowly saved from capture by Aztec warriors intent on dragging him off for the supreme sacrifice to their gods. Even so, the baleful temple drums beat often enough over a sacrificed Spaniard. Inch by bloody inch, destroying as they advanced, leveling the city block by block, filling the broad streets and canals with Aztec dead, the able Spaniards and their allies battered their way back in. Finally, too weak from hunger to fight on, the Aztec garrison gave up. Cuauhtémoc, trying to make off in a canoe, was captured. Brought before Cortés, he said: "I have done all that I could to defend myself and my people." Then, pointing to a dagger, he said, "Better dispatch me with this and rid me of life at once."

Instead, Cortés kept Cuauhtémoc by him as hostage against any rising by the Aztec remnants. Three years later, while marching to

Honduras, Cortés made the charge that the Indians were plotting a rising against him. Cuauhtémoc acknowledged that the Indians had sometimes talked of an uprising but he himself had discouraged it as hopeless. Cortés ordered him hanged from a *ceiba* tree.

Aztec civilization died with Cuauhtémoc, and Spanish speech, religion and government were imposed on his realm. But the Aztecs (as well as the Maya) remain: one third of all Mexicans are pure-blooded Indians, and today, after four centuries of wars and revolutions, Indian blood is a thing of pride in the Spanish-speaking republic. Cuauhtémoc is revered as a national hero. But in all the land, there is not a monument to Cortés. The name of Cortés' mistress has passed into the national vocabulary: a *malinche* is one who sells his country or favors foreigners at the expense of his countrymen. Such was the fate of the triumphant, tragic figures of the Aztec downfall. But in a thousand Mexican villages may still be heard the pat of Indian hands shaping *tortillas* as they did in these same villages 20 centuries and more before the Spaniards first voyaged to America.

ARCHAEOLOGICAL DIVER seeks Maya relics in the hot, sulphurous waters of Guatemala's Lake Amatitlán. To placate the gods, the Maya threw incense burners, pottery vessels and sculptures into lakes they considered sacred.

A NOBLEMAN'S PORTRAIT adorns a 1,700-year-old clay jar found on the north coast of Peru. The vessel probably dates back to the Mochica culture, one of the civilized precursors of the Inca empire that ran from Colombia to Chile in the Andes. The Inca were the last in a long line of Andean peoples whose impressive achievements in the fields of art, agriculture and politics forged the third of the New World's three great native civilizations.

THE IMPERIAL INCA OF THE ANDES

The organizing genius of the Inca crowned a succession of civilizations that flourished for 2,600 years in Peru

OF the big civilizations of the New World, the Maya, one of the first in Middle America, had to cut its way out of the jungle. The Aztecs had to conquer their way through Mexico. Far to the south, other mighty civilizations, the Andean, thrust upward through some of the world's most forbidding terrain: the towering mountains and desert coast of Andean Peru. The empire of the Inca, which crowned these early civilizations of the southern half of the globe, ruled from a capital 11,000 feet in the clouds.

Andean civilization seems to have centered far more than that of Middle America on the material techniques of life: planning big cities and irrigation works, building highways and a network of communications, perfecting the domestic arts of weaving and pottery making. The Inca passion for organization in every field seems to have extended even to their art work. But the best in Andean art was produced by American peoples who preceded the Inca.

Civilization around the world traces its origins to the time when men settled down and started cultivating rather than hunting their food. The early South Americans showed a versatile talent for domesticating plants, many of them unknown in the Old World. Some 4,500 years ago they were already cultivating squash, peppers, gourds, beans and cotton on the coast of Peru. By the time of the Spanish conquest, the early South Americans were probably better farmers than their European contemporaries. They had domesticated the potato, the tomato, the yam and the lima bean. They found a source of wool by taming the llama and the alpaca. They terraced the mountainsides and built vast irrigation systems. Since about 900 B.C., when corn appeared, apparently brought from Middle America, Peruvian agriculture had been disciplined and well developed. Early American civilization, north and south, grew up with corn as its basic food crop.

Since the ancient South Americans never developed writing, all that is known of their early progress is what archaeologists have been able to find out. After a half century's excavations, scholars now trace six distinct cultural stages in the evolution of Andean civilization. The earliest of these, named for Chavín de Huántar, a 2,800-year-old ruin in the remote northern highlands of Peru, lasted from about 1200 to 400 B.C., and is the one period in Andean prehistory when religion seems to have absorbed all high culture as completely as it did among the Maya. At their huge ceremonial center, the Chavín people created a resplendent temple and powerful stone carvings that Dr. Junius Bird, a leading expert on Andean civilization, calls superior to later Inca art.

In the second of these eras, starting in 400 B.C. and lasting until about 400 A.D., the Paracas people, named for the south coast peninsula where their tombs and other remains were found, flourished. They wove textiles that have seldom been surpassed by civilized man. In the third period identified by the experts, the Nazca culture succeeded the Paracas in southern Peru while the so-called Mochica people arose on the north coast. Subduing their neighbors in the nearby river valleys, the Mochica people evolved a complicated class society, laid roads and invented other sophisticated techniques that were adopted by the later Inca. Their pottery is the finest made by early Americans.

Up to this point in history, no one culture had spread over the whole of Peru's arid coasts and high mountains. In the fourth stage of prehistoric Andean civilization, about 1000 A.D., a single culture originating around Tiahuanaco in the southern Andes imposed its leadership in art and in war throughout most of Peru. The evidence of the archaeological record indicates that the spread of this fourth culture was not long-lived and may not even have been accomplished altogether by one people. A fifth era opened, and new forces sprang up again along the coast, notably the Chimu people in the north. This last development set the stage for the Andean drama so long in the building: the emergence by conquest and ruthless annexation of the New World's only completely unified state—the Inca empire.

MIGHTY MASONRY at the Inca city of Machu Picchu is constructed of blocks of granite. The Inca fashioned their blocks without metal tools of any kind, and their stone walls were put together without any cement or sealer.

TRAPEZOIDAL DOORWAYS and a similarly shaped wall niche in the distance line up evenly in the well-engineered city of Machu Picchu. Before beginning work on large buildings, Inca architects made detailed clay models.

LUSTROUS FIGURINES, silver representations of an alpaca, a llama and a woman, are religious offerings that were frequently used by the Inca nobility. The llama, more than nine inches high, is inlaid with gold and cinnabar.

THE GREAT ENGINEERS

AS imperial organizers, the Inca rate with the Romans. These warrior people took over the last of a 2,600-year-old series of cultures and reshaped the roads, religion and government they inherited.

The Inca excelled at engineering. They built roads 3,250 miles long, piped irrigation water through mountain tunnels, hung 200-foot suspension bridges across Andean canyons. The Inca were masters at shaping and fitting stones. A militant, conquering people, they built their most spectacular monuments in places already fortified by nature. The main fortress protecting Cuzco, their imperial headquarters in the southern Andes, was built out of rock and defended by a thick wall 1,600 feet long. Machu Picchu, another Inca stronghold, is a condor's nest of a city possibly built to protect the empire's eastern flank against Amazonian raiders, and so ingeniously adapted to the site that it seems a part of the mountains.

The Inca organized their five million subjects into "the land of the four quarters," each ruled by a noble. They also divided their capital city of Cuzco, with its neatly gridded streets, into four quarters, and required visitors from the provinces to stay in their own appropriate sections. Taking an empire-wide census, they appointed subordinate officials right down to the precinct level: the highest held responsibilities over 10,000 men, the next over 1,000, the next over 500, and the lowest over groups of 50 and 10. All except the last two ranks were rated as Inca nobles. Each reported to his superior by state couriers, who dashed in relays up and down the mountainsides on the emperor's paved roads.

The Inca also created a rigid caste system. From one end of the Andes to the other, the state ran factories for making all the cloths, ceramics and gold ornaments required for ceremonial use and for the nobility. Ordinary people were required to contribute either labor or goods to the state. In every sizable town and at intervals along the main roads were large stone warehouses which the state required the population to keep stocked against a local shortage or an imperial requisition. The Inca also exacted tribute from everybody they conquered, keeping track of their accounts by a system of tying knots in a set of colored strings called the *quipu*.

In this totalitarian society everyone knew his place. Education was strictly for the young nobles who would command armies and govern provinces. These were mainly the members of the Inca royal clan, but sons of conquered rulers were also sometimes taken into the governing caste. These nobles wore rich fabrics, bright feathers and gold ornaments, but by rigid rule the commoners had to dress in simple fashion. The emperor himself wore clothes of the finest vicuña wool that were meticulously disposed of at the end of a single day's wear. He was lord over government, army and priesthood, the sun god's divine son. To keep the bloodline pure, the emperor usually married only his sister, though it was possible for him to have as many as 700 concubines and any number of natural children.

A FORTRESS CITY built on a series of levels, Machu Picchu straddles a mountain ridge 8,000 feet above sea level. The site has more than a hundred stairways, some of which have as many as 150 steps. Outside the city, agricultural terraces were built so that crops could be raised on the hillside. Today the city is a 27-acre ruin of once-gabled houses, temples, barracks and palaces interconnected by narrow streets and the steep stone staircases.

A LEERING FELINE with bared fangs decorates a temple built by Chavín people about 2,500 years ago. The stone head, which is fixed to the wall with a tenon, represents the cat god that pervaded most of the Chavín art.

WORSHIP OF FELINES

THE world the Inca conquered in the 14th and 15th Centuries was already an area of high cultures of some 25 centuries' standing. In the 16th Century, the Inca gave the Spanish invaders the impression that they had created everything themselves. But archaeologists, through the years, have slowly peeled back layer after layer of a past in which many of the features of Inca life are anticipated by a thousand years or more.

The time of great cultural advance in Peru began soon after 1000 B.C. at Cupisnique on the coast and Chavín de Huántar in the highlands. Tombs beneath the sands have yielded thick Cupisnique stirrup-spout jugs and highly decorated clay jars. Chavín is a major center of the northern highlands that has given its name to the entire first era of Andean civilization. Today a massive stone temple, the Castillo, 246 feet square, dominates the site. Pyramidal platforms, paved terraces and plazas surround the low monument. The temple, three stories high and honeycombed with stone-lined passages and rooms, has a special system of ventilating shafts and is a remarkable piece of complex architecture. But the most important features of Chavín are the grotesque stone sculptures and carved slabs that are set into its laboriously smoothed walls.

These massive, monstrous carvings have a special style. Whether they represent men, animals or birds, the figures are shown with a feline mouth. This mouth, which might be that of a jaguar, puma or cat, is everywhere. On one monster figure it is affixed at 12 different places on the body. On a condor it is shown as a continuation of the beak. It glares from the head and tail of a snake. Though this image is found in early American art from Mexico to Bolivia, nowhere else is it depicted with such power. Obviously it is a symbol that conveyed to ancient Peruvians the idea of supernatural power, and its appearance on men and other creatures was enough to make them supernatural.

Not many people seem to have lived continuously at Chavín. No graves have been found there. The symmetrical layout, the careful construction and the nature of the carvings strongly imply that Chavín was a religious center. Scholars believe that Chavín, like the modern Bolivian town of Copacabana, was a center to which pilgrims made their way at a certain season each year from all parts of the land. While the people were assembled, they may have been put to work in a community project, dragging together stones and putting some of the larger slabs in place. Then, when the ceremonies were over and the pilgrims returned to their distant homes, specialized artisans may have carried on the building and carving with the help of local laborers. At all events, the feline element in art—and probably in religion—spread far and wide from Chavín; its influence is to be seen in the continuing preoccupation of later generations of Peruvian artists with the figure of the puma, the jaguar and the cat.

A CRUMBLING ENTRANCE to a temple at Chavín de Huántar is guarded by eight-foot pillars decorated in the intricate low-relief style of the Chavín era. Circling the pillar at the right is the figure of the ubiquitous feline.

A SEATED GIRL is a 2,500-year-old jug made by a potter at Cupisnique during the Chavín period. The Cupisnique culture originated in the Peruvian coastal valley where men began cultivating crops at least 4,000 years ago.

Throughout all Chavín relief work, the feline motif is repeated again and again as a key element of the design. The temple, which is part of a huge ceremonial center, has other cat-figure carvings inside its windowless galleries.

A DRINKING JUG from Cupisnique is a forerunner of later notable masterworks of Andean ceramics. The clean-lined jar's cleverly contrived combination handle and spout give a massive quality to this eight-inch piece.

A CAT MAN holding a human trophy head (*above*) is painted on the border of a mantle which the ancestor-worshiping people of Paracas wove for their dead. This fragment was preserved for 2,000 years in a bone-dry burial vault.

A SHIRT OF MANY COLORS, a poncho two and a half feet in length (*opposite*), is painstakingly embroidered with feline figures to form a symmetrical pattern. The cloak was a grave offering found in the Paracas burial vaults.

AN EMBROIDERED FACE, a border decoration for a Paracas altar cloth, is shown in detail here. Embroidered wool, dyed gold, forms the eyes.

THE COASTAL PEOPLES

STARTING about 400 B.C., a strong and distinctive culture began to take form in three small river valleys on the virtually rainless coast south of what is now Lima. In this new society, which produced no known large buildings, ancestor worship seems to have been the overriding theme of people's lives. It is called the Paracas culture, after the modern name of the desert peninsula on which its richest burial vaults were found.

These people wove magnificent clothes for their dead. More than 350 Paracas mummy bundles have been dug up, containing mantles buried with the dead. After 2,200 years, the ancient colors still glow with beauty. So fine is the weaving that threads run up to 500 to the square inch. Some mantles have been painted with feline faces that recall the Chavín motif. Others are embroidered with such bizarre figures as winged men with snakes coiled around their eyes, split-headed condors gobbling fish, and cat-faced men with knives.

Whole communities evidently worked in their spare time to make these death clothes. Some of the dead were warriors and priests with especially rich mantles and copper battle-axes and gold ornaments at their sides. But because they are found buried with others of lesser rank—men and women together—it is believed that this was a society in which class distinctions had not yet become important.

A ROTUND WOMAN in a poncho is the figure on a funeral jug made some 1,500 years ago by a Nazca potter. The nine-inch-high vessel has the characteristic high polish, bright colors and globular shape of most Nazca ceramics.

A WIDE-EYED FISHERMAN adorns a clay jar dating back to the early Nazca period. The crude, incised crosshatching on the design probably represents the net he has thrown over his head as he uses his hands to carry his catch.

233

THE DYNAMIC MOCHICA

THE first six centuries A.D. were one of the most creative times in the life of ancient Peru. The so-called Mochica people who dominated the river valleys of the north coast appear to have been a dynamic, original, almost aggressive people who worked out many of the social patterns later taken over in the political empire of the Inca. Their society seems to have been based on large-scale exploitation of mass labor. The Mochica built by far the biggest monument to be found on the coast: the Pyramid of the Sun near the modern city of Trujillo, estimated to contain 130 million adobe bricks. Evidently they had evolved a status society, in which a small, aristocratic class managed the lives and work of the rest. Their graphically painted pottery vessels show bejeweled chieftains borne about on litters. Guests of inferior rank dine at a lower table than the chiefs. Artisans were probably full-time specialists in their crafts, and one pottery picture shows a line of weavers working away under a foreman's eye in what looks like mass production of textiles.

In all these Mochica pottery pictures there is an earthy preoccupation with material things. Men are seen farming, fishing, hunting and waging war. The time of the Mochica seems to have been a kind of morning for the Andean imagination. Historians compare the pottery of these north coast people with the art of classical Greece.

GOLDEN EARPLUGS are deftly inlaid with shell and turquoise. They were worn 1,700 years ago by one of the Mochica nobility. Decorated with the figures of warriors wielding mace and shield, the earplugs are four inches wide.

A PINK FIGURE, modeled in a naturalistic style, is part of a clay jar once used for Mochica burial rites. The turban was standard Mochica headgear. Natural clay gives the vessel its pink tone. Mochica potters were masters in the New World at creating lifelike representations, and undoubtedly modeled portraits of actual people on their clay effigy vessels. Probably only a person of the nobility would have had his portrait done in this manner.

BEAN WARRIORS vigorously trade mace blows on the buff-colored surface of a Mochica jar. The painted bean figure is a conventional motif in Mochica decoration, but the maces, round shields, darts and conical crested helmets represent actual fighting gear of the Mochica warrior, who held a high rank within the society. Skilled at rendering movement and action in their painting, Mochica potters decorated their vessels with detailed scenes of daily life.

A BOLD EYE dominates this detail from an abstract design created with feathers. After 900 years, the colored feathers, taken from gaudy birds, stay bright because they had been placed in a burial site in a dry area.

Workers in the Tiahuanaco period used feathers from brightly plumed birds found in the distant Amazon rain forest. Feathers were either cemented on or attached to yarn and then stitched to the fabric row by row.

236

A LONELY REMNANT of the once great ceremonial center of Tiahuanaco is the 10-foot-high Gateway of the Sun, now restored. The free-standing slabs near the carved gate are remains of a wall that once bounded the sides of a vast courtyard on this 13,000-foot-high plateau. Never completed, Tiahuanaco's main structures covered an area of about one sixth of a square mile. The widespread Tiahuanaco style undoubtedly originated in this area.

GATEWAY OF THE SUN

HIGH on the treeless plains just south of Lake Titicaca, the world's highest navigable lake (12,506 feet), stand the windblasted ruins of Tiahuanaco. The small community of Bolivian Indians who pasture llamas near them today gives little clue to the city's onetime grandeur. But 1,000 years ago, Tiahuanaco was a great ceremonial center to which thousands thronged from all over the Andes in periodic pilgrimages, much as their predecessors of northern Peru had flocked to Chavín de Huántar. It is too bleak a place to support a large permanent population, and digging has not disclosed that many people lived there. Scholars think it may have been the pilgrims, marshaled by supervisors as masterful as the later Inca, who built the monumental structures of Tiahuanaco.

Stone buildings and giant statues dot the plain, one an unfinished pyramid whose ground plan is only slightly smaller than that of the Great Pyramid of Egypt. Restored is Tiahuanaco's famous Gateway of the Sun, a doorway carved in a 10-foot block of andesite and decorated with a frieze in a boldly abstract style that was popular in Andean Peru. It shows a two-foot figure that may be the Creator God, Viracocha, surrounded by numbers of small, stylized puma heads and geometrically patterned figures of winged men with weapons running toward the deity.

Until the Tiahuanaco era, doubtless because of the difficult mountain and desert terrain of Peru, no single culture had been able to spread over and dominate the whole of the area. With the rise of Tiahuanaco, such a domination was accomplished, and during this period the stylized designs that are the symbols of the Tiahuanaco cult were repeated on ceramics, woodcarving and metalwork throughout most of Peru. Experts doubt that all of the Tiahuanaco expansion took place through military conquest, though no one really knows.

THE PUMA, here pictured formally and in profile, is a decoration motif that the potters of Tiahuanaco made popular throughout the Central Andes area 1,000 years ago. This graceful beaker is a typical Tiahuanaco work of art.

237

THE LURE OF GOLD

WITH the establishment of Inca rule, Andean civilization entered its final, imperial phase. In the world of the Inca, a man's status was clearly shown by what he wore. Only members of the nobility or the royal family could wear elaborate ornaments of gold and precious stones. The most socially significant of all such ornaments of rank were earplugs, a particularly gaudy kind of male earring.

One of the high points of a well-born Inca's life came, after a rigorous schooling in the manly arts of wrestling, boxing, fighting and long-distance marching, when a teen-age novice knelt before the emperor himself to have his ears pierced by a gold dagger. When the youth rose, having uttered no cry, he was a man. Gradually the hole was made big enough to bear the weight of the nobleman's huge earplugs. Some of the pendants were enormous, and before many years the young nobleman's earlobes might droop nearly to the shoulders with the weight of gold. The Spanish were so shocked and impressed by the custom that they called the Inca *orejones* (big ears). The Inca regarded the earplug as a thing of great beauty.

The art of working in precious metals was highly advanced in Peru long before the Inca. Some of the finest gold objects, in fact, date from the time of the Mochica people, who knew how to hammer, cast, gild and solder expertly a thousand years before the Inca set up their empire. But the Inca went in for mass production of gold, and it was the lure of all that gold that drew Francisco Pizarro and his 170 conquistadores to scale the Andes in 1532, kidnap the emperor and overturn his empire and the whole edifice of Andean civilization.

A WEALTHY CITIZEN, accompanied by a llama, decorates a clay vessel that was made by a North Highland potter. The man wears the outsize earplugs and headdress that make it plain he is one of the Andes' well-to-do nobility.

ANDEAN GOLD is the chief interest in this museum exhibition of items assembled from Peruvian cultures. Suspended in the center are a plumed crown, earplugs, epaulettes, a necklace and a 17-inch collar—ornaments worn by a

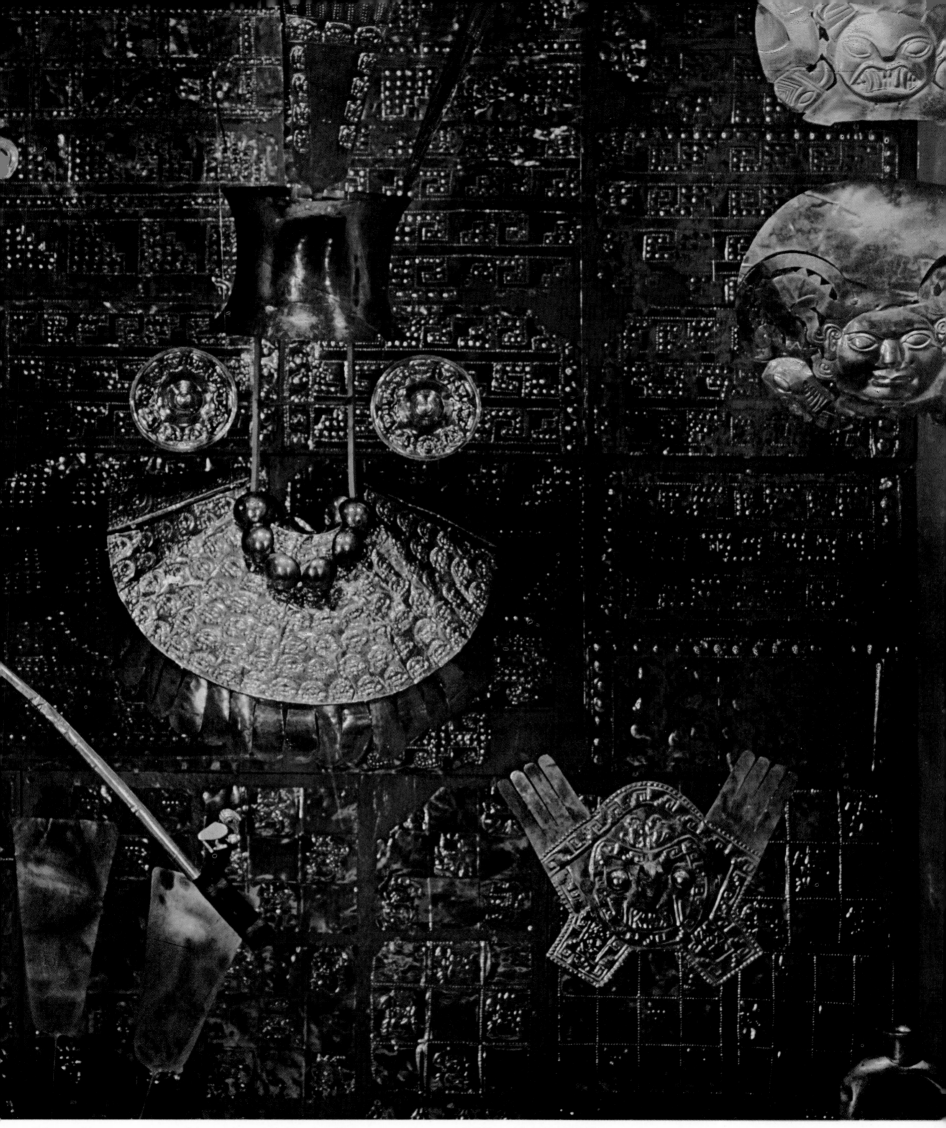

Chimu nobleman on ceremonial occasions. Mochica headdresses appear at the right and lower left. Also at the lower left is a 10-inch Chimu earring. Above, at upper left, is an elaborate Chimu breastplate and mummy mask.

Gold was commonly used for personal and ceremonial ornaments as far back as Chavín times. When rumors of an Andean "Kingdom of Gold" reached Francisco Pizarro in Panama, the fate of the Inca empire was at last sealed.

239

THE WORLD OF
THE AMERICAN INDIAN

IT took the Spaniards longer to find the Inca empire than the Aztec. But in 1532, when Francisco Pizarro and his band of 180 marched ashore at Tumbes, in northern Peru, they drove to a triumph swifter and even richer than Cortés won.

Learning that the Inca emperor Atahuallpa was encamped in the northern highlands, Pizarro boldly marched up the Andean precipices. When Atahuallpa came to meet him, Pizarro treacherously seized the emperor. In the regimented, antlike society of the Inca, the trick worked better than it had in Mexico. The government was so dependent on orders from the top that when the emperor was captured, there was little resistance left. Atahuallpa offered to fill a room with gold and silver as high as he could reach if Pizarro would free him. The efficient Inca organization rounded up the ransom—worth an estimated $8.3 million—but Atahuallpa was murdered. Pizarro rode as a conqueror into Cuzco, the capital city; the Inca ruling class was ruthlessly exterminated, and the whole Inca world collapsed.

With the disappearance of the Inca as well as the Aztec empires, not much was left of the New World's greatest cultural achievements. The Andean and Middle American civilizations were the upper crust of the western world, and when the Spaniards wiped them out, all that remained throughout the Americas for the most part was a sort of substratum of primitive peoples, the barbaric hinterland of the Indian civilizations.

Wherever they lived, these people had one thing in common. The ancestors of all Indians, civilized or not, had come at different times across the Bering Strait land bridge from Asia to Alaska, and filtered south as far as Cape Horn. They were not a lost tribe of Israel, a tribe out of ancient Wales or children of the lost Atlantis—though all these fanciful explanations have been put forward to account for their having reached America before the white man.

Many evidences of the first big-game-hunting Americans have been dug up in the western United States dating from 15,000 to 24,000 years ago. One of the most spectacular is a man-made implement found at Sandia Cave, New Mexico, together with mammoth and mastodon bones. Remains of early hunters some 10,000 years old have been found in the Argentine pampas and in Patagonia. Early Americans are believed to have begun cultivating the first root crops in the tropics of South America 4,000 years ago, and at Bat Cave, New Mexico, scientists have unearthed two-inch-long corncobs shown by carbon 14 measurements to date back to 2500 B.C.

AS things turned out, it was south of the Rio Grande that civilization flowered. Farther north, in the Great Plains and Canada, the Indians remained mostly nomadic gatherers rather than cultivators of food. But the big centers of civilization in Middle America generated a considerable influence, and were no doubt responsible for the fact that some of the most advanced Indian societies in what is now the United States were those nearest to Mexico and Central America.

Such cultural influences can be traced far back. More than 1,500

PERU'S FOREMOST ARCHAEOLOGIST was Dr. Julio Cesar Tello, a full-blooded Indian who is best known for his discovery of the 2,000-year-old Paracas culture. The ceremonial vessel he is showing is of Nazca manufacture.

years ago, Indians of the so-called Basket Maker culture of the U.S. Southwest were already living in village societies like those created considerably earlier in Middle America. They were cultivating maize, beans and other crops that had been developed first in Middle America. At ancient Hohokam Indian sites in southern Arizona, diggers have uncovered ball courts, for some form of ball games, like those found in Yucatán and central Mexico. In the 14th Century a cult existed in southern Alabama and Georgia much like the cults of the early Mexicans. In the 15th Century A.D., peoples in the lower Mississippi valley built pyramidal mounds with temples on top that suggest a borrowing of ideas from the Maya. The structures are even lined up to north and south, east and west, in Maya fashion. The largest surviving monument ever made by the Mound Builders is Mississippi's Emerald Mound, 35 feet high and covering seven acres.

By the time of Columbus, the basic Middle American pattern of garden agriculture based on maize was to be found in many parts of

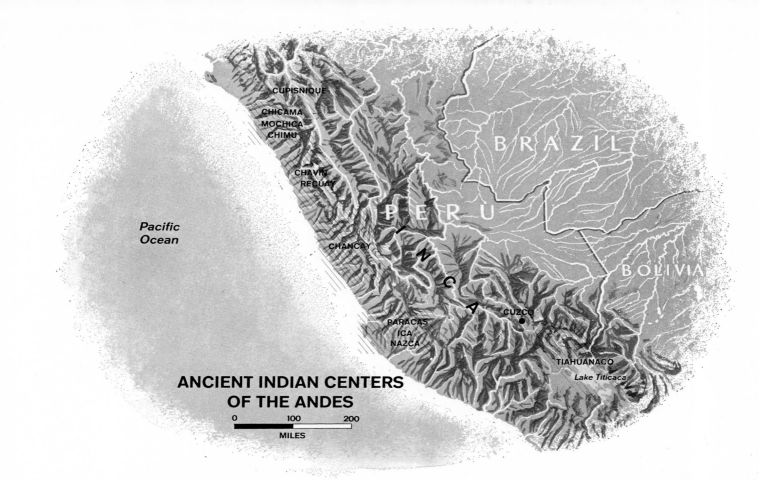

ANCIENT INDIAN CENTERS
OF THE ANDES

0   100   200
MILES

Pacific
Ocean

CUPISNIQUE
CHICAMA
MOCHICA
CHIMU
CHAVIN
RECUAY
CHANCAY
PARACAS
ICA
NAZCA
TIAHUANACO
Lake Titicaca
CUZCO

BRAZIL
PERU
INCA
BOLIVIA

what is now the United States. But, except for the people living nearest the Middle Americans, Indians north of the Rio Grande lived in relatively less established, less highly organized communities. They numbered perhaps 900,000 in all, split up among some 350 different tribes speaking 350 different tongues. The densest settlement was in California (112 per square mile), where tribes found shellfish in abundance. They also ground a fairly nourishing flour from the acorns of live oaks near Santa Barbara and San Francisco. Farther north, around Puget Sound, salmon fishing, sealing and whaling supported a population nearly as large and a culture famous for its totem poles and other wood carvings.

In the Southwest the Pueblo maize planters led settled agricultural lives like the Indians of Mexico. But instead of worshiping at pyramidal altars, the Pueblos dug holes in the ground for their religious rites. Oraibi, a Hopi Pueblo village in Arizona dating from A.D. 1150, is probably the oldest continuously inhabited place in the U.S. Mesa Verde and other famous cliff colonies, built 850 years ago when barbaric Navajo and other tribesmen began drifting into Pueblo country, were abandoned long ago. The Navajo invaders, discovering a source of both food and clothing in the sheep they stole from the Spaniards, settled down as shepherds. Today they are the most numerous of all U.S. Indian tribes.

The Plains Indians also gained from the Spaniards when some of the horses the conquistadors had brought to the New World got away and the Plains people caught them. Overnight the fortunes of the Dakota, the Cheyenne, the Pawnee, the Sioux and the Comanche were transformed. Slung bareback on his pony and armed with a white man's rifle, the feathered red raider of the television show came briefly into his own. Galloping after buffalo, smoking before his tepee, snatching the scalps of the other tribes—this was the Indian who captured the world's imagination, though his kind never numbered more than a fifth of all U.S. Indians and in any case never hit the warpath until the battle was all but over.

IN the Southeast the most advanced tribes were those like the Creeks and the Cherokees, who lived in settled bark-house towns, and the Natchez, who may have been the last survivors of the original Mound Builders. The Natchez had an absolute ruler called "the Sun," who was decked out like an Aztec in an elaborate feathered coat. North of them lived the Iroquois, who banded together in a league called the Six Nations, the most advanced political organization north of Middle America. These tribes, noted for their skills in fortification and housing, left most of the fighting to the Mohawks, who played a role something like that of the lords of the Marches in medieval Europe, raiding the surrounding tribes. Their accustomed victims were most often the Algonquin-speaking Indians—hapless, wigwam-dwelling hunters who had been pushed back to the Atlantic by the warlike and better-organized Iroquois, and were now ground to extinction between the Iroquois invaders in the mountains

and the European settlers who had pre-empted the land on the coast.

In both North and South America, the "undeveloped" Indian peoples died or submitted to colonial rule. Sixty years ago the Indians of the United States seemed on their way to extinction. But since then their number has almost doubled—in 1960 there were 523,591 Indians, an increase of more than 45 per cent in the last 10 years. Today they are more than holding their own. Many of the men who rivet the steel frameworks of skyscrapers high above Manhattan are Mohawks, who work in groups recruited by leaders and periodically retire to upstate reservations with their loot—or wages—just as parties of raiding Mohawk braves always have done.

South of the Rio Grande, the Spanish civilization of Cortés and Pizarro has imposed both its speech and religion. But the faces in the streets of Guatemala City today are faces that might have been copied from the frescoes now being uncovered in the jungle sites of Bonampak. More than three million Andean Indians still speak the Quechua language of the Incas. The emancipator of Mexico was Benito Juárez, a full-blooded Zapotec Indian who saved his country from the foreign rule of Emperor Maximilian in the 1860s.

Some of these peoples are like survivals out of the past; others clearly belong to ancient societies in the process of changing to new ways. Today it is the Mexico of the eagle and the serpent, not the New Spain of Cortés, that strives to become an industrial country and takes its place in the councils of the world's nations. In Latin America, as in other awakening regions, the most revolutionary of the new aspirations are those stirring the oldest societies of mankind.

LOOKING FOR RELICS, Dr. Junius B. Bird (*left*), an authority on Andean civilization at the American Museum of Natural History in New York, and Dr. Helge Larsen of Denmark dig in a cave at Bear Mountain, New York.

AN ABORIGINE of northern Australia returns from the day's hunt bearing a wallaby, a small kangaroo. The Australian Aborigine, like Stone Age man, is marvelously skilled at stalking game, alternately creeping forward and freezing motionless, until he gets within spear-throwing distance. Then he hurls his weapon. Hunting and gathering are the Aborigine's only ways of providing his subsistence, as they are for other Stone Age people today.

STONE AGE CULTURES TODAY

Living in remote and harsh areas, Australian Aborigines and some Caribou Eskimos have held to primitive ways

THE mainstream of human life, after flowing so evenly through about 16,000 generations of man, has accelerated enormously in the last 160, which is the period since history began. It has borne men swiftly past a procession of landmarks: in energy sources, from the first kindled fire to the unlocked atom; in transport, from the first wheel to the space vehicle; in communications, from the first written word to the commonplace of world-wide television. But not all of mankind has been traveling in this mainstream. Left behind, in stagnant cultural pools, are peoples who still exist on the Paleolithic, Mesolithic and Neolithic levels. "It is clear," anthropologist Carleton S. Coon observes, "that all parts of the world, all of the members of the human family have not participated equally in the events that have marked the main line of human progress. . . . There are still marginal regions . . . where simple Stone Age hunters are suddenly confronted by strangers carrying rifles, where Neolithic garden-cultivators are trading their stone axes for steel ones and their pottery water jugs for discarded oil tins."

These bypassed peoples are fascinating subjects for study by scientists reconstructing mankind's buried past. For there are only two sources of deductive information available for this reconstruction. One lies in actual relics left by early men: their paintings, implements of stone and bone, sculpture, graves and other mute traces of their tenancy on earth. The other derives from analogies found in the life patterns of those contemporary peoples who have never emerged, so to speak, from prehistory. These are people of the 20th Century who still hunt, eat, and obey codes and taboos just as all men did in the Stone Ages.

The term Paleolithic or Old Stone Age refers, strictly speaking, not to a fixed interval of time but to a stage of culture whose boundaries in time vary from place to place. Thus in Europe the Paleolithic ended around 8000 B.C., but in remote places such as the Andaman Islands in the Bay of Bengal and the desolate hideaways of the African Bushmen of the Kalahari Desert, it is still going on. Similarly, some of the Caribou Eskimos of Canada's interior have never found a way out of the Mesolithic or Middle Stone Age, and the Berbers of Morocco's mountain fastnesses still follow a way of life that resembles that of the Neolithic or New Stone Age.

Of modern-day Paleolithic men, the most numerous and best known are the 70,600 Aborigines who live on Australia's inland desert and on isolated reservations along the coastline. To be sure, it is never possible to draw absolutely exact parallels between one time and situation and another. Geography and climate often dictate ways of life. Thus the people of Europe's late Old Stone Age faced the challenge of a bitter glacial epoch when great ice sheets reached down to the heartland of their continent. The vegetation of that time resembled that of northern Canada and Siberia today—a combination of taiga and tundra flora, clumps of evergreen and a carpet of dwarf birch and willow, lichen and reindeer moss. In winter, deep snow blanketed the land. Man had to cover his shivering body with the furs and hides of animals. He lived in rock shelters and the outer chambers of caves, and for warmth he ate fat and burned wood and the oily bones of the beasts whose flesh he gnawed.

Superficially the life of the Australian Aborigine today appears vastly different. Dwelling in coastal savanna and in inland desert areas that are extremely hot most of the year, he requires no clothing and wears none, save in a few regions where he has copied the Malayan loincloth. For the most part he sleeps in the open, though occasionally he erects temporary lean-tos of grass, bark, leaves or sapling boughs as a shelter against the tropic sun and rain. But like Paleolithic man of Europe, Paleolithic man of present-day Australia is a nomad who lives off the land. His basic implements are largely the same: he has digging sticks and fire sticks, some stonecutting tools and wooden spears tipped with stone points. He is living in the 20th Century, but he has not yet discovered the bow and arrow.

A STONE-TIPPED SPEAR is aimed by an Aborigine. It is equipped with a spear thrower, a short shaft with a projection that fits into the butt end. Upper Paleolithic men in Europe used devices of this kind 10,000 years ago.

A PAINTED ROCK above an inland plain, bearing the likenesses of lizards, is visited by a desert tribesman. To the Aborigine, ritual rock paintings of the animals that he hunts, executed by his predecessors, are sacred relics.

A SUCCESSFUL HUNTER holds two lizards, much smaller than those painted on the rock at left, which he has captured in the forest. He will broil them over a fire that he will start by twirling a drill stick in powdered charcoal.

THE ENDLESS HUNT

THE Aborigine does not till the soil. So, like all Paleolithic people, he must make the business of finding food his full-time occupation. Hence hunting, and the animals he hunts, are bound into the ritual structure of his life. As was doubtless the case with early Stone Age people, the work involved in this endless search for food is divided between the sexes: the men are the hunters, the women are the gatherers. Every day, while the men are away on their long and arduous journeys in quest of kangaroos, lizards, emus, alligators and fish, the women trudge through the forest gathering more accessible foods—wild figs, berries, grass seed, yams, the nuts of cycad palms, small reptiles, wood grubs, snails, water lilies and wild honey.

What the women find they carry back to the campsite in palm-leaf bags or wooden bowls chopped with stone flakes from the hollow trunk of a gum tree. What the spear is to the hunter, the wooden bowl is to his woman; it is her prime possession, the product of painstaking toil and assiduous craftsmanship, which may serve as a container for food and water, as a cradle for a baby or as a carryall. Year in and year out, it is the women who are the most consistent providers. Although the Aborigine hunters are skillful at finding game in the harsh reaches of their land, they sometimes return empty-handed to women who always have something to assuage their hunger—even if it is only edible roots dug from the ground with a stick.

SETTLING A FEUD, a killer stands near his witness (*right*). The dead man's clan will insult the killer, throw spears at him—which he can dodge—and then give him a symbolic nick in the thigh. With that, the quarrel ends.

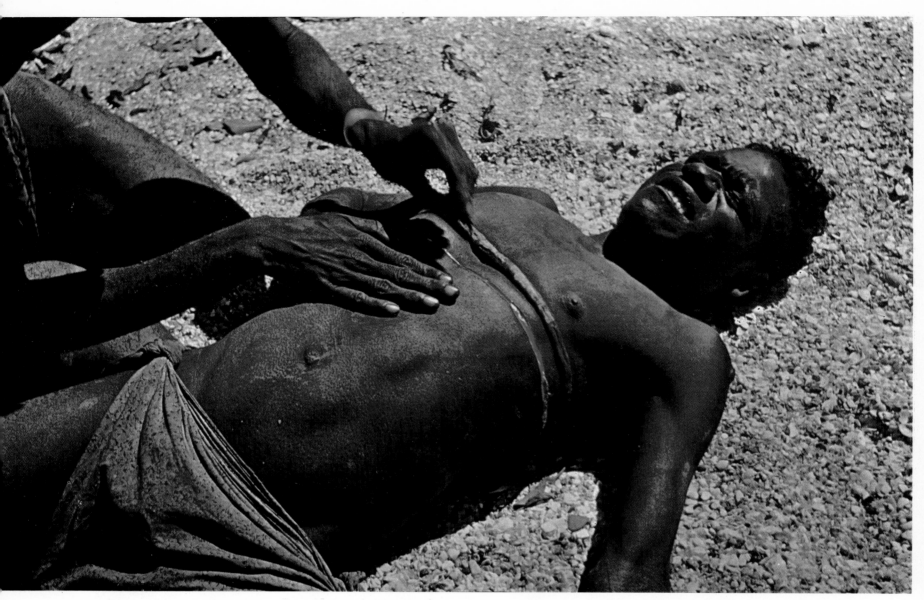

A DECORATIVE SLASH is incised on the chest of an Aborigine youth. His wounds will produce scars that are considered manly and attractive. Among some Aborigines, body scarring is one of a number of ordeals—including circumcision, bloodletting, knocking out teeth—in what scholars call a "rite of passage" that initiates a boy into adulthood and integrates him into the social order. The boy is also instructed in the myths and codes of his clan.

A WOMEN'S DANCE, perhaps performed to encourage successful hunting, is represented in this painting from the northern coast of Australia. The artist used ocher on a three-foot strip of bark peeled from a eucalyptus tree.

TOTEMS AND DANCERS

IN a material sense the Aborigines are among the poorest people in existence, yet the religion by which they live is one of rich complexity. This religion, like that of prehistoric man, is based on a belief in an unseen spirit world from which all living creatures came and to which in death they will return. Both the phenomena of nature and the destinies of men and animals, in this view, are governed by powers in the spirit domain that may be influenced by man if proper reverence is accorded them through sacred symbols, shrines and rites. To Australia's Stone Age tribesmen, life is a reciprocal partnership between man and nature. If man does his part, the spirits that activate the natural world will cooperate with him. But his part requires ritual as well as reverence: he can best aid the spirit forces by repeatedly re-enacting in symbolic ritual the deeds of his ancestral spirits. The rituals are of two kinds: "rites of passage," which qualify the individual to take a part in the clan's secret life, and "rites of intensification," in which, by acting out the exploits of the clan's legendary heroes, he preserves all its ancient traditions and expresses the unity of the clan.

Involved in every aspect of the Aborigines' religion and social life is the unifying strand of totemism—the belief that every person and group from family to tribe is the guardian of mythological symbols and is spiritually allied with, and dependent on, some animal or plant species. The totemic animal or plant is more than a mascot; it is believed to share fully in human feelings and reactions. Since a man may owe allegiance not only to his own totem but to his kin's and to his clan's as well, the totemic system is infinitely elaborate. The system does much more than regulate education, marriage and every other relationship: it insures that no man need feel alone.

A WALLABY DANCE celebrates the allegiance of a northern tribe to its totemic animal. To this particular group the wallaby is a spiritual ally, and the dancers execute a circular movement that is supposed to imitate the wallaby's distinctive hop. The Aborigines consider the dance a means of cooperating with nature and an acknowledgment of the bonds between their workaday world and the realm of nature. It is not meant to produce a magical result.

MESOLITHIC WEAPONS used by the Caribou Eskimos of northern Canada are a leister for spearing fish and a spear for killing caribou. Though both have metal parts, the designs have not changed in thousands of years.

THE CARIBOU ESKIMOS

DWELLING in the lake-pocked tundra west of Hudson Bay in northern Canada, the Caribou Eskimos present a closer analogy to the Mesolithic or Middle Stone Age period than any other people now alive. They sustain themselves like their ancient counterparts, by hunting, fishing and fowling. They grow no crops. They rely heavily on implements of antler and bone and of wood from stunted evergreen and willow. Their traditional weapons are the spear, the fishhook and the leister, or fish spear; their vehicle is the one-man kayak. Their only domesticated animal is the dog, their principal social unit the family.

The Caribou Eskimos lived in virtual isolation until 1949. Then a new radio station established by the Canadian government at Ennadai Lake brought those who lived there into closer contact with the outside world. In 1957, the way of life for many of the Caribou people changed abruptly. The herds on which they depended so heavily had become seriously depleted. In part, commercial hunting was to blame, but there were natural causes as well: many caribou were killed by tundra and forest fires; severe springs were responsible for the death of newborn calves, and the herds also suffered from disease. The government finally felt obliged to move the Caribou Eskimos. A good number of them were resettled in communities where they could be better cared for. The pictures here, taken prior to that transplanting, stand as a record of patterns of living little changed from those evolved by Mesolithic man 10,000 years ago.

There are some notable differences between the life of the Caribou Eskimos and that of Mesolithic man in Europe many thousands of years ago. Where Mesolithic hunters roamed the temperate European forests, stalking the solitary deer, the Eskimos pursue migrant herds of caribou that traverse the tundra. Where the warmer climate of the European Mesolithic produced an abundance of nuts, fruits, seeds and wild grain, the Eskimos find no edible plants on the bleak tundra save berries. They get added vegetable sustenance by eating the caribou's stomach contents, homogenized and rich in vitamins. Nevertheless, in their basic lines, the social and economic patterns of the Eskimos and those of Mesolithic man show striking parallels.

ANOWTELIK AND IYA are contemporary representatives of a Mesolithic culture. They married young. Iya, here shown when she was in her teens, is the eldest daughter of a tribe leader of her encampment (*below, right*); her

A SKILLED FOWLER uses a bow made from a caribou antler and strung with sinew cord. It shoots a wooden arrow. The Eskimos are handy with firearms, but skilled marksmen still bring down birds with bow and arrow.

husband is in his late twenties. They are dressed in caribou skins, short-haired and chestnut brown, indicating that the animals were killed in early autumn. Anowtelik, Iya and their children live in her father's double tent.

PADDLING A KAYAK, a young hunter maneuvers his craft along a rocky shore. The kayak is used mainly for hunting. When a hunter paddles his kayak within range of a swimming caribou, he kills it with his spear.

CHECKING A NET, a fisherman takes a flapping pike out of the water. The nets, made of twine, are also tended by the women. The lakes abound with fish, but the Eskimos fish only when caribou meat is running low.

AN ESKIMO ELDER, Owlijoot, repairs his kayak after a collision with a swimming caribou. He is bending a branch of arctic willow into a new rib for the boat. The skin covering has been slipped off and lies behind him.

249

CARIBOU MEAT is sliced thin by a young Eskimo woman, who will hang it in strips on the racks above her for drying. Caribou is the mainstay of the people's diet and they consume virtually the entire animal, even the blood.

A HIDE newly stripped from a caribou carcass is folded for the trip back to camp. The hunter's kayak is poised where the caribou cross, ready for immediate launching if more animals should start swimming from the far shore.

CARIBOU BONES provide a mid-morning snack for an expectant mother. She uses a splinter of rib to extract the marrow from an ankle bone. The bone pile is more than a month old, but cold weather keeps it from spoiling.

WET SKINS are pegged down to dry in the sun (*right*). Slivers of wood and of rib furnish the pegs. At the peak of the caribou run, in the autumn, the ground around a camp is covered with a crimson carpet of drying skins.

FOR A KNIFE HANDLE a caribou antler is bored with a bow drill. The drill differs from Mesolithic tools: it has an iron point.

FOR A FISHING LINE caribou sinews from the animal's sturdy back are braided by an Eskimo woman. Shorter strands of sinew lie in her lap, waiting to be twisted into the line.

FOR A MITTEN a piece of caribou hide is scraped to proper thickness. It will then be made soft and workable by being chewed.

FROM THE SHORE of Ennadai Lake, a family watches its men depart in kayaks. The hunters paddle a few miles to a point where migrating caribou swim across the lake. After spearing the animals, they tow them ashore.

AT THE TREE LINE near the lake shore two Eskimo women gather branches for firewood. The deadwood they find is brittle and light. For a hotter but smokier fire, the resin-rich green branches of dwarf arctic spruce are cut.

ON THE TUNDRA a woman picks wild cranberry leaves, which will be dried for smoking. The country offers the Eskimos little food from plants, though in summer they gather handfuls of blueberries to augment their meat diet.

A WARM FAMILY LIFE

THE Caribou Eskimos have developed practically no tribal organization. Their social structure is simple, like that of Mesolithic man: the family is its basic unit, and several families compose a camp. But the grouping of families, like the location of a camp, is temporary. Since food is largely communal and nobody owns land, there is no economic hierarchy. And since everyone shares the same background, there is no basis for social status except that created by respect for age, wisdom or skill as a hunter-fisherman. There are no tribal chieftains, but the camp's wisest hunter is treated as a headman, while the magic healer, or shaman, may exert a kind of dominance through fear of his power to cast and undo evil spells. The religious concepts are limited. There is a god named Pinga who lives in the sky, guards the souls of men and beasts and after death reincarnates them in other bodies. But neither god nor shaman governs the caribou migrations. The caribou's good will is courted by observance of many hunting taboos, and the good will of one's neighbors is more precious to the individual than private possessions. Ostracism —being ignored by the members of the camp—is the direst punishment, prescribed for such grave crimes as murder.

Labor is divided between the sexes, as in Mesolithic cultures. The man hunts and fishes, and works in bone, antler and wood. The woman pitches tents, tends the fire, collects berries and leaves, cooks, sews, gathers wood and prepares skins and meat for drying. The differentiations are not hard and fast; on occasion the man may take a turn at darning and cooking and his wife may hunt caribou.

Marriages can be contracted by parents for their children at an early age. In exchange for a daughter's hand, a father may receive a kayak and a sled. Polygamy is practiced, and the Eskimos also exchange wives among friends. The most striking feature of Eskimo family life is the intense and indulgent love for children. The existence is hard but has its diversions, notably long evening songfests and drum dances in dimly lit tents. A typical song proclaims:

> *I have been hunting caribou*
> *And I killed them all:*
> *Three of them, down by the lake.*

Every man has a song that is his own. It is unchanged from the time he composed it in his youth, and it is sung to the chant of women.

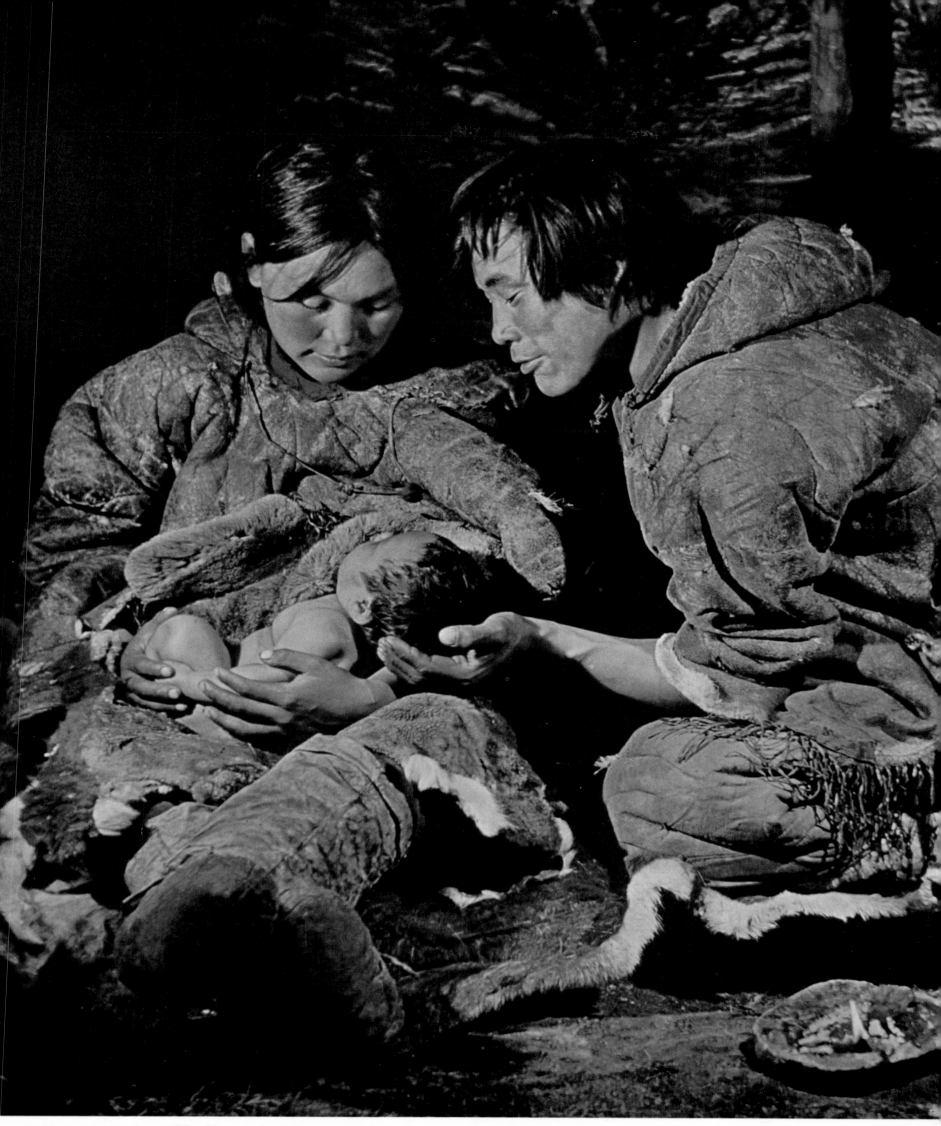

GENTLE PARENTS, Anowtelik and Iya care for their new son in the family's caribou-skin tent. Babies are treasured among the Eskimos, and every child is pampered beyond any heights of affection commonly reached in western cultures, for the birth rate here is low and infant mortality is high. Whatever a child wants, he gets. If he cries, all family activity stops until he is solaced. Scolding and punishing a child are unheard of, no matter what the offense.

THE STONE AGERS' STRUGGLE FOR SURVIVAL

THE origins of the Aborigines and Caribou Eskimos are unknown. The Aborigines do not even fit comfortably into any of the three main categories of existing man: they are not Negroid, Mongoloid or Caucasoid. On the basis of such facial characteristics as a receding forehead, beetling eyebrow ridges and prognathous jaws, they were once grouped by anthropologists with Neanderthal man. Some anthropologists related them to Cro-Magnon man, whose appearance in Europe roughly coincided with the Neanderthals' extinction there. More recently the Aborigines have been accorded a special category of their own: the Australoid.

One theory suggests that the Aborigines may be descended from an ancient people, perhaps akin to Solo man of Java, who migrated from the Asiatic mainland many millenniums ago, when the ocean levels were lower and the water gaps between land masses shorter. It is clear from the similarity of early Paleolithic implements in Europe, Africa and Asia that during the Old Stone Age early man traveled from continent to continent. Then, as the glaciers melted and the waters rose and the land causeways sank beneath the sea, the prehistoric migrants to Australia (who probably got there by way of the Malay Peninsula and the East Indies) were isolated. Through the

intervening centuries they retained unchanged their Paleolithic type of existence. One reason why a primitive Australian culture was slow in coming may be found in the inhospitable environment of the island continent's interior, which did not provide a variety of native plants or native animals suitable for domestication. Hence the first requirements for civilization—agriculture and animal husbandry—were lacking.

Only in recent years has the intricate intellectual-emotional edifice of the Australoids' religion been investigated and recognized. Their elaborate social structure, with its kinship groups and taboos, is one of the most complicated in the world, governing every one of life's activities. Their language as well has been found to be a sophisticated structure. While it has no written form, it has ample range to express subtle variations in meaning, and is rich not only in concrete terms but in abstract concepts.

In the impressive context of their cultural life, the Aborigines no longer appear so primitive to scholars as they once did. "We are very apt to underrate the philosophical powers of primitive people," says anthropologist A.P. Elkin of the University of Sydney, "but the absence of clothes and complicated economic systems does not imply an absence of thought."

THE genealogy of the Eskimos is obscure, and no one can say for certain when they first appeared on the North American continent. It is believed that during European Mesolithic times, the only inhabitants of the Western Hemisphere were a generalized Mongoloid people resembling modern American Indians, who probably had crossed the Bering Strait much earlier, when a land bridge connected Siberia and Alaska. The Eskimos, who are also Mongoloid but differ physically from the Indians, presumably followed these first pioneers across the strait in several waves, possibly from as early as 1500 B.C. to as late as the time of Christ.

Culturally, the Caribou Eskimos differed from the Greenland, Alaskan and other Canadian Eskimos in their dependence on the caribou and in their adaptation to the rigors of inland life. Their differing economy resulted in different hunting tools and techniques, and differences in clothing, shelter and religion. Because of their isolation in the inhospitable tundra, hundreds of miles from the nearest outpost of any other culture, they were not deeply affected, as the coastal Eskimos were, by any proximity to civilization.

It was not until the mid-1940s that the inland people began to have any sustained contact with the outside world and started to trade pelts for rifles, ammunition, tobacco and tea. Until then their Mesolithic way of life had remained virtually unaltered since its initial development in some unknown corner of the prehistoric world. Its persistence was a magnificent example of the durability of the human species, which nowhere on earth has ever been subjected to more rigorous conditions of existence. But the swift destruction of the Caribou Eskimos' antique world in the brief years since their

IN AUSTRALIA, on the Arnhem Land reservation, a policeman seeking clues to a band of crocodile poachers, talks with Aborigines. Crocodiles are highly prized for their skins, and by law they can be hunted only by Aborigines.

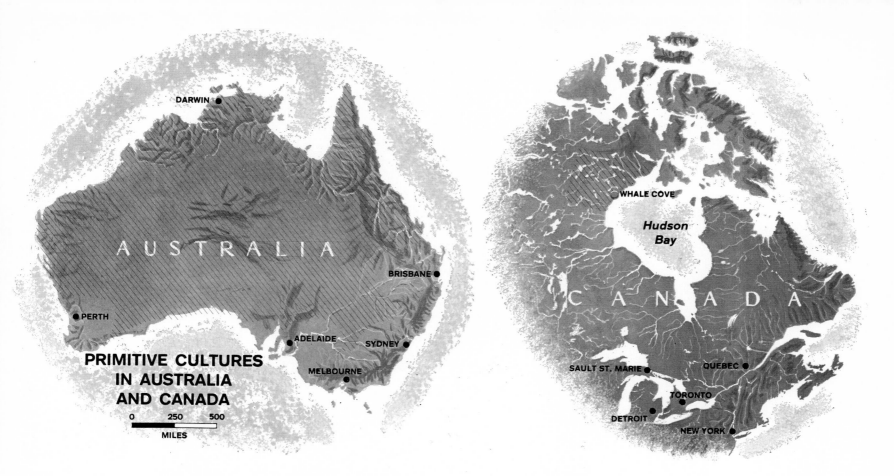

PRIMITIVE CULTURES
IN AUSTRALIA
AND CANADA

0   250   500
MILES

isolation was penetrated is an impressive example of what happens when the only basis for an economy begins to disappear and a more aggressive and prosperous culture comes on the scene.

The seeds of this destruction were sown in the last century, long before most of the Eskimos ever saw a white man. Hundreds of miles to the south of the barrens, the forest abodes of the caribou were cut, cleared and burned ahead of civilization's advance. In time, the herds themselves—once as uncountable as the buffalo had been on the American plains—were depleted by both natural disasters and the marksmanship of hunters. For the first time in Eskimo memory there were seasons when the caribou came out of the south as a trickle instead of a torrent, or failed to appear at all. The Eskimo hunters were baffled, and the shamans' magic proved impotent. Knowing no other prime food source to turn to, many people died. Explaining how essential the caribou were to the Eskimos, Richard Harrington spelled out the consequences in his book, *The Face of the Arctic:* "No caribou means no dogs, they die of starvation. It means no food, no new clothing. It means hungry people that catch any germ that comes along."

Direct exposure to the white man, when it finally came, also brought exposure to his diseases, but not enough access to his medical resources. Tuberculosis, influenza, poliomyelitis and pneumonia all took their turn in scourging the Eskimo camps. The introduction of firearms, which immediately advanced the efficiency of the hunters by thousands of years against the dwindling caribou, proved an illusory blessing. For there were seasons when no cartridges for the rifles ever reached the lakes at the far end of the supply lines; and a man grown accustomed to a gun does not easily revert to the spear.

By the time the Canadian government recognized their plight and came to their rescue, disease and starvation had reduced the Caribou Eskimos from an independent society of several thousand people to a remnant of a few hundred. The total impact of this century reduced them from hardy self-sufficiency to the level of beggarhood.

TO some observers, at this late stage, it appeared that where many original Mesolithic peoples learned to provide for the future, the Eskimo holdovers remained essentially improvident. Given a temporary opulence of caribou meat or a pound of lard or tea, they would consume it in a day, even if this meant they went hungry the next day. They seemed unwilling or unable to take present action for future needs. But such observations could not have been made until the past few years. All through the millenniums before modern men upset the balance of nature in the north, the Eskimos were anything but improvident. In the natural deepfreeze of the tundra, they cached piles of caribou carcasses between seasons, and sliced and dried other parts of their kill, as is shown in the photographs on the preceding pages of this chapter. In good times, they provided for lean times because their survival depended on it.

But in the middle of the 1950s there were only lean times. Deprived of their immemorial livelihood and dependent on handouts from the invading society that had helped take it away, the Eskimos behaved as any people may who do not know where their next meal is coming from, or whether it will come at all.

The people of Ennadai Lake emigrated to the Henik Lake Region, where they found too little game to support their hunting and trapping economy, so they moved another hundred miles to Eskimo Point on Hudson Bay. During this last trek, several of them died from exposure and lack of food. About two years after they had left Ennadai, they were finally moved to Rankin Inlet, to a spot about a mile from a small community where most of them were employed by a Canadian government project. They were put to work hunting, fishing and constructing buildings, and at various handicrafts. By 1961 most of the Rankin Inlet Eskimos had moved on to Whale Cove, about 50 miles south, where they are still able to hunt caribou as of old but are not solely dependent upon it.

Today the Caribou Eskimos' tundra home is inhabited by less than a thousand of these people, who make a hard living hunting or fishing. Only about 300 of them make their living by hunting caribou.

IN NORTHERN CANADA, near Ennadai Lake, photographer Fritz Goro feeds oatmeal to an Eskimo child. The youngster is wearing a parka made by the mother (*center*) from felt that is provided by the Canadian government.

255

BEJEWELED AND MASCARAED, a Berber girl holds the knife she uses to cut brush for fuel on the mountainside above her village of M'Semrir. She is wearing a thick application of eye shadow made of grease and antimony, which the Berber women consider medicinal as well as fashionable. Gathering fuel, the hardest of a woman's labors in this survival of Neolithic culture, will occupy half her time, from spring through fall, all her life.

NEOLITHIC LIFE OF THE PRESENT

In a remote mountain valley, Berber tribesmen follow the ways of their ancestors more than 5,000 years ago

HIGH on the southern slopes of Morocco's Atlas Mountains, in a fertile valley north of the parched plain of the Sahara, live a few thousand Berbers whose way of life has been little changed from that of prehistoric times. Like the precursors of civilization in Sumer and in Egypt long ago, these tribesmen are herders of sheep and tillers of the soil. The center of their existence is a river, the small rushing Dadès, whose waters they divert through irrigation ditches to fields of wheat and barley. In their houses of pressed mud, in their crude pots and looms, they repeat a pattern of settled life, innocent of cities, which compares closely to that of their Neolithic ancestors.

Only recently discovered by the outside world, the Berbers of the Dadès are still little known. They share an indistinct heritage with the millions of other Berbers—one tradition has it that the name derives from the Greek word for "barbarians"—who populate the North African mountains and scattered oases in the Sahara. All Berbers are descendants of the first known white settlers of North Africa, a people who began migrating from the Middle East as early as 7000 B.C. And all of them speak a dialect of the Berber language, which is a Hamitic tongue, as opposed to the Semitic tongue spoken by the Arabs around them. But over centuries of virtual isolation, the Berbers of the Dadès valley have retained customs and developed characteristics peculiar to themselves. Insulated by hundreds of miles of rugged mountains, they were left untouched by wave after wave of invaders who conquered major groups of Berbers to the north and diluted their culture. Only the Arabs, whose itinerant teachers brought Islam to the Dadès less than a thousand years ago, had the slightest influence upon Berbers there. Not until the French came a half century ago was any concerted effort made by outsiders to govern the Berber stronghold in the High Atlas, and not until 1934 was the region even nominally subdued.

The inhabitants of the Upper Dadès valley are members of two tribes, the Aït Hadiddou and the Aït Morrhad. Occasionally, they join forces for defensive purposes, but generally they go separate ways in following the seasons in an ageless pattern. As the ewes lamb and the spring rains begin, the Berbers start to work their neat little fields. Within a month their crops are planted, and the men and boys lead their flocks far up into the High Atlas, to tribal pasturelands turned green again by melted snow. Here they remain, living in black goat's-hair tents, drifting on a traditional course from pasture to pasture until the summer begins to cool. They return to the valley in time to help bring the harvest in. Late in September the Aït Hadiddou travel over 50 miles to Sidi Hmid u l'Mghanni and attend the great regional market, a three-day hubbub of sharp trading, folk dancing, religious festivals and mass marriages. Work and custom have made autumn the marriage season of the Berbers, and few marry at any other time of year. Then winter takes hold. In February, when the men's work is slackest, tribal councils are held. A month later the rains begin, the ewes lamb and the earth is broken for springtime planting.

So the seasons pass, as they have passed for centuries, while the tribesmen remain resolutely unchanged. They profess Islam, but they also perform still older rites of nature worship. They have no written language and no history beyond word-of-mouth tales and traditions. They have no art beyond traditional tribal songs and the simple tribal patterns they weave into their cloth and bake into their pottery. They still cultivate with spade and hoe and the power of their own muscles; the plow they disdain as an unnecessary gadget. They do not have the arch or the true wheel or draft animals of any kind. Yet their society is effective and responsible. In their councils every February the Berbers elect chieftains, mayors and judges by democratic processes. The assets and resources that are vital to them—water, irrigation ditches, granaries and pasturelands—are owned in common and are collectively maintained. And within the tribe—often within the family unit itself—they produce everything they need to survive.

RETURNING home at the end of the day, Berber herdsmen (*above*) guide their sheep and goats to the fortresslike village of Aït M'Hand.

IN SPRING Berbers preparing for the planting season (*left*) work their fields late into the afternoon. Beyond them rises the village of Aït Attiq.

HERDING AND PLANTING
IN THE DADES VALLEY

THE Upper Dadès lies 250 difficult miles east of the market center of Marrakesh. To the north, tiers of bleak mountains, some with snow-clad 13,000-foot summits, separate the Dadès fields and dozens of small villages from the fringe of civilization along the coast of Morocco. In an arc to the south stretches the vast Sahara. Cut into the High Atlas, the valley itself is only 15 miles long and nowhere more than three miles wide. In this narrow trough, treeless except for a few birches along the clear green Dadès River, there is enough arable land to grow a subsistence crop, but little more. After the bitter winters,

the rains of April barely moisten the soil for springtime planting. But through the blazing hot summers the *targa*, the canals of the Berbers' ancient irrigation system, sustain their fields of wheat, barley and vegetables.

With only two and a half acres in the average family holding, the Aït Hadiddou and the Aït Morrhad—these tribal names mean "the people of" Hadiddou and of Morrhad—look beyond their valley to the patchwork of tribal pasturage staked out by their ancestors long ago in other valleys and on mountainsides beyond other tribes. Thither they send part of each family to herd their precious flocks through the summer; back in the home valley during the winter they feed the animals on the stalks and hulls of their meager harvest. In their semi-nomadic economy these Berbers must both farm and herd in order to survive; their livestock—sheep and goats and a few cattle—give them a little surplus with which the tribesmen can purchase a few luxuries and amenities, such as sugar, cloth for women's dresses, and beads.

INTRICATE HAIRCUT of a shepherd boy conforms to tribal style. The pattern of braids and shaved spots indicates his family saint. At puberty his head will be completely shaved to mark the estate of Berber manhood.

"IT IS THE CUSTOM"

A MIXTURE of tribal customs, blood relationships and rudimentary democratic processes controls the life of the Dadès communities. Fields and livestock are privately owned; granaries and grazing land are communal property. It is the responsibility of everyone to protect the granaries and maintain the irrigation ditches.

The smallest political unit in this society is the *ighs,* a group of related families often representing five generations descended from a common male ancestor, whose members live together in a single village. Several villages make up a clan, several clans a tribe. The confederation, largest unit in the Berber society, is a loose organization of tribes brought together for a special purpose, usually for defense or to combine their common grazing lands. The confederation lacks the strong, long-standing allegiances that hold the tribes together. Typically, the Aït Hadiddou and the Aït Morrhad joined a confederation to fight another collection of nearby tribes, but once the issue was decided they separated.

In recent years the tribesmen have relied on more peaceful methods of settling disputes. Criminal cases, from petty theft to rape and murder, are brought before a *jemaa n'lorf,* or court of customary law, consisting of seven judges elected for a three-year term (*opposite*). The court also sits in civil actions involving property or inheritance rights. In these cases the judges make it their goal to arrive at a decision satisfactory to all parties. They generally succeed. Deadlocks and hot tempers they treat by the simple expedient of adjournment—if necessary for as long as 20 years.

In the tribal councils held each February, the men cast their vote for political officers as well as judges. Each village elects a *mokallif,* or mayor, to serve for one year. Each tribe elects an *amrhar,* or chieftain, to serve for a year; in order to rotate the office among the clans an *amrhar* may not succeed himself.

With infinite embellishments and very few changes, these institutions have sufficed for countless centuries. As the tribesmen like to say with a shrug of the shoulders, *"Aya d'asrif"*—"It is the custom."

TATTOOED HADIDDOU, a young girl of Aït Tilmi, carries her baby brother papoose-fashion in a fold of a blanket. Her hair was cropped in childhood; now she wears bangs in front and pigtails, all covered by a headdress.

260

HADIDDOU TRIBESMAN, Sa'id u Muha (*opposite*), holds a month-old kid in the doorway of his house near the village of Aït Tilmi. His single earring shows he was born on Wednesday, a lucky day to the Hadiddou.

THE COURT OF CUSTOM of the Aït Hadiddou (*above*) hears a witness testify in a rape case. The elected judges, who are guided by ancient tribal lore, found the witnesses contradictory and acquitted the accused man.

TENDING SHEEP, an eight-year-old boy stands watch amongst the graves of a burial ground. The burnoose he wears is made of homespun woven by the women of his family. He is held fully responsible for the flock under his care and may be severely punished if an animal is lost.

BUILDING A HOUSE, tribesmen dump mud into a wooden mold. The mud is pounded down; more is added and pounded until the mold is full. Then its sides are removed and the mud hardens. Houses of this type are quickly built, quickly damaged by rain and always being fixed.

BAKING POTTERY, a craftsman refuels his fire with brush. In his kiln, which is made of pressed mud, shards of old pots hold new pots in place.

DOING LAUNDRY, a Berber tribesman and his wife trample their soaked garments on a flat rock above an irrigation ditch. The man washes only his heavy burnoose; his wife launders all the lighter clothes. Among the tribes of the Upper Dadès valley, all work is precisely divided between the sexes. After finishing his stint and smoking a pipe of *kif* (hashish), the man will ride a mule back home. His wife will follow him on foot with the laundry.

MAN'S WORK
IN A MAN'S SOCIETY

AMONG the tribes of the Upper Dadès, only a few men are afflu-ent—i.e., they have more than one wife in their home or more than 50 to 100 sheep in their flock. The rest live out their lives just above the subsistence level. While trades like pottery making (*opposite*) have a few practitioners, the work of the community is mostly general in character. In the traditional division of labor between the sexes, the men carry the lighter share of the day-to-day work, though much of the heavy seasonal work is theirs.

Very much master in his own house, the tribesman spends most of his time outside it. In addition to herding, he is responsible for house-building and repair, for guarding the communal granaries against marauding nomads from the desert, for irrigating the fields and for maintaining the *targa,* through which water from the Dadès flows in three stages to his individual plot. He also hoes the hard rocky earth each spring, a labor that requires all his strength. And he is on hand to harvest in the fall.

A Berber's work is highly seasonal, and a tribesman need not be a wealthy man to have his leisure. In the winter, in the uplands in summer, on many afternoons in early spring and late fall, and all day at the markets he has plenty of time for visiting and chatting, drinking the treacly mint tea the Berbers love and smoking *kif*.

IRRIGATING THE FIELDS, a Berber opens a primary ditch, letting precious river water flow into secondary channels below. Completely dependent on irrigation for their crops, tribesmen water each section on a strict schedule.

HOMEWARD BOUND with brush, three Hadiddou women dogtrot across barren slopes, bent double under their 100-pound loads. Coarse grass is the only fuel in this land, where trees are too scarce to be burned. The women set out from their village before dawn to gather the brush in the mountains. With their towering burdens balanced and held down by stones, they fight their way home through blustery winds in time to prepare the midday meal.

WOMAN'S WORK

THE life of a Berber woman in the valley of the Upper Dadès is changeless years of heavy labor. From the age of eight—as soon as she is strong enough to carry brush or dexterous enough to braid grass mats—she toils. The men till the fields in spring and help with the harvest in fall, but the tribeswomen remain responsible for the fields, cultivating early and late through the scorching summers. They also spin and weave, cook and bake, milk the livestock and mill the grain. Their most onerous task is the gathering of brush. By dawn each morning they are on their way from the valley to the mountains. Hurrying from slope to slope they crop the fibrous quick-burning grass with sickle-like knives. As the season's work strips nearby hills, they have to forage farther. By late autumn they may have to trot as far as 10 miles home, bent double under their towering burdens, and their houses are crammed upstairs and down with brush stored up against the winter cold.

Women may not be seen in the "shameful" act of riding a mule or a donkey. They may arrange to buy, sell or trade, but only their men may complete transactions. A widow may inherit property, but a close male relative of her husband is appointed by the court of custom to administer it. The widow may not sell her land without the executor's permission; for handling the sale he receives—and thus keeps in the family—a third of the land. The patrilineal tradition is strong: on marrying, a woman does not take her husband's surname but retains her father's.

The Aït Hadiddou are probably the most conservative of the Moroccan Berbers, but they allow women to participate in the festivities of the fall market, which also functions as a "marriage mart." Then mass weddings are performed, after which the new couples spend their first night together in a great connubial tent. And a Hadiddou woman may divorce her husband simply by moving out of his house.

SPINNING YARN in Neolithic fashion, a Saharan Negro woman adopted by the Aït Morrhad winds tufts of wool onto a spindle weighted with a whorl.

AT MARKET, three women in the tribal striped blankets of the Aït Hadiddou await a buyer for their cow. The market, a small *souk* at the village of Aït Tilmi, is held every Friday. For the men it is a day of social pleasures with interruptions for business. The women, who come only for business but cannot complete a transaction, summon their men to haggle over the price.

WEAVING A BURNOOSE, two Berber women work together at a loom, an early Neolithic invention. Strands of wool strung vertically on the frame form the warp, through which the women weave the horizontal strands of the woof. It will take 10 days to complete the garment. They stop on Fridays, for to work with wool on the Moslem Sabbath is considered bad luck.

GRINDING GRAIN between Neolithic millstones, two sisters chat gaily as they work. Aïcha M' Bark, the girl at the left, is 14 years old and wears the simple scarf headdress of a virgin. Her sister, Itto M' Bark, 16, shows she is married by wearing a more elaborate headdress, which reinforces her braids with wooden frames; but she retains her father's surname according to tribal custom.

BREWING TEA, a tribesman (*center*) offers hospitality to a neighbor in his family's second-floor living area. His 13-year-old daughter (*left*) shapes a flat loaf of bread while his younger daughter brings fuel from a brush pile in the background. To combat the winter cold, the Berbers build their houses with a few tiny windows that admit only thin shafts of light. The body heat of sheep and cattle, quartered on the ground floor, helps warm the house.

THE DADES BERBERS AND OTHER NEOLITHIC PEOPLES

TODAY the Aït Hadiddou and the Aït Morrhad, including tribal segments living outside the Dadès valley, number about 30,000. This represents a population rise of 10 per cent since 1955 and keeps the pressures among the Berbers increasing apace with pressures from the outside world. More and more often, the old and new now meet in the lost valley; after many encounters, progress sometimes makes a small net gain.

The Berbers' first real introduction to modern ways came from the French Office of Indigenous Affairs. While France had purposefully kept the mountain tribesmen insulated in the so-called "Zone of Insecurity," using them as a counterbalance to the more advanced and nationalistic Arabs, Indigenous Affairs officers initiated some measures aimed at raising the tribal standard of living. Since Morocco became independent in 1956, the Moroccan government has carried this program further among the Berbers. A school-building program is accompanied by efforts to create pupils by curbing child labor. But with their livelihood—indeed, their very survival—depending on the flocks, the tribesmen cannot spare their shepherd sons, least of all during the half year they must spend in mountain pasturage. To shorten this seasonal absence, the government is trying a plan to install local fodder storehouses, but the cost of fodder and of transporting it to the inaccessible valley is discouragingly high. A paved road is being built into the heart of Aït Hadiddou country that would reduce the cost of fodder imports, but the road is far from complete. To reduce the need of fodder imports, new pastures in the arid perimeter of the valley itself are being developed, but this means drilling water holes and paving the irrigation ditches to save waste, both costly operations. Thus the crux of the problem—that the semi-nomads must be permanently settled before they can make any sustained progress—is far more complicated than breaking down other old tribal traditions.

The tribesmen themselves have recently shown a growing interest in doing something about bettering their lot. The spark was kindled by the local elections of May 1960—the nation's first. In these elections, communes were set up, each with its own budget, to manage local affairs. A system of regional administration links the communes to a governor at Ksar es Souk. Now that they have a voice in their own affairs, tribesmen are eager to discuss and even suggest improvements. Their new attitude has yet to be tested by deep and sweeping innovations. But the tribesmen of the Rif Mountains to the northeast 40 years ago accepted the abolition of the collective oath, a timeless Berber institution that permits male relatives of an accused man to exculpate him by swearing his innocence in public.

While government technicians work to draw the tribesmen into the present, scholars in increasing numbers try to figure out the pattern of the Berber past. Anthropologists believe that the coastal Berbers had reached a Neolithic level some 3,000 years before the Roman conquest about 150 B.C., and that people from the eastern Mediterranean were common ancestors to many of the present-day tribesmen. These migrants from the east, who settled along the North African coast over the centuries after 10,000 B.C., were the main

NEW GUINEAN with ritual ax and feathered nosepiece cultivates taro and yams on his poor hilly land.

FINNISH LAPP, hooded nomad of the Arctic tundra, depends on reindeer for food, clothing and shelter.

TODA HERDSMAN, whose people believe some buffaloes to be sacred, ekes out a living in southern India.

AINU CHIEFTAIN in robe of woven bark heads hunting and fishing tribal community in northern Japan.

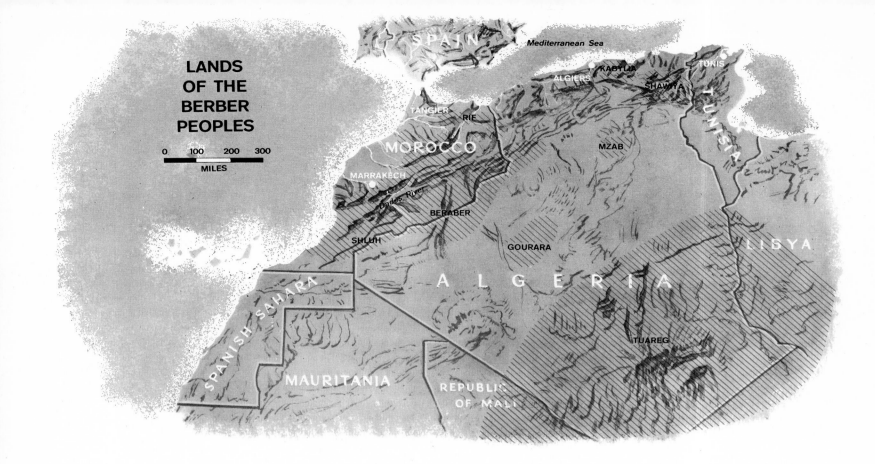

LANDS OF THE BERBER PEOPLES

0 100 200 300
MILES

settlers of the area. They drove out or so completely absorbed the indigenous aborigines as to leave little trace of them. There is speculation that this early intermingling of peoples created local variations in stock that became fixed when the various tribes, displaced by waves of invaders, isolated themselves in mountain valleys and desert oases. Thus the Aït Hadiddou and Aït Morrhad bear little resemblance to the plump, pallid Mzabites, the Berbers of the "desert within a desert in central Algeria." Both seem unrelated to the lean, long-boned Tuareg people, once fierce warriors now reduced to breeding camels. With the major Berber groups also showing great variations of blond and red hair, blue and green eyes, broad and small faces, the noted French sociologist G. H. Bousquet asserts that there is no Berber people; there are only Berber-speaking peoples.

But in language the Berbers are fully as complex as in racial stock. While a Berber language is spoken by about 7,000,000 people from the Atlantic coast of Africa to the Libyan Desert, many speak Arabic as well as Berber, and some speak Berber dialects, unintelligible to Berbers from other regions. The percentage of Berbers speaking Arabic is on the increase. Basic to the lag of Berber speech is the lack of a written language: only the dialect of the Tuareg has its own script. Without a script applicable to all dialects and acceptable to all groups, it is only a matter of time before the Berbers lose the last link to their common past and their main claim to a national identity.

The Berbers are only a small fraction of the peoples all over the world who have progressed not much further than the agricultural revolution; and daily, as the modern world encroaches closer upon them, these Neolithic peoples grow in importance. Each society, created in the image of its own land, differs as sharply as the Berbers do among themselves.

SOME groups, like the Toda of southern India and the Lapps, are herders but not farmers. Tribes in extreme climates such as the Camayura Indians of Brazil and the Ainus in northern Japan have never passed the most primitive steps toward a food-producing economy: the Camayura grow a little tobacco and occasionally plant some corn; the Ainus cultivate only meager gardens and also still depend on hunting and fishing, but with domesticated dogs to help them. Some New Guinea tribes preserve one of the earliest forms of agriculture, planting taro until the soil is exhausted, then moving on to new fields. They are among the few food producers who are classically Neolithic; that is, utilizing polished stone implements.

Like the Berbers of the High Atlas in Morocco, most peoples otherwise at a Neolithic level, such as the Polynesians, have long since received iron and steel tools from more advanced cultures superimposed on their own. Before this happened in America, Indians such as the Pueblo tribes had achieved advanced agricultural techniques with a complex irrigation system and lived in equally advanced settled communities on a level similar to that of the Berbers. The iron hoes and flashlights trickling into the Dadès valley have done fundamentally little to change the life the Berber tribesmen have lived for centuries.

OLD POLYNESIAN belongs to an island people who are famed seamen with a still primitive economy.

PICURI FARMER of the American Southwest lives in a pueblo settlement supplied by irrigated gardens.

PREPARING FOR WRESTLING MATCH, Camayura Indians of Brazil's Mato Grosso bind protective fibers around their knees and ankles. Hunters and fishermen, they also plant with primitive implements in poor jungle soil.

269

BHAIRAB THE TERRIBLE ONE, glaring from a shrine in the city of Kathmandu, receives an offering in the mouth of a serpent that forms a necklace around the statue. Bhairab, an incarnation of the Hindu god Siva, is worshiped by Buddhists as well as Hindus, and is one of hundreds that pervade the daily lives of the Nepalese and dominate their culture. The offering was made at the festival of Indra Jatra, celebrating the fall harvest.

16

ANCIENT WAYS
IN KATHMANDU

The cities in a sheltered valley of Nepal perpetuate living patterns similar to those of early civilizations

BETWEEN India and Tibet is a narrow strip of mountain-bound land that has for centuries been inhabited by millions of people. This is the Kingdom of Nepal. Most of the Nepalese live in scattered settlements and herd flocks on the plunging slopes of the Himalayas or farm fields that range from poor and rocky plots to fertile plainlands. In Nepal's Kathmandu Valley, however, there persists a civilization which in complexity of structure and elaborateness of religion is reminiscent of Sumer at the dawn of history and of ancient Egypt. Three cities of the valley carry on this civilization. They are the capital, Kathmandu, Patan and Bhatgaon, all over a thousand years old.

Kathmandu Valley is the fertile centerpiece in a string of Middle Himalayan valleys that stretches east and west through the 500-mile length of the kingdom. Northward the mountains rise and thicken into a great white wall that includes nine of the world's 14 highest peaks. To the south the way is barred by a belt of rugged hills, forested and choked with 15-foot elephant grass, and tangled jungles made dangerous by tigers. On every side, access to the inner kingdom is so hard and precipitous that for centuries the only goods to reach or depart from Kathmandu were carried on the backs of porters.

Despite its geographic defenses, Nepal fell often to peoples of determined strength. Its southern barrier was probably the first to be penetrated—by a Negroid people thought to be the original settlers of the Indian subcontinent. Mongolian peoples followed, some of them driven north by Indo-Aryans expanding their foothold in northern India. The Indo-Aryans themselves arrived in Nepal between 1000 and 700 B.C. In the Seventh Century A.D., an invasion force from Tibet overran Nepal on the way into India. In the 14th Century came a new ruling dynasty, the Malla kings; and in 1769 the fragmented realm of the Mallas was conquered by Gurkha warriors, themselves then being driven out of India by the Moslem invaders. From all

comers the civilization of Kathmandu Valley borrowed and adapted. It absorbed rather than being absorbed. The Newars, the people primarily responsible for developing the civilization, emerge indistinctly out of Nepalese legend. It is not known exactly where they came from or when they arrived, but it seems likely that their culture was established in Kathmandu Valley by 563 B.C., when the founder of Buddhism, Gautama Buddha, was born in what is now southwestern Nepal. The Newars showed at a very early date unusual talent as organizers and craftsmen. They etched out the irrigation net that crisscrosses the valley floor, and here, ever since, Newar farmers have been planting rice, their main and ritual food. They cut terraces into the dizzying hillsides and planted fields, which were watered by the monsoon rains. Their wood carvers fashioned Hindu and Buddhist gods; their architects designed temples to house them; their builders erected the temples in wood, stone and brass. They used brick for the many-storied homes of the huge Newar families. The three Newar cities of Kathmandu, Patan and Bhatgaon rose less than seven miles apart. In the face of war, occupation and earthquake, these cities have come through the centuries largely unchanged. They are the nucleus of a medieval state only recently opened to the modern world outside.

Short and tan-skinned, the people of these cities dwell among soaring temples and monoliths, locked into their past as into the valley by the compass of mountains around them. They adhere to the Buddhist and Hindu faiths, and many of them practice both in common rites. They painstakingly observe an intricate caste system, based on traditional family trades and crafts, which divides them into innumerable social compartments. Despite the diversity of their gods, these people are practically united in worship; and for all the strictures of caste, they are tolerant of exceptions and social climbing. A life rich in ceremony and a society satisfying in its firm order sustain them as the modern world impinges on ancient Nepal.

IN KATHMANDU VALLEY, whose northern rim is overhung by 20,000-foot peaks of the Himalayas, the capital city of Kathmandu is surrounded on all sides by irrigated fields. The tall white column at right, sometimes called "Bhim Sen's Folly" after the prime minister who built it in the 1820s, stands 150 feet high. Beyond it lie the vast Singha Durbar Palace, which is the seat of Nepal's government, and Tri Chandra College. In the old quarter, to the

left of the column, most of the city's 105,000 people live crowded together in shapeless squares and narrow streets among golden-roofed temples. The rambling white structure in the old quarter is the former palace of the Malla kings.

BEARING SUPPLIES, Nepalese porters plod past a village reservoir. For centuries, trade in and out of Kathmandu Valley has depended on the sure step and strong backs of these porters. Some can carry 160-pound loads.

TRADE AND THE CITY

SHAPED like a maple leaf and surrounded by mountains almost a mile high, Kathmandu Valley contains 209 square miles of fertile land and more than 400,000 people. Farming is the basic work of the valley, and it is carried on intensively by the large clan-like families that are the basic unit of the valley society. Each day members of a farming family go out to work their plot, which is usually rented and often as small as one tenth of an acre. The other members remain at home plying the traditional trade or craft that long ago determined their caste. A farmer's home may be one of the scores of thatch-roofed hamlets that dot the rice fields. But the valley's three cities—Kathmandu, Patan and Bhatgaon—lie within easy walking distance of most fields, and many members of the population are city dwellers as well as farmers.

Inside the cities, the complex interchange of goods and services that helped to create them in the first place, centuries ago, goes on in coin and kind in the caste-prescribed way. The pottery makers work in their workshops, the oil-pressers in their *sah,* and the priests officiate in their temples. Innumerable religious holidays that are always marked by lavish ceremonies, the costs of which sometimes keep people in debt for a year, supplement the bustle of commerce. The three cities, less than seven miles apart, have long since outgrown the walls that were built to defend them in the 18th Century twilight of the Malla kings, when each was a tiny kingdom at war with the others. They continue to thrive in the heart of the mountain valley.

IN THE STREET OF TEMPLES at the center of Patan's main square (*above*), citizens gather in knots to watch preparations for a celebration. The oldest city in the valley, a mile and a half southeast of Kathmandu, Patan reached its prominence as a Buddhist city, though its outward appearance and most of its 41,000 people are Hindu. Around the colonnaded temple of Krishna (*above, left, and below*), vendors hawk guavas. In the foreground at the right

IN AN ORNATE WINDOW built out over the street, a girl of Patan gazes from her tile-roofed home. The triple-arched frame and latticework screen were handmade by Newar craftsmen, who became famous throughout Asia.

above, along the wall of the Old Palace, craftsmen are painting the figures of the gods in brilliant colors. Under the tiered eaves, which are common to Patan's scores of temples, statues of mythological animals line the street.

SHRINES OF MANY GODS

ACCORDING to Nepalese legend, in 250 B.C. the Indian emperor Asoka visited his northern realm and built five stupa shrines, four at the cardinal points of the compass and one in the center. Thus he founded the city of Patan in the form of the Buddhist Wheel of the Law. In legend, too, Bhatgaon was built in the hourglass shape of the drum of the Hindu deity Mahadea, and Kathmandu in the form of the sword of the goddess Devi. As temples, shrines and monoliths arose to honor the gods, the cities grew up around them. About the Sixth Century A.D. the tiered-roof pagoda style (*above*) was developed by Nepalese architects for the temples. Their fame spread abroad, and in the 13th Century a troop of Nepalese temple artists was summoned to build a shrine of gold for the fabled Kublai Khan, Emperor of China. Many of the early Nepalese temples, as well as the original five at Patan attributed to Asoka, are still standing.

DEVIL DANCERS in grotesque masks, who act out the battles of the gods, march into Bhatgaon's Durbar Square. They have just come from a nearby temple where a buffalo was sacrificed for the spring festival of Holi.

275

A SHERPA PORTER, a tribesman of the Great Himalayas (*below*), hefts a load near Pokhara, west of Kathmandu Valley. Sherpas haul for caravans that trade across the mountains and act as porters for mountain climbers.

A NEWAR PEASANT, preparing to weave cloth for a skirt, plays out yarn on a wooden frame in the courtyard of her Kathmandu home. All Newar women wear full-length, plain black skirts with one band of color around the bottom.

TAMANG GIRLS wearing holiday silks and traditional jewelry (*above*) pause in their tour of Kathmandu city to enter a temple in the marketplace. They are wearing long Tamang pigtails, and their nose rings and sunburst headpieces, made of gold by Tamang smiths, are also traditional. These girls live in the Great Himalayas to the northeast of Kathmandu Valley; they were making one of their infrequent visits to town to attend the king's coronation.

A MELANGE OF PEOPLE

AT least 10 broad ethnic groups and many smaller ones can be distinguished in Nepal, each with its own combination of physical traits and cultural characteristics. Showing Tibetan influences, the Nepalese along the northern border—peoples like the Tamang and the Sherpa (*above and left*)—are generally short, yellow-skinned and Buddhist, and they speak Tibeto-Burmese dialects. Under Indian influences, the Nepalese along the southern border tend to be relatively tall, dark-skinned and Hindu; they speak Indo-Aryan dialects. Between the two bands, in the valleys of the Middle Himalayas, the tides of migration have produced a zone of great mixture, which shows its most spectacular results at the focal point, Kathmandu Valley.

Typical of the admixture in Kathmandu are the Newars, whose ancestors initially developed the valley civilization. In coloring and in height the Newars are somewhere between the Mongolian and the Indo-Aryan; they speak Newari, which is a Tibeto-Burmese language, and write in a Sanskrit script, which is Indo-Aryan; and they are both Hindu and Buddhist. Because of the Newars' predominance and because their culture is so deep-rooted, their name has become almost synonymous with Kathmandu Valley, and outsiders are inclined to regard all its residents as Newari. The various tribesmen who have filtered into the valley after them follow many of their own distinct cultural patterns, as do the ruling-class Gurkhas. But all live in the shadow of the Newar civilization as it evolved in the ancient past.

TRANSPLANTING RICE, a Newar woman with her sleeping baby bound to her back plucks young shoots from the family field near her house. In Kathmandu, men do the plowing and delegate planting and weeding to the women.

IN THE KITCHEN on the third floor, two women of the Prajapati family heat milk on a hearth. The family's servants are casteless Untouchables whose contact is thought to pollute the food, so they are barred from the kitchen.

IN THE QUADRANGLE of the Prajapati's 80-year-old home, newly made pots are set out to dry. In front of the five-story wing of the house (*left*) stand a low utility shed (*center*) and a small shrine (*right*) that is open to the public.

AT THE TEMPLE OF RAM, Rudra Bahadur Prajapati, the headman of the pottery-making family whose members surround him, flings a handful of festive red Holi powder at a hired musician. To celebrate Holi, a feast of fun

A FAMILY OF POTTERS

THE joint or extended family unit, whose members are related on the male descent side and live together in one home, exists at all caste levels in Kathmandu Valley. Typical of the institution, but far wealthier than most families, is the large clan shown on these pages. The Prajapati are pottery makers, a subcaste of the agriculturists' caste. In their quadrangular compound on the outskirts of Bhatgaon, six miles east of Kathmandu, live 60-year-old headman Rudra Bahadur, his second wife, his five sons and their wives, his three unmarried daughters, his three younger brothers and their wives, and dozens of grandchildren and great-grandchildren—80 members in all. They work together, worship together, keep all their funds in a common coffer and devote countless hours to safeguarding their caste status by following the rules of ritual cleanliness. The Prajapati have lived in Bhatgaon since 1324, when their ancestors arrived from India. Their affluence dates back 50 years to Rudra Bahadur's grandfather, who conducted a surveying mission for the prime minister and received as a reward all the precious valley land he could see from his house —26 acres. Since then the family has bought 660 acres of farmland along Nepal's southern border, where 35 of its members now live. Over three quarters of the family income is derived from land rentals, but the Prajapati continue to practice their traditional craft.

that falls late in February, the family sacrificed a goat. For the ceremony they went to a temple dedicated to Ganesh, the elephant god, son of Siva. After the sacrifice, their musicians led them homeward in a gay procession, singing and playing *bhajans* (religious songs). They paused on the way to offer a prayer at the temple of Ram, built by Rudra Bahadur's grandfather. At temples devoted to the Hindu god Ram, animal sacrifices are prohibited.

SHAPING A POT, Radha Krishna Prajapati, a 14-year-old with three years' experience in the family's traditional craft, spins the wet clay vessel on a potter's wheel. After the pot dries, baking turns it a soft reddish brown.

TAKING LESSONS from a Brahman tutor, a practice favored by the well-to-do, children of the family study Nepali and English before leaving for public school. They are not taught to read or write Newari, their speaking language.

BATHING IN HOLY WATERS, devout Hindus worship at Pashupatinath, the shrine of the Lord of Beasts, on the Bagmati River outside the city of Kathmandu. The river is revered by Hindus as a source of the sacred Ganges.

Behind the bathers at the left stand two boothlike *ghats* in which members of royalty are cremated. On the waterside steps at the center sick people wait to die while touching the river. They thus try to prevent reincarnation.

THE TEMPLE OF BODNATH, strung with Buddhist prayer flags, towers over Kathmandu Valley. A favorite wintering place for Buddhist pilgrims who come to it from the north, Bodnath has a Tibetan lama as its chief custodian.

A BLENDING OF FAITHS

OF Kathmandu Valley's more than 2,500 shrines, only a few—the ones on this page are examples—remain purely Hindu or purely Buddhist. In the distant past, the faith of the valley people reflected the religious developments that took place to the south in India. First came Hinduism. This was based on worship of a wide proliferation of gods, adopted from primitive nature worship and summed up in one eternal spirit called Brahma. Hinduism also had rigid racial and class barriers—a caste system—established by its Indo-Aryan founders to differentiate themselves from the indigenous Negroid population of India. It was partly to reform the caste system of early Hinduism that Buddha began his teachings. During the following centuries, when Buddhism reached the valley, most of the people became Buddhists. In the struggle for popularity, Buddhism developed a new and less austere school, but the enormous pantheon of Hinduism claimed more adherents and assimilated the competitive gods of the new Buddhism as rapidly as they arose. A so-called tantric cult, based on magical formulas, among other things, spread after the Seventh Century A.D., winning followers among Hindus and Buddhists alike and thus Hinduizing Buddhism even further. In India the contest between the two major religions ended about a thousand years ago with the virtual extinction of Buddhism. Only in Kathmandu Valley did the two live on together, side by side and strangely intermixed.

A CLASSIC BUDDHA in the posture of enlightenment (*right*) is attended by sacred monkeys. This is one of six Buddhas that guard the steps leading up a hill to the temple of Swayambhunath, holiest Buddhist shrine in the valley.

GIANT BUDDHAS brought from temples in and around Kathmandu (*above*) await the coronation parade under fringed sunshades, symbolic of majesty. They have been given places of honor even though the king is a Hindu.

GLIMPSING THE GOD-KING, a Nepalese (*below*) outside the palace clasps his hands in *namaskara*, the posture of reverence. The king, emerging to begin his coronation parade (*opposite*), is revered as Vishnu in human form.

KING AND LIVING DEITY

AS godhood and mankind met in ancient Egypt in the person of the pharaoh, so they meet today in Nepal in the person of Mahendra Bir Bikram, ninth king of the Shah Dynasty. The king is worshiped by his people as the representative of Vishnu on earth, and through a system of district administrators he rules areas very remote indeed from his central government. Though he was king in fact for a year after his father's death, Mahendra did not begin his reign officially until 10:43 a.m. on May 2, 1956, the precise moment selected by his royal astrologers, when the helmetlike crown of state was placed on his head by his Hindu priests. That colorful ceremony, together with the festive aftermath shown on these pages, attracted world-wide attention and hastened the emergence of Nepal from isolation and from the past.

Kingship in Nepal has a history as murky and violent as the legends of the gods, and Mahendra is only the second monarch in modern times to wield his full powers as "King of Kings, Five Times Godly, Valorous Warrior and Divine Emperor." Modern Nepal was created and Mahendra's line installed on the throne in 1769, when the Gurkhas united by conquest the three warring realms of the Mallas in Kathmandu Valley. But the Shah kings soon fell under the sway of the aristocratic Rana family. Through 104 years marked by court intrigue, the Ranas ruled the land as hereditary prime ministers while the kings remained virtual prisoners in their gilded palaces. Finally, in 1950, King Tribhuvana staged a *coup d'état*, declared a constitutional monarchy and opened his country to visitors from the outside world. Mahendra is following his father's progressive policies.

THE NEWLY CROWNED KING rides an elephant in splendid array through Hanuman Dhoka, the square of the Monkey God, in the heart of Kathmandu. A servant trots alongside carrying the ladder that King Mahendra and Queen Ratna Devi will use to dismount from their golden howdah after they tour the temples. The procession is led by the royal guard and soldiers of the regular Nepalese army, uniformed in the style of the British.

THE NEW PROBLEMS
OF AN OLD KINGDOM

NEPAL is not yet an effective nation. It is Kathmandu Valley and a map-maker's line drawn around thousands of primitive, isolated settlements, many of them overpopulated and most of them underfed. The some nine million Nepalese have no tradition as a nation and no common national culture. Nepal does have a national language now spoken by much of the population. This is Nepal as it has been for centuries—a group of tribal societies variously stratified by caste and barren of the arts, architecture and literature of Kathmandu Valley.

Nepal brings into the modern world a staggering catalog of problems—problems as old, varied and complex as the civilization of Kathmandu Valley. Over three million Nepalese along the southern border are at times disastrously flooded. The rate of literacy is low—somewhere between 2 and 9 per cent. King Mahendra has made himself a model for monogamy, but polygamy still exists. Many ancient customs persist. Girls are sometimes "married" first to trees, so that they may not suffer the disadvantages of widowhood should their human husbands die before them. Pockets of slavery still persist. Bartering is still the main method of trade and payment. Rails and paved roads are so rare that the first wheel seen in Nepal, besides those used for making pottery, appeared as late as 1950 on an airplane flown in from India to relieve a local shortage of rice. The cost of living is high and, with an average per capita income of about $30 a year, the standard of living is wretchedly low. Only slightly more than 10 per cent, or 6,476 square miles, of Nepal's total area is under cultivation, but this is practically every inch of the rugged country's arable land. The Nepalese take extreme measures to utilize the land: they terrace hillsides, using hand tools, to a height of 10,000 feet above sea level. The steadily increasing population has produced subdivision and redivision of land, about two thirds of which is cultivated by tenant farmers under various systems. Farms of half an acre are self-sufficient and farms of over two acres may produce a marketable surplus. But while great landlords own up to a million acres, private or rented holdings of less than half an acre continue to be the rule despite attempted land reform. The economy stagnates because there is no middle class to moderate the extremes of wealth and poverty. The country is so drastically cut up by mountains that it takes three weeks to travel some 300 miles from the central capital in the Valley of Kathmandu to the end of the kingdom.

THE valley continues to be the substance of the kingdom, and it is here that the changes that have affected Nepal are most evident. Pushed by influences from the outside world, Kathmandu in modern times is entering a phase that resembles the breakdown of feudal society in Europe. The structure of ancient family life is slowly weakening. The extended family unit, traditionally an independent, self-sufficient economic body that produced most of the needs of its members, is splitting into smaller components as more and more people buy the things they recently made for themselves at home. Manu-

factured goods from outside are crowding out the products of local craftsmen; cash sales are increasing and trade in kind declining. Group worship and celebration are losing ground to individual pursuits, including such garish western innovations as movie theaters and other diversions of the valley's three towns. The basic fact of valley life is that there are too many hands for too little land. Drifting south as mobility increases, the labor surplus, together with the 25,000 Nepalese troops serving with the British and Indian armies, makes manpower Nepal's most lucrative export. Public education, even in its painful

RULER OF NEPAL, King Mahendra Bir Bikram is shown with Queen Ratna Devi on a state visit to the United States in 1960. A constitutional monarch, King Mahendra ascended the throne in 1955 as the ninth of his line.

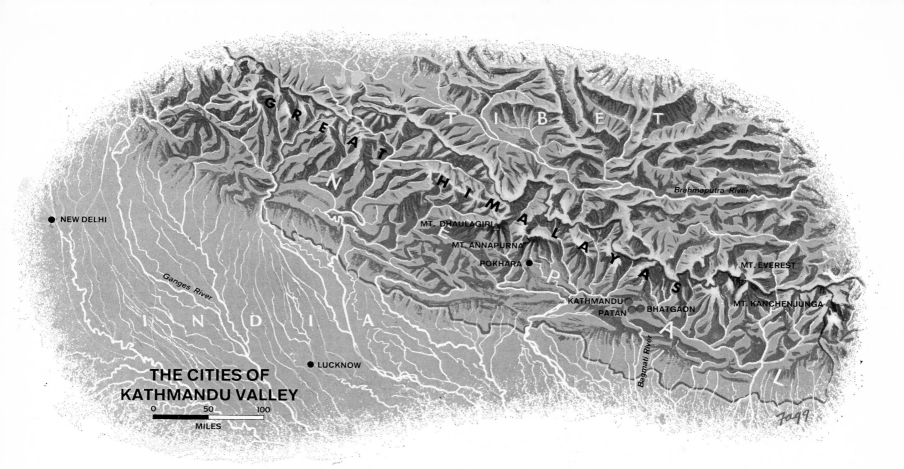

THE CITIES OF
KATHMANDU VALLEY

0   50   100
MILES

beginnings, has proved a galvanizing force in the present as well as the main hope for the future. More than a dozen political parties politick earnestly, although in 1960 they were banned by Mahendra for "obstructing progress." All the political parties—even the well-organized and growing Communist contingent—advocate nationalism, democracy and a higher standard of living. Thirteen Kathmandu newspapers, most with a circulation of less than 1,000, remind readers daily of Chou En-lai, Nehru, the outside world and the United Nations, which Nepal joined in 1956. But many of the changes in Nepal and in the outside world are a long way from touching the peasant in his rice paddy.

IT was not until the mid-1950s, after the power of the Rana family of prime ministers was overthrown, that foreigners were permitted access to Kathmandu Valley. Though tourists may now visit Kathmandu, it still requires special government permission to travel outside the valley into other parts of Nepal. In 1956 the face of Nepal began to be altered when the valley was finally connected by paved road to India. American technicians are installing a tele-communications network, building roads and airstrips for expanding air transport. The Indians are working on educational and health programs, huge power and flood-control projects. The Russians are building a cigarette factory and a hydroelectric installation; the Chinese, cement and paper factories. Progress is slow, and the natural difficulties of change have been compounded by endless differences among Nepalese politicians about how it should be attained. Some have criticized locations chosen for U.S. aid projects, yet American steel for many footbridges has rusted in the hills while the government debates where the next one shall be located. In their political immaturity and very much aware of their strategic geographical position between India and the Red Chinese in Tibet, the Nepalese veer before each political wind, trying to stick to their avowed course of neutralism. They are so determined to show their independence of India that they keep the Nepalese clock 10 minutes ahead of Indian time, and yet they are enthusiastic and eager to please every nation that is working to help them.

Millions in foreign aid lie untouched awaiting the planners, plans and skilled cadres to put them to work. Specialized factories cannot be built before the demand for their products and the power to purchase them have been created. The health and sanitation of the country is deplorable; yet a sudden, substantial improvement without modernization of the economy could, by dropping the death rate, plunge Nepal into a serious food shortage. While some impatient supernationalists may argue in terms of overnight miracles, responsible Nepalese realize that their country is too deeply rooted in the past to expect dramatic turns for the better over any short run. Nepal's text for the future was written in a Himalayan cave by Milarepa, the 11th Century Buddhist poet: "Hasten slowly and ye shall soon arrive."

The Nepalese are not quite ready to cope with the tremendous problems that face them. But in the light of their history, it is not unlikely that they will cope. Though their civilization—the civilization of Kathmandu Valley—is a strange relic, it has survived. Perhaps it has survived partly because of, rather than despite, the waves of migration and invasion that have swept the land since prehistory. The very process of assimilating the new peoples into the valley society may have kept it from attaining the final rigidity that characterized some of the defunct civilizations described in the middle section of this book. At least there is good reason to believe that the Nepalese will absorb—rather than be absorbed by—modern technology.

BEST-KNOWN NEPALESE to the outside world is Tenzing Norgay, the famous Sherpa guide. As a guide for the 1953 British expedition, Tenzing accompanied Sir Edmund Hillary on man's first conquest of Mount Everest.

285

BAREFOOT INDUSTRIAL LABORERS. Indian women wearing traditional saris, shovel coal by hand from a freight car at the newly modernized, $800,000,000 Tata Steel Mill, located at Jamshedpur. Modern mass production and great demands for factory labor are disrupting India's ancient craft trades and village customs. Until the advent of modern industry, most Indians and many people in many other parts of the world followed a Neolithic way of life.

THE COURSE OF CIVILIZATION

Heir to a long past, modern technological civilization is impinging upon the people of less advanced cultures

SOME scraps of bones, a broken figurine, a cryptic notation carved in stone—in the light shed by such relics, *The Epic of Man* has traced man's journey through the darkness of the distant past up to the flowering of his first civilizations. Some civilizations, like the magnificently planned cities of the Indus Valley, arose, flourished and disappeared, leaving behind only vague influences. But almost every culture, as related in Section II, had a formative role to play in the human adventure. In Asia, the Shang, powerful hordes of horsed archers, set patterns for Chinese culture. In the Middle East, the Sumerians developed writing, the idea of money, and a decimal system. The culture of imperial Egypt, especially in government and science, was one of many whose influence was spread through the Mediterranean by traders and colonizers like the Phoenicians. The greatness of Greece was importantly based on the culture of the Minoans and Mycenaeans. The monotheism and ethic of the Hebrews were embodied in the traditions of Christianity and Islam. The modern Romance languages began when the migrating Celts mixed their language with the Latin of the Romans. The record, incomplete and sometimes hard to read, indicates that some civilizations grew out of others and faded into newer cultures. Some seem to have developed without antecedents, and to have vanished without heirs.

To reach the state of civilization, man spent over 400,000 years in the process of experiment and growth reconstructed in Section I. But as man's culture accumulated, his progress accelerated; and by the 20th Century, less than 5,000 years after the dawn of civilization, he had developed a technology that was shrinking distance, minimizing political boundaries, extending his life span and increasing his very potential for greater progress. But this modern technological civilization, now shared by at least a billion people, had bypassed about two thirds of the world's population; and of that two thirds, half—or about one billion—were following an essentially Neolithic or even more primitive way of life. The chapters of Section III demonstrate how these bypassed peoples around the world have followed their ancient ways into the present. In recent years, confronted with the sudden onslaught and sheer speed of technological civilization, they have endured dislocation, upheaval or strife. For societies as primitive as that of the Caribou Eskimos of Canada, the shock has been so great that many disintegrated. When they first came in contact with technology, old, rigid societies, like that of the Berbers of Morocco's Atlas Mountains, have tended to resist, to fight against change, to cling to the old hardships along with the old ways. Societies with the distinct civilization of Nepal's Kathmandu Valley may accept the need for change but lose their cultural heritages as a result of change. This confrontation of old and new, a process as old as civilization itself, is shown in the pictures on the pages that follow.

As Dr. Loren Eiseley notes in the introduction to this book, it is always man's hope "that by a true knowledge of the past he will wander less blindly among the shards and attic rubble of past failures." *The Epic of Man* sets forth, as well as scholars have been able to reconstruct it, the early life of man on this earth. What does it tell of the future course of civilization?

Mankind's future yields no more to the measurements and projections of scientists than it did to the oracle bones of the Shang divinators. But a study of the story of the past does reveal something of the nature of mankind's progress. Writing of the Greeks and Romans, through whom so much of the early civilizations was transmitted to the western civilization of today, the classicist Gilbert Highet says: "Those who are most easily depressed about the precarious future of Western civilization are usually people who do not know the full history of its past. . . . Progress has not been continuous throughout the last three thousand years of our history—nor the last three hundred; nor even the last thirty. . . . We, who stand lower than the Greeks and Romans in some things and higher in others, can and should look toward them constantly, in order to interpret our own destinies."

LEAPS TO A NEW AGE

LARGE areas of the world remained virtually untouched by the Industrial Revolution for nearly two hundred years after its beginning in England. Then the urge to catch up, to modernize, began to be felt in country after country. Nations that had been colonies of industrial powers now wanted to provide for themselves the goods of the 20th Century, and Neolithic peoples sought to transform their economies overnight. Some underdeveloped countries, like China, were willing to utilize the most primitive manufacturing methods as one means toward achieving an industrial revolution, as they expressed it, in "the leap forward." Others, like the Indians, sought and obtained assistance from more advanced nations in building an industrial base of factories, dams and steel mills. Wherever underdeveloped societies sought to move ahead abruptly, the city became the symbol of change, and the city grew rapidly. In new African metropolises, primitive, crude huts were clustering near elegant skyscrapers.

SHANTIES AND SKYSCRAPERS are not far apart at Dakar. Located in the native quarter of this West African metropolis, the shanties are roofed with corrugated metal and walled off into crude compounds. The skyscrapers are in the downtown area. Despite the squalor and the overcrowding of Dakar's shantytown, rural Senegalese by the thousands continue to flock into the city, pulled from their tribal moorings by the magnetic lure of modern city life.

A CRUDE IRONWORKS at the Shiu Shin commune in China uses a battery of brick blast furnaces and small air blowers to turn ore and scrap into pig iron. The furnaces, laboriously fed by hand, were built by the men, women and children in all communes during a drive to industrialize in 1958. Communist China plans to become a leading industrial nation in the world of today by an efficient use of materials and a ruthless use of its tremendous manpower.

JET PLANES AND OXCARTS, centuries apart in the history of transportation, are both employed at the Hindustan Aircraft Factory in Bangalore, India. The scoop-shaped carts, built to a pattern unchanged for over 5,000 years, are used in construction work. The low-lying factory, which covers more than two square miles and employs 15,000 people, turns out railway cars, buses and civil and military aircraft, including the British-designed

OXCART TO JET:
THE GREAT SPEED-UP

THE upheavals and transformations that shook the modern world were speeded up tremendously by the phenomenon of speed itself —by electronics in communications and the jet in transportation. All of mankind, it seemed, was being pushed under one roof. A politician's speech in Southeast Asia could upset ministries in northwestern Europe. A radio broadcast in Cairo could start riots within the hour in remote Persian Gulf ports. A dance invented in the Caribbean got

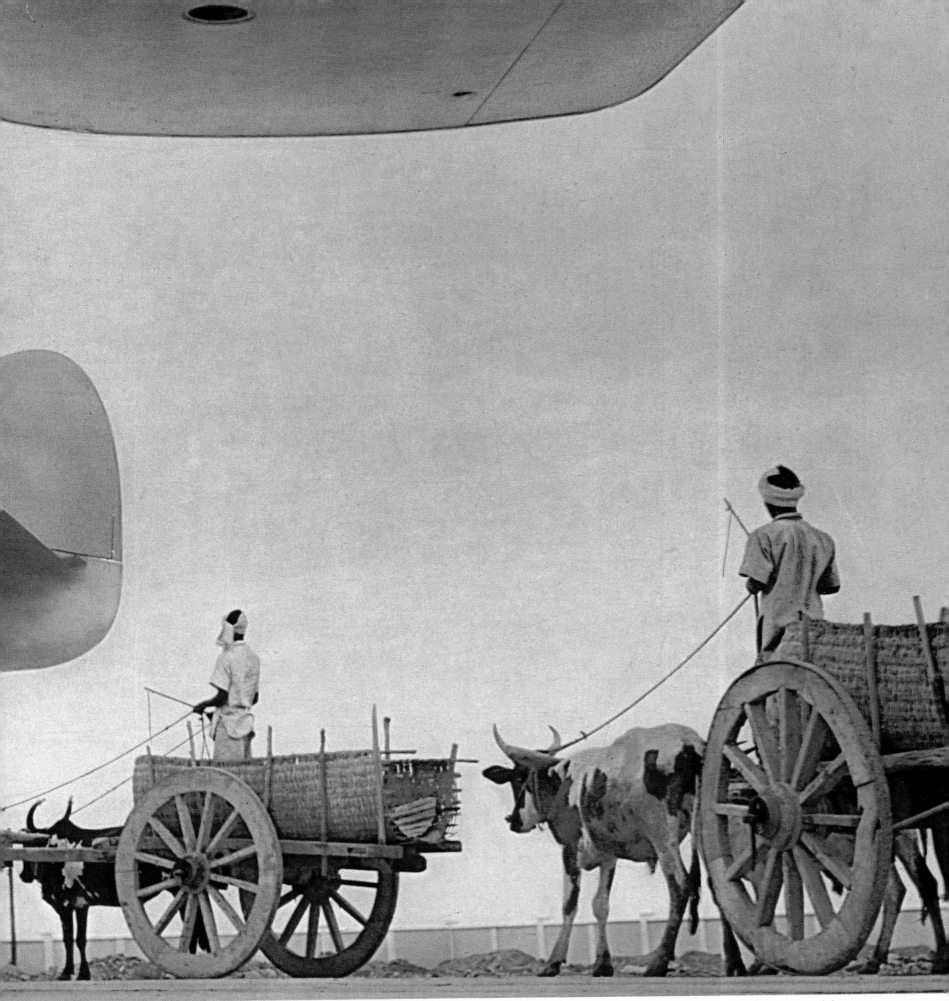

Vampire fighter planes, parts of which are visible in the photograph above. Although 15,000 miles of highway and over 500,000 motor vehicles crisscross the subcontinent, about 10,000,000 oxcarts still bear a major part of India's transportation load. Also holding back India's progress are social customs and caste taboos which, despite government attempts to rectify them, deny equal rights to work and education to large segments of the population.

banned in Djakarta. A popular soft drink in one country became an international symbol—and the subject of nationalistic argument.

So eagerly taken up were technological innovations that people like the Brazilians moved straight from horse-and-buggy transport to airliners, skipping much of the rail and road development common in older industrial nations. Devout North African Moslems dismounted from their camels at planeside and finished their pilgrimage to Mecca by air. In many lands, the centuries seemed to be running side by side. In India the turbaned driver and his straining beasts labored to build the factories which would make them obsolete if they were successful as planned. In many parts of the world the airplane was the only available means of travel in addition to draft animals and bicycles. As a result, some widely separated cities were actually closer to each other than to many cities in their own rural districts.

OLD FAITHS, NEW GOALS

LEARNING ABOUT A FOREIGN FAITH, Nigerian pupils in Zagun listen to an American Baptist missionary read the story of Daniel in the lions' den. Zagun has three clinics, one for lepers, which are run by the Baptist mission.

THE earnest college students at the new university in the newly independent country of Nigeria spent most of their study hours on western subjects, and their purpose in life was to become professional or scientific men and women on the European model. But they were wearing traditional West African garments as well as European clothing, and African culture still played an important part in molding their minds. The education of more and more young Africans greatly speeded up the adoption of 20th-Century technological culture—a process that had begun in the past when far-ranging traders and colonizers brought with them many products of industry—clocks, rifles, tools, stoves and sewing machines.

One of the exports of modern nations was religion. When two faiths met in the far corners of the world, the result was not necessarily a clear-cut dominance of one over the other. In Latin America, from Mexico to Peru, human sacrifice was abolished by the Roman Catholic Church, but the Indians were allowed to make their gods into saints. In 1947, the establishment of the Moslem state of Pakistan helped in some degree to resolve the age-old conflict between Islam and Hinduism on the Indian subcontinent. In many other places, old faiths have remained the same in the midst of rapid industrial growth.

MEMBERS OF A NEW ELITE, Nigerian collegians wearing European and traditional West African clothes, lounge outside a modern sun-screened building, the library of University College, Ibadan. Opened in 1948, the college today has more than 1,200 students. College graduates are desperately needed in the newly independent country, but so far they make up a mere .05 per cent of Nigeria's population. They man almost every high office in the government.

CONTINUING A PAGAN RITE, descendants of the Maya in Chichicastenango, Guatemala, burn incense on the steps of a 400-year-old Roman Catholic church before going in to Mass. The smoke carries their prayers upward to the souls of good men who will intercede for them with the almighty spirit. The modern Maya's blend of pagan and Catholic elements is viewed by local priests as a necessary compromise with the stubborn, ancient Maya tradition.

293

TRIBES INTO NATIONS

FATHER and son, the Alake of Abeokuta and Sir Adetokunbo Ademola, portrayed in the photograph on the opposite page, were important men in Nigeria. The father, as paramount chief of the Yoruba, was continuing a tradition that had endured unchanged even after the white man had come to rule the region. But with independence in 1959, Nigerians took over many governmental functions, and the son, Sir Adetokunbo, became the country's chief judicial officer.

Nigeria was one of the new nations that crowded onto the world stage and clamored to be heard after World War II. In many of the newly independent lands the only effective political organization was primitive tribal grouping, and their leaders had to instill in them a sense of nation almost overnight. Where the colonial powers had prepared their wards for independence, through education and by permitting them to take on the responsibilities of government, the transition to nationhood went smoothly. But where education was inadequate and the take-over of power abrupt, bloody chaos resulted.

A NEW SPOKESMAN for new nations is Ghana's delegation to the U.N. Granted independence by Britain in 1957, Ghana joined the United Nations as its 81st member and quickly became prominent in the Afro-Asian bloc.

UPHOLDING DIFFERENT TRADITIONS, a Nigerian father and son (*opposite*) wear official robes. The Alake of Abeokuta is head chief of the Yoruba; Sir Adetokunbo Ademola is Chief Justice of Nigeria's Supreme Court.

FORGING NEW UNITY, a government education officer in Ghana (*above*) urges village chiefs, seated under an umbrella, to organize construction of a dance floor. This was the first inter-village enterprise in local history.

"INTERWOVEN,
INTERCONNECTED"

IN a group of Polynesians gathered on the porch of a general store in Tahiti could be read one of the truths of the time. As anthropologist Margaret Mead has observed, mankind was "moving toward an interwoven, interconnected world." Instead of their traditional sarongs and wrap-around skirts, many of the Tahitians were wearing print dresses, sport jackets and hats made in factories thousands of miles away. Like their forefathers, the men still ventured far out into the Pacific in outrigger canoes. But they were spending much more time at home on their island, where they farmed and fished—and welcomed tourists borne by jet from another land and another culture.

THE TIMES OF MAN

DATES	AMERICA	EUROPE	AFRICA-MIDDLE EAST	ASIA
70,000,000 First primate				
30,000,000 Anthropoid apes				
700,000 Ice ages begin			600,000 Zinjanthropus	500,000 Java man
500,000-100,000 Acheulian age			400,000 Chellean man	360,000 Peking man
250,000 Homo sapiens		250,000 Steinheim and Swanscombe men / 150,000 Fontechevade man		
100,000-35,000 Mousterian age		100,000 Neanderthal man / 75,000 Fourth ice age begins		
35,000-8000 Upper Paleolithic (Europe)	20,000 Ancestors of American Indians cross Bering Strait from Asia	35,000 Combe Capelle man	23,000 Rhodesian man	
35,000-28,000 Lower Perigordian		28,000-14,000 Cro-Magnon man		
28,000-21,000 Aurignacian				
21,000-18,000 Upper Perigordian		18,000 Fourth retreat of glaciers		
18,000-14,000 Solutrean		14,000-8000 Magdalenian man		
14,000-8000 Magdalenian				
8000-5000	8000 Human settlements extend to Strait of Magellan		8000 Neolithic revolution takes place in the Middle East / 8000 Founding of Jericho	
5000-4000			4500 Farming starts in Egypt / 4500-2900 Rise of civilization in Sumer	
4000-3000			3500-2500 First cities rise in Nile and Tigris-Euphrates valleys / 3100 Menes unites Egypt	3500-2500 First cities rise in Indus valley
3000-2000	2500 Farming under way in Middle and South America	3000 Neolithic farming starts in Europe	2700 Old Kingdom begins in Egypt / 2600-1200 Egyptian dominance in Syro-Palestine / 2500 Sumerian Royal Tombs built at Ur, Bronze Age begins / 2360-2180 Semites establish Akkadian Empire / 2160 Fall of Egyptian Old Kingdom / 2100-2025 Ur-Nammu unites Sumer and Akkad. Period of Sumerian renaissance / 2050 Start of the Middle Kingdom in Egypt	2500 Farming begins on the North China plain / 2500 Start of Indus Valley civilization / 2500 Mastery of the horse in central Asia
2000-1000	1500 B.C.-300 A.D. Maya Pre-Classic age	2000-1400 Minoan civilization in Crete / 1900 Mycenaeans reach Greece from the north / 1450-1150 Mycenaean maritime domination / 1450-1400 Mycenaean rule in Knossos / 1400 Start of metallurgy in northern Europe. Bronze Age begins	2000 Abraham leaves Haran in northern Mesopotamia / 1900 Hittites conquer north-central Anatolia / 1728-1686 Rise of Babylon. Hammurabi issues Law Code / 1567 New Kingdom begins in Egypt / 1400 Hebrews invade the land of Canaan / 1370 Akh-en-Aton tries to convert Egypt to monotheism. Hittites move into northern Syro-Palestine	2000 Height of Indus civilization at Harappa and Mohenjo-daro / 1700-1100 Shang civilization. Bronze Age begins in China

Early Evolutionary and Cultural Periods

1000-700 Indo-Aryans migrate to Nepal

800 Huns retreat from China

6th Century Rise of Iron Age cities of the Ganges valley
563 Siddhartha Gautama, founder of Buddhism, born

550-485 Persian Conquests Under Cyrus II and Darius I

500 Buddhism comes to Nepal via India

5th Century Scythian burials at Pazirik, Siberia

221-206 Unification of China under the Ch'in Dynasty. Great Wall built

B. C.

A. D.

7th Century Nepal overrun by Tibetans

14th Century Malla kings reign in Nepal

1300-1100 The age of the Sea Peoples
1286 Hittites defeat Ramses II of Egypt at Kadesh
1198 Ramses III and the end of the Egyptian Empire
1100-600 Phoenician maritime supremacy
1020-922 Hebrews united under Kings Saul, David and Solomon
1000 Start of the Iron Age in Syro-Palestine

950 Carthage founded by the Phoenicians

883-612 Assyrian domination of Syro-Palestine and Egypt

700 Iron Age begins in Egypt
700 Scythians move into Black Sea region

612-538 Neo-Babylonian Empire

332-323 Alexander The Great

146 Carthage falls to Rome
100 Scythians fade into obscurity
30 Egypt becomes a Roman province

622 Mohammed's *hegira*. Start of the Moslem era

1453 Fall of Constantinople to the Turks

1194-1184 The Trojan War

1100 Gadir (modern Cadiz) founded by Phoenicians

850 Halstatt Iron Age in central Europe, first major signs of Celtic settlement
800 Homer's *Iliad* and *Odyssey*
800 Rise of Etruscan urban society

776 First Olympic games
700-500 Etruscan expansion

616-510 Etruscan kings rule in Rome
600-300 Greek Golden Age

510 Romans oust Etruscans, establish Republic
500 Start of La Tène Iron Age in western Europe

5th Century Herodotus writes his *Histories*

490-479 Persians fail to conquer Greece
400 Celtic expansion begins

4th Century Huns sweep from Asia into Europe

3rd-1st Centuries Etruscan civilization disappears as a separate entity, traditions carried on by Rome
55 Julius Caesar invades England

1st-5th Centuries Roman rule in Gaul and England
2nd Century Roman sea trade with India and southeastern Asia

mid-7th Century Saxons gain control in England
750-1000 Khazar Empire in southern Russia
800 Charlemagne founds Holy Roman Empire
878 Oleg captures Kiev, which becomes nucleus for Russian state

1017 Danish rule established in England
1066 Norman conquest of England

1450-1500 Culmination of the Renaissance

1000 Rise of Cupisnique and Chavín de Huántar pre-Inca cultures in Peru

Ceremonial center built at Chavin in Peru

400 B.C.-400 A.D. Height of Paracas culture in Peru

1st-5th Centuries Nazca culture in coastal southern Peru, Mochica in northern Peru
300 Start of Maya Classic age, Tikal becomes ceremonial center in northern Guatemala

10th-12th Centuries Height of Toltec civilization
900-1450 Maya Post-Classic period
1000 Spread of Tiahuanaco culture throughout Peru

14th-16th Centuries Height of Aztec and Inca civilizations

999-900

899-800

799-700

699-600

599-500

499-1

B. C.

A. D.
1-500

501-1000

1001-1500

BIBLIOGRAPHY

GENERAL READING

Bibby, Geoffrey, *The Testimony of the Spade.* Alfred A. Knopf, 1960.
Childe, V. Gordon, *What Happened in History.* Penguin, 1952. *New Light on the Most Ancient East.* Frederick A. Praeger, 1953. *The Dawn of European Civilization.* Alfred A. Knopf, 1958.
Coon, Carleton S., *A Reader in General Anthropology.* Henry Holt, 1954. *The Story of Man.* Alfred A. Knopf, 1954.
Cottrell, Leonard, *The Anvil of Civilization.* Mentor Books, 1959.
Frankfort, Henri, *et al., Before Philosophy.* Penguin, 1951.
Linton, Ralph, *The Tree of Culture.* Alfred A. Knopf, 1955.
Pritchard, James B., ed., *Ancient Near Eastern Texts.* Princeton University Press, 1950. *Ancient Near Eastern Pictures.* Princeton University Press, 1955.
Shapiro, Harry L., *Man, Culture, and Society.* Oxford University Press, 1956.

CHAPTER 1

Braidwood, Robert J., *Prehistoric Men.* Chicago Natural History Museum Press, 1959.
Howells, William, *Mankind in the Making.* Doubleday, 1959.
Le Gros Clark, W. E., *History of the Primates.* Phoenix, Chicago Press, 1959.
Oakley, Kenneth P., *Man the Tool Maker.* British Museum of Natural History, London, 1956.
Von Koenigswald, G.H.R., *Meeting Prehistoric Man.* Harper, 1956.

CHAPTER 2

Bibby, Geoffrey, *The Testimony of the Spade.* Alfred A. Knopf, 1960.
Breuil, Abbé H., *Four Hundred Centuries of Cave Art.* Trans. by Mary E. Boyle. Centre d'Etudes et de Documentation Prehistoriques, Montignac, 1952.
Graziosi, Paolo, *Paleolithic Art.* McGraw-Hill, 1960.
Maringer, Johannes, *The God of Prehistoric Man.* Alfred A. Knopf, 1960.
Maringer, Johannes, and Hans-Georg Bandi, *Art in the Ice Ages.* Frederick A. Praeger, 1953.
van Gennep, Arnold, *The Rites of Passage.* University of Chicago Press, 1960.

CHAPTER 3

Braidwood, Robert J., and Bruce Howe, *Prehistoric Investigations in Iraqui Kurdistan.* University of Chicago Press, 1960.
Kenyon, Kathleen M., *Digging up Jericho.* Frederick A. Praeger, 1957.
Lee, Norman, *Harvests and Harvesting Through the Ages.* Cambridge University Press, 1961.
Lhote, Henri, *The Search for the Tassili Frescoes.* E. P. Dutton, 1959.

CHAPTER 4

Frankfort, Henri, *The Birth of Civilization in the Near East.* Doubleday, 1959.
Kramer, Samuel Noah, *Mythologies of the Ancient World.* Doubleday, 1961.
Woolley, C. L., *The Sumerians.* Oxford University Press, 1928. *The Royal Cemetery* (2 vols.). University of Pennsylvania Museum, 1934. *The Ziggurat and its Surroundings.* University of Pennsylvania Museum, 1939. *Excavations at Ur.* Thomas Y. Crowell, 1954.

CHAPTER 5

Gordon, D. H., *The Pre-Historic Background of Indian Culture.* N. M. Tripathi Ltd., Bombay, 1958.
Piggott, Stuart, *Prehistoric India.* Penguin, 1950.
Subbaro, B., *The Personality of India.* M. S. University of Baroda, 1956.
Wheeler, Sir Mortimer, *The Indus Civilization.* Cambridge University Press, 1953. *Early India and Pakistan.* Frederick A. Praeger, 1959.

CHAPTER 6

Gardiner, Sir Alan, *Egypt of the Pharaohs.* The Clarendon Press, Oxford, 1961.
Glanville, S.R.K., *The Legacy of Egypt.* The Clarendon Press, Oxford, 1942.
Hayes, William Christopher, *The Scepter of Egypt.* Harper, 1953.
Smith, William S., *The Architecture of Ancient Egypt.* Penguin, 1958.
Wilson, John Albert, *The Burden of Egypt.* University of Chicago Press, 1951.

CHAPTER 7

Albright, William Foxwell, *The Archaeology of Palestine.* Penguin, 1960.
Ceram, C. W., *The Secret of the Hittites.* Alfred A. Knopf, 1956.
Hitti, Philip K., *History of Syria.* Macmillan, 1951.

CHAPTER 8

Kenyon, Kathleen M., *Archaeology in the Holy Land.* Frederick A. Praeger, 1960.
Moscati, Sabatino, *Ancient Semitic Civilizations.* G. P. Putnam's Sons, 1960.
Warmington, B. H., *Carthage.* Robert Hale, 1960.
Wright, G. Ernest, *Biblical Archaeology.* The Westminster Press, 1957.

CHAPTER 8

Chadwick, John, *The Decipherment of Linear B.* Random House, 1958.
Cottrell, Leonard, *The Bull of Minos.* Rinehart, 1958.
Marinatos, S., *Crete and Mycenae.* Harry N. Abrams, 1960.
Mylonas, George Emmanuel, *Ancient Mycenae.* Princeton University Press, 1957.
Pendlebury, J.D.S., *Archaeology of Crete.* Methuen, London, 1939.

CHAPTER 9

Bloch, Raymond, *The Etruscans.* Frederick A. Praeger, 1958.
Pallottino, Massimo, *The Etruscans.* Trans. by J. Cremona. Penguin, 1955.
Randall-MacIver, David, *Etruscans.* Oxford University Press, London, 1927.

CHAPTER 10

McGovern, William M., *The Early Empires of Central Asia.* University of North Carolina Press, 1939.
Powell, T.G.E., *The Celts.* Frederick A. Praeger, 1958.
Rice, Tamara Talbot, *The Scythians.* Frederick A. Praeger, 1958.
Rostovtzeff, Mikhail, *Out of the Past of Greece and Rome.* Yale University Press, 1932.
Vernadsky, George, *History of Russia,* Vol. I. Yale University Press, 1957.

CHAPTER 11

Chêng Té-k'un, *Archaeology in China,* Vols. I and II. Heffer, Cambridge, 1959-1960.
Creel, Herrlee Glessner, *The Birth of China.* Frederick Ungar, 1937.
Li Chi, *The Beginnings of Chinese Civilization.* University of Washington Press, 1957.
Reischauer, Edwin O., and John K. Fairbank, *A History of East Asia Civilization,* Vol. I. Houghton Mifflin, 1960.
Watson, William, *Archaeology in China.* Max Parrish, London, 1960.

CHAPTER 12

Morley, Sylvanus Griswold, *The Ancient Maya.* Stanford University Press, 1958.
Prescott, William H., *The Conquest of Mexico and The Conquest of Peru.* Random House.
Rivet, Paul, *Maya Cities.* G. P. Putnam's Sons, 1960.
Thompson, J. Eric S., *The Rise and Fall of Maya Civilization.* University of Oklahoma Press, 1954.
Vaillant, George C., *The Aztecs of Mexico.* Penguin, 1960.

CHAPTER 13

Bennett, Wendell C., *Ancient Arts of the Andes.* The Museum of Modern Art, 1954.
Bennett, Wendell C., and Junius Bird, *Andean Culture History.* The American Museum of Natural History, 1960.
Bingham, Hiram, *Lost City of the Incas.* Duell, Sloan and Pearce, 1948.
Bushnell, G.H.S., *Peru.* Frederick A. Praeger, 1957.
La Farge, Oliver, *A Pictorial History of the American Indian.* Crown, 1956.
Mason, J. Alden, *The Ancient Civilizations of Peru.* Penguin, 1957.

CHAPTER 14

Elkin, A. P., *The Australian Aborigines.* Angus and Robertson, Sydney, 1938.
Harrington, Richard, *The Face of the Arctic.* Henry Schuman, 1952.
Mowat, Farley, *People of the Deer.* Little, Brown, 1952. *Desperate People.* Little, Brown, 1959.

CHAPTER 15

Bousquet, G. H., *Les Berbères.* Presses Universitaires de France, Paris, 1957.
Coon, Carleton S., *Caravan: The Story of the Middle East.* Henry Holt, 1958.
Gerster, Georg, *Sahara.* Coward-McCann, 1961.

CHAPTER 16

Karan, Pradyumna P., *Nepal.* University of Kentucky Press, 1960.
Landon, Perceval, *Nepal* (2 vols.). Constable, London, 1928.
Sekelj, Tibor, *Window on Nepal.* Robert Hale, London, 1959.

ACKNOWLEDGMENTS

The editors are indebted to DR. CARLETON S. COON, Curator of Ethnology and Professor of Anthropology, and ROBERT H. DYSON, JR., Assistant Curator, of the University of Pennsylvania Museum, for their help and guidance in the preparation of *The Epic of Man* and to the other authorities and institutions listed below. However, the editors assume responsibility for the selection and arrangement of all material in the book and for the viewpoints expressed.

ACKERKNECHT, DR. ERWIN—University of Wisconsin
ADAMS, ROBERT—Oriental Institute, University of Chicago
AL-ASIL, HIS EXCELLENCY DR. NAJI—Director General of Antiquities, Iraq
ALBRIGHT, WILLIAM F.—Johns Hopkins University
AMADON, DR. DEAN—American Museum of Natural History
AMER, DR. MUSTAFA—Department of Antiquities, UAR
AMERICAN GEOGRAPHICAL SOCIETY
AMERICAN SCHOOL OF CLASSICAL STUDIES—Athens
ARJAL, NARAYAN P.—First Secretary, Nepal Mission to the U.N.
ARONSON, DR. LESTER—American Museum of Natural History
BARNETT, R. D.—Keeper of Western Asiatic Antiquities, British Museum
BASMAJI, DR. FARAJ—Curator, Iraq Museum
BERNDT, RONALD and CATHERINE—University of Sydney
BIRD, DR. JUNIUS—American Museum of Natural History
BLEGEN, CARL—University of Cincinnati
BOTHMER, DR. BERNARD—American Research Center, UAR
BRAIDWOOD, ROBERT J.and LINDA—Oriental Institute, University of Chicago
BREUIL, ABBE HENRI—Musée de l'Homme, Paris
BRITISH SCHOOL AT ATHENS
BROMAN, VIVIAN—Oriental Institute, University of Chicago
BROOKLYN BOTANIC GARDEN
CARTER, T. DONALD—American Museum of Natural History
CASSON, DR. LIONEL—New York University
CHEHAB, EMIR MAURICE—Director, National Museum of the Lebanon
CHESTER, KATHLEEN—British Museum of Natural History
CHICAGO NATURAL HISTORY MUSEUM
CHILDE, V. GORDON—Archaeological Institute, University of London
CLARK, DR. J. G. D.—Cambridge University
CLARK, T. W.—University of London
COONEY, DR. JOHN D.—Brooklyn Museum
DANISH NATIONAL MUSEUM—Copenhagen
DEEVEY, DR. EDWARD—Yale University
DELOUGAZ, PINHAS—Oriental Institute, University of Chicago
DEPARTMENT OF NORTHERN AFFAIRS AND NATURAL RESOURCES, CANADA
DEPARTMENT OF TRANSPORT, AIR SERVICES, CANADA
DIMBLEBY, DR. G. W.—Oxford University
DRAR, DR. MOHAMMED—Egyptian Agriculture Ministry
DRURY, DR. WILLIAM—Harvard University
DUNN, DR. LESLIE—Columbia University
DUPREE, LOUIS—American Museum of Natural History
EDGERTON, DR. WILLIAM F.—Oriental Institute, University of Chicago
EDWARDS, DR. I. E. S.—British Museum
EHRICH, ROBERT—Brooklyn College
EKHOLM, DR. GORDON F.—American Museum of Natural History
ELKIN, A.P.—University of Sydney
ELLISON, THE REVEREND ALFRED—Northern Territory, Australia
EMERICK, RICHARD—University of Pennsylvania
EMERY, DR. WALTER—London University
FISCHER, DR. HENRY G.—Assistant Curator, Department of Egyptian Art, Metropolitan Museum of Art, New York
FRASER, F.C.—British Museum of Natural History
GLASTONBURY LAKE VILLAGE MUSEUM—England
GLUECK, DR. NELSON—President, Hebrew Union College—Jewish Institute of Religion
GODWIN, DR. HARRY—Cambridge University
GOODWIN, GEORGE—American Museum of Natural History
GORDON, DR. EDMUND—University of Pennsylvania Museum
GOTHENBURG MUSEUM—Sweden
GUTERBOCK, DR. HANS G.—Oriental Institute, University of Chicago
HARRIS, THE REVEREND DR. ERDMAN—Yale University
HART, DAVID M.—University of Pennsylvania
HAYES,DR. WILLIAM C.—Metropolitan Museum of Art, New York
HELBAEK, HANS—Danish National Museum, Copenhagen
HENCKEN, HUGH—Peabody Museum, Harvard University
HISTORICAL MUSEUM—Lund University, Sweden
HOWE, DR. BRUCE—Harvard University

HOWELLS, DR. WILLIAM—Harvard University
HUGHES, DR. GEORGE—Oriental Institute, University of Chicago
JACOBSEN, THORKILD—Oriental Institute, University of Chicago
KANTOR, DR. HELENE J.—Oriental Institute, University of Chicago
KAROUZOS, DR. CH.—Director, National Museum, Athens
KELLEY, HARPER—Musée de l'Homme, Paris
KENYON, DR. KATHLEEN M.—Director of the British School of Archaeology at Jerusalem
KRAMER, DR. SAMUEL NOAH—University of Pennsylvania Museum
KUHN, DR. EMIL—University of Zurich
KWANG-CHIH CHANG, DR.—Peabody Museum, Harvard University
LANTIER, RAYMOND—Musée des Antiquités Nationales, St. Germain-en-Laye
LEAKEY, DR. L. S. B.—Coryndon Memorial Museum, Nairobi
LEET, DR. L. DON—Harvard University
LENZEN, HEINRICH—University of Berlin
LI CHI, DR.—Academia Sinica, Taipei, Formosa
LINES, JOAN—Metropolitan Museum of Art, New York
LOCKER, FREDERICK—U.S. Operations Mission to Iraq
McCOWN, DR. DONALD
MARINATOS, SPYRIDON—Director, Department of Antiquities, Greece
MATSON, FREDERICK R.—Pennsylvania State University
MAYER, DR. JEAN—School of Public Health, Harvard University
MAYR, DR. ERNST—Harvard University
MEAD, DR. MARGARET—Associate Curator of Ethnology, American Museum of Natural History
MOVIUS, DR. HALLAM—Harvard University
MYLONAS, GEORGE E.—Washington University, St. Louis
NATIONAL AUDUBON SOCIETY
NATIONAL MUSEUM—Helsinki
NATIONAL MUSEUM OF ANTIQUITIES—Edinburgh
NATIONAL MUSEUM OF IRELAND
NEW YORK BOTANICAL GARDEN
OAKLEY, DR. KENNETH—British Museum of Natural History
OKADA, DR. FERDINAND—U.S. International Cooperation Administration
O RIORDAIN, SEAN—University College, Dublin
PAPADEMETRIOU, DR. JOHN—Ephor of Antiquities of the Argolid, Greece
PARIBENI, ENRICO—Director, Foro Romano, Rome
PIGGOTT, DR. STUART—University of Edinburgh
PLATON, NICHOLAS—Director, Heraclion Archaeological Museum, Crete
PORADA, DR. EDITH—Columbia University
QUIRING, DR. DANIEL—Western Reserve University
RAFFIEUR, JOAN—Museum of Fine Arts, Boston
REDLICH, DR. FREDERICK—Yale University
REED, CHARLES A.—University of Illinois
RIEFSTAHL, ELIZABETH—Brooklyn Museum
ROBINSON, J. T.—Transvaal Museum, Pretoria
SAFAR, FOUAD—Iraq Museum
SATTERTHWAITE, DR. LINTON—University of Pennsylvania Museum
SCHORGER, DR. WILLIAM—University of Michigan
SCHULTZ, DR. LEONARD—Smithsonian Institution
SMITH, DR. WILLIAM S.—Museum of Fine Arts, Boston
SOUSA, DR. AHMED—Director General of Agriculture, Government of Iraq
SPAHNI, JEAN-CHRISTIAN—Granada
STEARNS, DR. CHARLES—Tufts University, Medford, Mass.
STEVENSON, DR. LEWIS—New York City
STRAHLER, DR. ARTHUR—Columbia University
STRAUS, DR. WILLIAM—Johns Hopkins University
STRONG, W. DUNCAN—Columbia University
TACKHOLM, DR. VIVI—Cairo University
THENIUS, DR. E.—University of Vienna
THEPENIER, JEAN—Captain, Office of Indigenous Affairs, Morocco
THOMSON, DR. DONALD—University of Melbourne
UNIVERSITE DE LYON
VARAGNAC, ANDRE—Musée des Antiquités Nationales, St. Germain-en-Laye
WACE, ALAN J. B.—Cambridge University
WARD, LAURISTON—Harvard University
WELLS, THE REVEREND EDGAR—Northern Territory, Australia
WHEELER, SIR MORTIMER—C.I.E., British Academy
WILSON, DR. JOHN A.—Oriental Institute, University of Chicago
WRIGHT, DR. GEORGE ERNEST—Harvard University
WRIGHT, HERBERT E., JR.—University of Minnesota
ZEUNER, F. E.—University of London
ZOOLOGICAL SOCIETY OF LONDON

PICTURE CREDITS

The sources for the illustrations in this book are shown below. Credits for pictures from left to right are separated by commas, top to bottom by dashes.

INDEX

Shiloh, 129
Shinar, land of, 67
Shiu Shin commune, China, *289
Shrines, Upper Paleolithic, 31
Shu, *112
Shu Ching, 195, 207
Shub-ad, 71, 73, 79
Sickle, Neolithic, *54
Sidi Hmid u l'Mghanni, 257
Sidon, *123, 132, 133, 134, 136
Signoretti, Alfredo, 174
Sinanthropus. See Peking man
Singha Durbar Palace, *272
Sioux Indians, 241
Siva, 92, 270
Sivapithecus, 13
Slavery:
  beginnings of, 67
  laws of, in Sumer, 81
Sled, invention of, 49
Smith, importance of, for Celts,
  *180-181
Social conscience, first stirring of, 108
Social organization, beginnings of, 47
Society:
  Berber, 260
  Caribou Eskimo, 252
  Etruscan, *164-165
  growth of, 47-65
  Inca, 228-229
  Shang, *200-201
Solo man, 254
Solomon, 123, *128, 129, 130
Solutrean stage of culture, 22, *23
South America, 209
Spearhead, *18
Speed, phenomenon of, 290-291
Sphinx, at Gizeh, *103
Sports, of Etruscans, *166-167
Ssu-ma Ch'ien, 200, 207
Star Carr factory, *48-50
Steinheim man, *13
Steinheim skull, 29
Step Pyramid, *104
Stereoscopic vision, 11,12
Stone Age. See Middle Stone Age;
  New Stone Age; Old Stone Age
Stone ax, hafted, 49, *52
Stone sculpture, of Shang, *202-203
Stonehenge sanctuary, 31, *43, *192
Sumer, civilization of, 67-81, 287
  art, wealth and death in, *78-79
  cities of, map 81
  city and temple in, *68-70

Sumer, continued
  crafts and business in, *71-73
  gods of, 68, *74-75
  legacies of, 80-81
  prosperity of, *76-77, *78-79
Sun:
  Gateway of, *237
  Pyramid of, *218-219
  Temple of, *212
Supernatural powers, 31
Swanscombe skull, 29
Syro-Palestine, 121, 123, 129, 136

T'a-chi, 200
Tabasco, 224
Tages, 170
Tamangs, *277
Tantric cult, 281
T'ao-t'ieh, *198, 199
Tarquinia, 175
Tarquins, 161, 175
Tata Steel Mill, *286
Tebennos, 164
Technology, development of, 287
Tefnut, 113
Teilhard de Chardin, P., 17
Tello, Julio Cesar, *240
Temple, and city, in Sumer, *68-70
Temple of the Giant Jaguar, *210-211,
  *212
Temple of the Masks, *210
Temple of the Sun, *212
Temple of the Warriors, *214
Tenochtitlán, 222, 224, 225
Teotihuacán, 217, 218, 219
Tepeyollotli, *222
Teutons, 193
Thebes, 139
Theseus, myth of, 139, 142, 148
Thucydides, 154
Thut-mose II, 111
Thut-mose III, *111
Tiahuanaco, 227, *237
Tiglathpileser III, 136
Tigris-Euphrates plain, *61, 63, 67, map
  81, 83, 121, map 122-123, 136
Tikal, *210-211, map 211
Time markers, of Maya, 211, *213
Tinia, 170
Tiryns, 139, 159
Titicaca, Lake, 237
Tlaxcala, 225
Tlaxcalans, 224
Toda, *268, 269

Toltecs, 209, 214, 217, 218, *220
Toolmaking, *18-23
Totemism, 246
Towns:
  Celtic, 179
  Neolithic, *61-63
Toynbee, Arnold, 83
Toys, of Indus, 90
Trade:
  in Kathmandu, *272-273
  of Phoenicians, *131-135
Transportation. See Air transportation
Tree-cult ceremony, *148-149
Tribhuvana, 282
Tri Chandra College, *272
Trojan War, 151, 154, 158
Troy, excavation of, 158
Truia, 166
Tuaregs, 269
Tuc d'Audoubert cave, 45
Tula, 220
Tule Springs, 209
Tumbes, 240
Turms, 170
Turshas, 174
Tut-ankh-Amon, *115, *118
Tyre, *120, *132-133, 134, 136
Tyrrhenians. See Etruscans
Tyrrhenos, 174

Ugarit, *122, 126
Umma, 81
Under-developed countries, 288
Uni, 170
Unicorn, worship of, 92
Union, idea of, 97
United States, 240-241
Upper Dadès. See Dadès Valley
Upper Magdalenian stage of culture, *24
Upper Paleolithic period, 18, 21
  art in, *32-33, *44-45
  shrines of, 31
Upper Perigordian stage of culture, *22
Ur, 67, 76, 81
  Great Death Pit at, 78
  Royal Cemetery at, 78, 79
Ur-Nammu, 81
Ursus spelaeus (cave bear), *38
Uruk, 67
Urukagina, 81

Vandals, 193
Ventris, Michael, 159
Vetulonia, 175

Vézère River valley, 44
Villages, Neolithic, *58-60
Viracocha, 237
Vishnu, 282
Vision, binocular stereoscopic, 11, 12
Vulca, 171
Vulci, 175

Wace, Alan J.B., 159
Wales, 193
Wallaby, *247
Warfare:
  of ancient Greeks, *154-155
  beginnings of, 67
  of Celts, *180-181
  of Etruscans, *172-173
  of Scythians, 188
  of Shang, *196-197
Wealth:
  in Indus, *88-90
  in Sumer, *78-79
Wen Wang, 206
West, shaping of, 139-159
  Minoans, *139-149
  Mycenaeans, *150-159
Whale Cove, 255
Wheel, invention of, *66
Wheeler, Sir Mortimer, 89, *94
Wind priests, 59
Women:
  Berber, *264-267
  in Egypt, 107
  Minoan, 146
Woolley, Sir Leonard, 78
Writing, invention of, *71, 73
  in Egypt, 118-119
  in Indus, *92-93
  Shang, 206
  in Sumer, 80-81
Wu-ting, 200, 207
Wu Wang, 206

Xiu, Eduarda, *224

Yadin, Yigael, *136
Yahweh. See Jehovah
Yellow River plain, 195
Yin, 195, 202
Yucatán peninsula, 209, 214, 217, 218

Zapotecs, 217, 218, 219
Zeus, 142, *147, 154, 170
Zinjanthropus, 29
Ziusudra, tale of, 81

TEXT PHOTOCOMPOSED ON PHOTON EQUIPMENT
IN THE EDITORIAL OFFICES OF TIME INCORPORATED, NEW YORK, NEW YORK

FOUR-COLOR SCANNED SEPARATIONS BY PRINTING DEVELOPMENTS INCORPORATED, STAMFORD, CONNECTICUT

FOUR-COLOR ENGRAVINGS BY R. R. DONNELLEY & SONS COMPANY, CHICAGO, ILLINOIS,
GRAPHIC COLOR PLATE, INC., STAMFORD, CONNECTICUT, AND LIVERMORE AND KNIGHT CO., PROVIDENCE, RHODE ISLAND
OTHER ENGRAVINGS BY THE BINGHAM PHOTO ENGRAVING CO., INC., NEW YORK, NEW YORK

PRINTED BY LIVERMORE AND KNIGHT CO., PROVIDENCE, RHODE ISLAND
BOUND BY R. R. DONNELLEY & SONS COMPANY, CRAWFORDSVILLE, INDIANA
PAPER BY THE MEAD CORPORATION, DAYTON, OHIO